GROWTH CENTRES IN THE EUROPEAN URBAN SYSTEM

Growth Centres in the European Urban System

PETER HALL
DENNIS HAY

 Heinemann Educational Books

Heinemann Educational Books Ltd
22 Bedford Square, London WC1B 3HH

LONDON EDINBURGH MELBOURNE AUCKLAND
HONG KONG SINGAPORE KUALA LUMPUR NEW DELHI
IBADAN NAIROBI JOHANNESBURG
EXETER (NH) KINGSTON PORT OF SPAIN

068818

British Library Cataloguing in Publication Data

Hall, Peter, *b. 1932*
  Growth centres in the European urban
  system.
  1. Cities and towns – Europe – Growth –
  History – 20th century
  I. Title   II. Hay, Dennis
  309.2′62′094   HT131

ISBN 0–435–35880–2

Typeset in 10 on 12pt Monophoto Baskerville
and printed in Great Britain by
Fletcher & Son Ltd, Norwich

To Our Scientific Collaborators

Contents

List of Tables

Appendix Tables

List of Figures

Preface

Like many good ideas, this study originated in a bar: in the Ginza Dai-Ichi Hotel in Tokyo, where an international group of urban researchers were gathered in June 1973 for a seminar on the International Comparative Study of Megalopolises under the auspices of the Japan Center for Area Development Research. At that seminar papers by Peter Hall and Brian Berry (Japan Center 1974) presented the advance results of studies in Britain and in the United States, which were published that same year: they delineated national urban systems for their respective countries, and analysed changes in them during the post-World War II period.

Discussing the implications with other researchers – Norman Glickman of the University of Pennsylvania, then beginning to work in Japan with Tatsuhiko Kawashima, and William Pendleton of the Ford Foundation – it seemed logical to try to set up a loose network of coordinated urban systems research in the main industrialised and urbanised regions of the world, using broadly similar concepts and definitions, and keeping regular contact so as to exchange results. Berry would continue to develop his American work; Glickman would collaborate with Japanese researchers, to produce parallel analyses there; and Hall would seek to extend the British work to continental Europe.

Later, through contact with Harry Swain – then transferred from Canada to direct the Human Settlements programme at the newly-formed International Institute for Applied Systems Analysis at Laxenburg, Austria – it seemed logical to develop the European side of the work there, in a centre that exists for scientific cooperation between eastern and western Europe and at which most European countries were represented. Initially, Peter Hall at Reading and Harry Swain at Laxenburg would collaborate in a preliminary study to define the urban systems of Europe and their boundaries. Later, the work would be concentrated at Laxenburg with a grant from the Ford Foundation. This was agreed after subsequent discussions among Hall, Swain, Pendleton, Glickman and Niles Hansen – then just about to move from the University of Texas at

Austin, to Laxenburg to take Swain's place on the International Urban Systems Study – in Ottawa, Canada in July 1975.

The work was launched at a conference in Laxenburg in December 1975; this was attended not only by European experts in urban analysis but also by Norman Glickman who was then beginning his parallel analysis of the Japanese urban system. Thence, as agreed, the first stage of the European work was divided between two centres. This involved primarily the work of reviewing data sources, of defining standardised urban regions and of providing a minimal data base for population and aggregate employment for the Census dates 1950/51, 1960/61 and 1970/71 (or their nearest equivalents). After discussion Hall, Swain and Hansen decided that this work should be done at the University of Reading, under Hall's direction, in respect of western Europe (Scandinavia, Great Britain and Ireland, the Low Countries, France, Iberia and Italy) and in Laxenburg under Hansen's direction for central and eastern Europe (the two Germanies, Switzerland, Austria and such eastern European countries as proved practicable to include). The work would be supported at Reading by a grant from the Ford Foundation international fund of the Centre for Environmental Studies, and at Laxenburg through the base grant from national academies of sciences. Throughout the project the Reading and Laxenburg research teams would maintain close contact in order to ensure standardisation and comparability.

Over a two-year period, work on the European study proceeded according to plan, through the parallel teams in Reading and Laxenburg. At Reading, Hall was assisted by research officers Dennis Hay, Caroline Young (who left the team in August 1976), Richard Linton (September 1976–November 1978) and Roger Sammons (December 1978–May 1979). At Laxenburg, Niles Hansen was assisted by Koren Sherrill. At the end of the parallel studies, in July–August 1977, Hay and then Hall joined Hansen and Sherrill to work together on marrying the data and analysing the results; Glickman and Kawashima, finalising the first stage of their work on the Japanese urban system, worked alongside them at Laxenburg during this period. Hansen and Sherrill then returned to their academic posts at Austin; Hansen's place was taken by Kawashima, working in the Human Settlements Systems Research Task at IIASA under the general direction of Andrei Rogers. Meanwhile, the Reading team had moved on to a second stage of the work, involving disaggregation of employment data for a sample of the European urban systems. This work, funded by the British Social Science Research Council, was completed in May 1979 and forms the basis of Chapter 6 of this book.

As will be explained more fully in Chapter 3, the Reading–Laxenburg analysis could be extended only to western and central Europe. It embraces Norway, Sweden and Denmark (but not Finland); Great Britain and Ireland; the Netherlands, Belgium and Luxembourg; France; Spain and Portugal; Italy; and certain minor countries (the Isle of Man, Channel Islands, Liechtenstein, Monaco, Gibraltar, Malta, Andorra, San Marino and the Vatican City) which have been incorporated in the data for the countries which adjoin or envelop them. In central Europe it embraces Switzerland, Federal Germany and Austria. Great efforts were made by the Laxenburg team to involve the cooperation of government statisticians and university scientists from eastern Europe. These finally resulted in a number of studies from eastern Europe – from Poland, Hungary, Romania, Czechoslovakia and the DDR – that use broadly similar concepts (Kawashima 1980). But, because the eastern European data base was not available during the timetable of this study, the analysis here does not include it.

Some Acknowledgements

So many acknowledgements are due that it is difficult to know where to begin. Logically, the first is to Eiichi Isomura and his colleagues at the Japan Center for Area Development Research, whose initiative and hospitality at the Tokyo seminar provided the catalyst for the start of the research. Second, thanks are due to the funding bodies whose generosity and understanding made the work possible: to the Ford Foundation (and especially to William Pendleton), to the Centre for Environmental Studies, to the Social Science Research Council of Great Britain and to the European Cultural Foundation who provided funds for the follow-up study at the University of Reading, partially reported in this volume, and to the International Institute for Applied Systems Analysis, for their hospitality, funding and generous aid with computing facilities.

Our greatest intellectual debt is to our many international scientific collaborators, to whom this work is dedicated. First, to the group of co-workers on the parallel studies, who have provided constant guidance and inspiration: Brian Berry, Norman Glickman and Tatsuhiko Kawashima. And in particular, because they are not immediately responsible for this report but provided an essential part of the methodology and data input, we thank Niles Hansen and Koren Sherrill at the University of Texas at Austin. Harry Swain, during his period at IIASA, was another vital catalyst without whose energy and inspiration the work might have floundered.

Then, in particular, we owe a debt to a group of collaborators in Europe, who have been unstinting in their aid on questions of technical detail. Many of them attended the workshop at IIASA in October 1975, at which the study was launched. They, and others, have provided a vital input at many stages of the study. In particular we would mention Professor Gunnar Törnqvist of the University of Lund and Inger Nybrant of the Statistika Centralbyrån, Sweden; Professor Barry Garner of the University of New South Wales (formerly of the University of Århus) and Sven Illeris of the National Agency for Physical Planning in Copenhagen, Denmark; Roy Drewett and Nigel Spence of the London School of Economics and M. Smart of the Department of Employment in Britain; Michael Bannon and Tony Parker of University College, Dublin, Garrett Carton of Donegal County Council, R. T. Herron and officials of the Central Statistical Office of the Republic of Ireland; Drs F. S. Schuurmans of the Geografisch Instituut, Rijksuniversiteit, Groningen and H. J. Raets, C. B. S. Voorburg, in the Netherlands; W. Van Waelvelde of the Institut National de Statistique, Brussels, Professor Dr H. Van der Haegen of the Katholieke Universiteit te Leuven, for Belgium; G. Als of STATEC, in Luxembourg; Professor Claude Chaline of the Université de Paris VII, J. G. Charré and L. M. Coyaud of the Centre de Recherche d'Urbanisme, Mme. Plas of INSEE, Paris, and a whole series of regional administrators of INSEE who provided much technical assistance; Dr Pierluigi Raule, Sr D. Fernando Fernandez Cavada, Luis-Felipe Alonso, Carlos Ferrán and his colleagues in the Ferrán–Mangada partnership and Juan Angelet Cladellas in Spain; Victor Pessoa, Mrs Maria Ceu Esteves (Mrs Pessoa) and Jose Henriques da Silva of the Centro de Estudos de Planeamento, Lisbon, Portugal; Paolo Costa and Umberto Piasentsin of the University of Venice and Dr S. Cafiero of SVIMEZ in Italy. In central Europe, our colleagues at IIASA received equally generous and powerful aid from Hellmut Ringli and A. Rossi of the Institut für Orts-, Regional- und Landesplanung (ORL) in the Eidgenössische Technische Hochschule, Zürich, and Walter Zust of the ORL, in Switzerland; from Herr Frosch and his associates of the Statistisches Bundesamt, in Wiesbaden, Federal Republic of Germany; and from R. Gisser of the Österreichisches Statistisches Zentralamt and H. Palme of the Interdisziplinäres Institut für Raumordnung, Hochschule für Welthandel, Wien, in Austria. Needless to say, though these collaborators were unstinting in providing advice – and, not infrequently, making generously available their own data banks – they are in no way responsible for any errors and omissions that may have crept into our analysis.

Lastly, we would want to thank a veritable army of technical collaborators. Caroline Young was our colleague for the first year of the Reading study and did much of the early definitional work on Great Britain and Belgium. Magdalena Hall was responsible for much of the detailed definitional work on France. Graham Chapman powerfully helped with the difficult task of interpreting Italian documents. Above all, Joy Liddell was a faithful and always accurate coder of masses of data.

The computing services of the University of Reading deserve special thanks. Tony Hewitt, then Computer Manager, Annette Haworth and Alan Thornton played a large part in setting up the basic data management system and also in assisting with the difficult task of translating IIASA files into Reading language. Equally, computer staff at IIASA worked heroically in July–August 1977 to translate Reading files into IIASA-compatible systems and then to process quite inordinate quantities of data. We would especially thank Bernhard Schweeger who aided in interpreting German and Austrian data used in earlier stages of the IIASA study. Above all, this work would never have been completed without the quiet efficiency and capability of Piotr Findeisen, who was responsible for creating the basic analytical programmes at Laxenburg. During summer 1977 Roger Sammons played a vital role in preparing computer output at Reading. A similarly crucial function was performed by Richard Linton, who joined the team at Reading in October 1977 and supervised the re-processing of the data there, as well as playing an important role in the follow-up study reported in Chapter 6. Thanks are also due to Carmen Hass-Klau, Walter Matznetter, Linda Mills, Linda Peake, Alan Ingram, Tina Ayres and Jenny Sitlington who assisted at various times with data collection or preparation. Additionally, John

Goddard and Mike Coombs of the University of Newcastle-upon-Tyne were kind enough to comment on earlier versions of the manuscript.

The maps were drawn by Sheila Dance and Brian Rogers of the University of Reading, Mrs M. Baker and Kathleen King. Their quality speaks for itself. And, finally, we are indebted to Mrs Pam Tovee who has spent many hours typing this manuscript, ably assisted by Bobbie Coussens and Andy Jackman.

A Brief Outline of the Book

The structure of this book is exceedingly simple. It consists of seven chapters. Chapters 1 and 2 are preliminary: Chapter 1 is an introductory overview of the current state-of-the-art in world urban systems research with particular reference to the studies which parallel and complement this present one and Chapter 2 succinctly sets out the objectives of the present book. Chapter 3 is a technical chapter, much or all of which may be skipped by a general reader; it discusses problems of area definition and of data availability and comparison for each of the European countries in the study. Chapters 4 and 5 present the main aspects of growth and change for Europe and its constituent parts and also examine the geographical patterns in more detail with the aid of maps; Chapter 5 goes into greater depth, presenting the results of statistical regression analyses that try to explain the patterns of growth and change in terms of a large number of possible explanatory variables. Then, Chapter 6 makes a more detailed analysis of the economic structure of selected urban systems. Lastly, Chapter 7 tries to bring together some of the more important general conclusions of the European urban systems study.

Logically, studies like this can never end. Pending some holocaust that sends us all back to the woods, urban systems in Europe will continue to evolve, thus requiring further analysis. Our academic colleagues may question the fact that this book appears nearly a decade after the end of the main time-span that is analysed. That, unfortunately, is inevitable: even in a computer age national Censuses take time to process, as witness the fact that some tabulations were not available when we were making our study. To parallel recent American work that has used post-1970 population estimates, we have supplemented the main analysis by a small comparison of trends between 1970 and 1975 based on annual estimates that are available from the Census and national statistical offices of some of the fifteen nations in our study.

The Working Output

Throughout the project, both the Reading and Laxenburg units communicated with each other – and with other members of the international scientific community – through the publication of working papers. They are listed in the Bibliography at the end of this book. Apart from two preliminary papers produced by IIASA before the study proper began, all are working output of the research. Thirteen papers – eleven from Reading, two from Laxenburg – describe, for each of the countries examined, the problems of data availability and of comparable area definition. They give full details of the composition of the areas used in the study. Though the essential details of methodology are summarised in Chapter 3, serious research workers may well wish to acquire a set of these working papers.

Additionally, at a concluding workshop held at Laxenburg in October 1978, papers were presented both by the Reading–IIASA team members and by co-operating East European scholars, as well as by other international experts. These papers, collected in the volume by Kawashima (1980), form an essential companion to the present book.

Peter Hall
Dennis Hay
Reading, May 1979

Chapter 1

World Urbanisation and Urban Systems: a State-of-the-Art Review

Europe did not invent cities, nor urban civilisation. Yet it was the continent that first experienced urbanisation *en masse*, and it was the first continent to develop a true system of cities. The Greeks introduced cities to Europe from their birthplace in the Middle East; the Romans, in the interests of territorial power, created the first continent-wide system of cities. That system almost – but not quite – faded during the Dark Ages: the period that Henri Pirenne described as one of an economy without markets. But soon the needs of defence and administration and trade again demanded towns, and by the end of the Middle Ages Europe had an even wider, more fully articulated urban system. Only in the far peripheries – of highland Scotland, of western Ireland, of northern Scandinavia – was this system fragmentary. Elsewhere, on the great trade routes that joined the oceans and seas across the fertile land basins, the cities that evolved then have provided the basis of the system we still recognise today.

One reason for this continuity is simple inertia. Towns are seldom located capriciously; their position reflects certain immutable facts of physical geography. Even if certain of their locational advantages weaken over time, this is seldom catastrophic enough to justify mass removal. There are, of course, exceptions: towns that died because nearby sites proved more conveniently located (as Roman Silchester was replaced by medieval Reading), towns that lost their function because of physical change (for instance, silting-up of the port of Bruges), cities that waxed or waned with the fortunes of empire (Naples, Vienna). But, for every one of these, there are a dozen cases of pure continuity. Many of the Roman cities of Europe are still among the high points of the urban hierarchy: London, Paris, Cologne, Rome itself. And hundreds of great medieval trading cities still perform the same functions for their rural hinterlands.

There is however a second, special reason. When the industrial revolution came to Europe in the nineteenth century, in general it created no fundamental break in locational patterns with the past. There were of course exceptions: in Britain coalfield areas like South Wales, Durham and Lancashire towns spawned almost overnight, and a century later there were similar urban creations in the German Ruhrgebiet and in Silesia. But in general, because (apart from Britain) the industry came after the establishment of a railway net, it located in the existing cities which logically became the main nodes of that network. So the principle of continuity persisted, and cities simply moved up – or, more rarely, down – the urban size hierarchy.

That principle has continued to operate down to the present day. Since 1945, indeed, it has been powerfully reinforced by two main events. The first, over a long period since World War II, has been a birth-rate remarkably high by the standards of the 1920s and 1930s (and now, by the standards of the 1970s). The period from 1950 to 1970, in most European countries, was one of buoyant natural increase of population, as Table 1.1 shows. The second was a very high rate of migration from the countryside to the cities – a product partly of the natural increase just mentioned, but more importantly of the rationalisation of land-holdings and agricultural methods that took place in most continental European countries during the 1950s and 1960s, coupled with the rapid growth of industrial demand for labour. So Europe, in the post-World War II period, has become if anything even more of an urban continent than before.

Table 1.1   Total and natural increase of population in selected European countries

	Total increase per cent per year				Natural increase per cent per year			
	1935	*1950*	*1960*	*1974*	*1935*	*1950*	*1960*	*1974*
Belgium	0.30	0.29	0.54	0.41	0.20	0.44	0.40	0.07
Denmark	0.74	0.97	0.75	0.60	0.72	0.94	0.70	0.40
France	−0.75	0.81	0.99	0.73	−0.05	0.78	0.66	0.48
West Germany	0.89	1.61	1.11	0,11	2.69	0.44	0.63	−0.16
Italy	0.87	0.64	0.63	0.84	0.93	0.98	0.88	0.61
Netherlands	1.06	1.59	1.18	0.74	1.16	1.52	1.36	0.58
Norway	0.58	0.96	0.84	0.76	0.48	1.00	0.82	0.50
Sweden	0.37	0.83	0.35	0.25	0.28	0.64	0.37	0.28
Switzerland	0.34	1.19	2.12	0.78	0.38	0.80	0.70	0.44
United Kingdom	0.58	0.58	0.73	0.09	0.31	0.44	0.60	0.11

Source: Hall (1977), based on UN Demographic Yearbook.

Just how urban, may be judged from official United Nations figures. The United Nations' *Demographic Yearbook* shows that at the last main Census date in most countries – 1970–1 – almost everywhere in western and central Europe between 70 and 90 per cent of the population was recorded as living in urban areas. (The percentages were 70 per cent in France, 77 per cent in West Germany, 78 per cent in the Netherlands and Britain, 81 per cent in Sweden and 87 per cent in Belgium [United Nations 1976].) In western Europe as a whole in

1969, according to Kingsley Davis of the University of California, 73 per cent of the population lived in urban areas; in northern Europe the figure was 75 per cent, in southern Europe 51 per cent and in eastern Europe 55 per cent (Davis 1969). In the rest of the world, only Japan, North America and Australasia have figures similar to those of western and northern Europe.

But, as urban analysts know, such comparisons are suspect. They depend on what Census statisticians define to be urban areas and urban population, and that can differ very radically from one country to another. (It is difficult to believe, for instance, that in 1970 Sweden recorded its population as 82 per cent urban, whereas the corresponding figure for neighbouring Norway was only 42 per cent) (United Nations 1976). Therefore, it was critical to impose uniform definitions based on uniform criteria. Kingsley Davis and his colleagues were among the first to try to do this, in studies published in 1959 and 1969; but, for much of the world, the paucity of published statistical sources makes rigorous comparison difficult.

In the more highly developed and highly industrialised countries, with good statistical services, it is much easier. So it is not surprising that in recent years, much work has been done on the delimitation and analysis of urban systems. As a preliminary to the account of the present study, it is important to present briefly this work, its research methods and its main conclusions.

Some Basic Concepts

First, some elementary distinctions are in order. The term *urbanisation* is ambiguous, but will be taken here to refer to a *state* of urban development; in contrast, the term *urban growth* will be taken to refer to a *process* of urban change. But both these words can be interpreted in at least three different ways, according to the definition of the root word *urban*; and these definitions tend to diverge over time.

The first of these is a *physical* meaning. That which is urban looks like a town: it has large numbers of buildings close together; they are functionally differentiated, with some used for residence, some for work, some for shopping, some for recreation; there is relatively little land that is not built on, and this land is specifically dedicated to recreation of either a public or private nature. The second meaning is a *functional* one. That which is urban functions like a town: its economic functions are manufacturing and the provision of services; the social functions are intercommunication and interaction on a large scale (Hall *et al.* 1973, p. 42). The third definition is *political* or *administrative*. That which is urban is governed as a town: it has its own city or town council; this may have different powers and responsibilities from other local administrations.

In the Middle Ages and even well into the nineteenth century, these definitions were for the most part reasonably coincident. But in the twentieth century, they have become more and more divergent. First, physical urban growth lapped beyond the administrative city boundaries, into physically contiguous suburbs which might however not be incorporated into the city. Then, more and more people began to live in a way that was functionally urban – in terms of the economic functions they performed and the social relationships they made – even though they might live in settlements that were physically not urban, such as villages or even isolated houses in the countryside. Indeed, in modern advanced industrial societies such as the countries of western Europe, virtually the whole population may become functionally urban, in the sense that it performs economic functions that are not related to the land, and in the sense that its way of life (its dwelling unit, its range and source of foods and household goods, its use of time and in particular of leisure time) is identical.

Unfortunately, in most countries official definitions of 'urban' and of 'urbanisation' are still based *faute de mieux* on administrative criteria which may bear little relationship to physical or functional reality; and the United Nations figures, which are based on these national definitions, are of little use for international comparative purposes. (For instance: their figures for 'urban agglomerations' for the United States are based on *Standard Metropolitan Statistical Areas*, a functional definition, but in Great Britain on *Conurbations*, a physical definition.) The problem therefore remains: how to produce one or more definitions, based on consistent criteria, that can be employed to reorder the very varied data bases of different countries and so produce some standard for internationa comparison?

Most attempts at standardisation so far have relied either on physical criteria or on functional ones. Physical definitions tend to be based either on analysis of land use from maps or air photographs or satellite imagery, or on some minimal density of residential population as a proxy for concentration of buildings. The British *conurbations* are an example of the first method, the American *Urbanized Areas* of the second. Because Census data are readily available and need less painstaking analysis than land use data, the second method has usually been employed – as in the agglomerations defined on physical–morphological criteria in the Dutch 1960 Census (Schmitz 1966). The United Nations standard for the definition of agglomerations, which used a criterion of less than 200-metre spacing between buildings, does however require land-use analysis and is now employed by a number of west European countries (Hall, Hay and Sammons 1979).

Functional definitions tend to follow the lead set by the United States Bureau of the Census, which has defined Standard Metropolitan Areas – latterly Standard Metropolitan Statistical Areas – since 1940 (Shyrock 1957; United States: Bureau of the Budget 1964). Except in New England the SMSA is built up from counties, and these must satisfy two criteria. First, there must be a city of a specified population, called a central city; the county containing this is called the central county. Then, contiguous counties are added which have metropolitan character and which also exhibit specific social or economic metropolitan integration with the central county or city. The most important of these criteria are minimum population of the central core city (usually 50 000), minimum non-agricultural labour force (75 per cent of total employment in the contiguous counties), minimum population density (150 persons per square mile in contiguous counties) and minimum commuting levels to the central city (15 per cent of workers resident in contiguous counties). Contiguous counties satisfying the criteria are then added to the central county, to constitute the SMSA. The boundaries are revised at each Census, and SMSA's may be added or (occasionally) dropped. In their totality, SMSA's by no means exhaust the territory of the continental United States (see Fig. 1.1).

The *Daily Urban System* – a term first coined by C. A. Doxiadis in 1967 (Berry 1973, I, II) – is slightly different. As adopted by Brian Berry for his exhaustive analysis of 1960–70 changes in the American system (Berry 1973), and as then adopted by the Bureau of Economic Analysis (BEA), it tends to extend to the farthest limits of daily commuting – and not infrequently beyond – to include the most likely prospective commuting areas within its limits. Thus the 171 Daily Urban Systems of the Berry–BEA scheme completely exhaust the territory of the coterminous, continental United States (Fig. 1.2); and each has a high degree of closure with regard to job and housing markets. In many cases the DUS's are based on SMSA's, but in most of the more heavily urbanised parts of the country a number of SMSA's have been aggregated into one DUS because of the high degree of connectivity between them. And, in the more rural areas, non-metropolitan cities have been used as the basis for delimiting DUS's, provided that they serve an area of at least 200 000 people and function as a wholesale trade centre for the surrounding area.

Thus both the SMSA's and the DUS's have similarities: both depend on some concept of central attractors or cores which form the heart of each unit, both depend on analysis of daily flows of people to and from these central cores (usually as commuters), and both may also employ other criteria such as character of employment or means of dissemination of media information. The difference is that the older SMSA concept is more firmly based on the traditional concept of core and surrounding suburban ring; the Daily Urban Systems are based on a more complex notion of closure within a space-economy where increasingly a core–ring distinction is seen as meaningless. Indeed, Berry's analyses (Berry 1970, 1973) suggest that growth in the American urban system has increasingly transferred itself to the extreme periphery, farthest from the metropolitan cores – and that these cores now threaten to become the declining parts of a system that has neatly reversed the traditional urban patterns of a generation ago.

Berry's major study (Berry 1973) thus focuses on a system of cities, arranged in a hierarchy according to the functions performed by each, and each having an area of influence (or urban field) around it. For the period 1960–70, he concludes that this system demonstrated quite striking variations in growth patterns. The median growth rate increased with size of DUS to a threshold of about one million population, then stabilising at about the national growth rate; this, Berry concluded, was consistent with the notion of self-generating growth above a threshold. Conversely, declining DUS's are disproportionately the smaller ones. Rather large DUS's – between 1 and 2.5 million – tend to include a quite high number with accelerated growth.

At least as important an explanation of differential growth is provided by

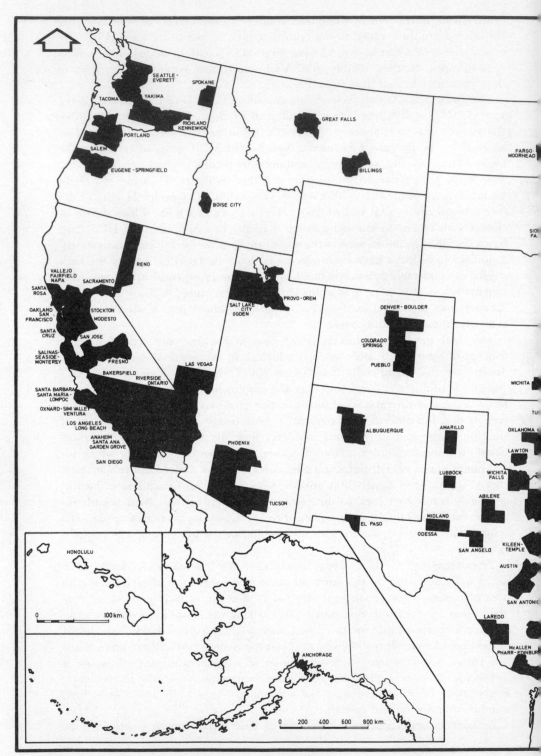

Fig. 1.1 USA: standard metropolitan statistical areas

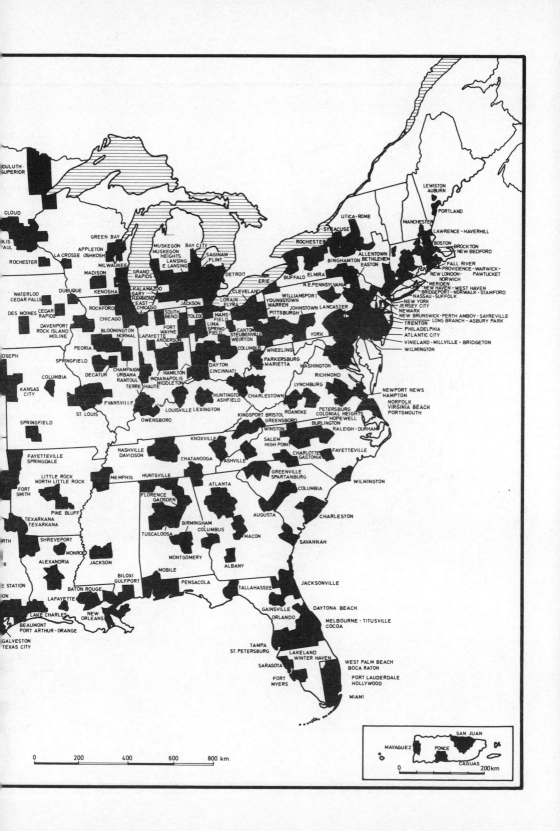

DULUTH-SUPERIOR

CLOUD

LIS-PAUL

ROCHESTER

WATERLOO
CEDAR FALLS

DES MOINES

OSEPH

KANSAS CITY

COLUMBIA

SPRINGFIELD

FAYETTEVILLE
SPRINGDALE

FORT SMITH

LITTLE ROCK
NORTH LITTLE ROCK

PINE BLUFF

TEXARKANA
TEXARKANA

SHREVEPORT

MONROE

RTH

ALEXANDRIA

JACKSON

R

E STATION

ON

LAFAYETTE

LAKE CHARLES

BEAUMONT
PORT ARTHUR-ORANGE

GALVESTON
TEXAS CITY

BATON ROUGE

NEW ORLEANS

BILOXI
GULFPORT

MOBILE

MONTGOMERY

PENSACOLA

ALBANY

TALLAHASSEE

GREEN BAY

APPLETON
LA CROSSE OSHKOSH

MILWAUKEE

MADISON

KENOSHA

DUBUQUE

CEDAR RAPIDS

DAVENPORT
ROCK ISLAND
MOLINE

PEORIA

SPRINGFIELD

DECATUR

ST. LOUIS

CHICAGO

ROCKFORD

BLOOMINGTON
NORMAL

CHAMPAIGN
URBANA
RANTOUL

TERRE HAUTE

EVANSVILLE

MUSKEGON
HEIGHTS
LANSING
E.LANSING

GRAND
RAPIDS

KALAMAZOO

GARY
HAMMOND
EAST
CHICAGO

LAFAYETTE

INDIANAPOLIS
MIDDLETON

SOUTH
BEND

FORT
WAYNE

ANDERSON

HAMILTON

LOUISVILLE LEXINGTON

OWENSBORO

BAY CITY

SAGINAW
FLINT

DETROIT

JACKSON

TOLEDO

LIMA
SPRING-
FIELD

MANS-
FIELD

DAYTON
CINCINNATI

MACON

ERIE

CLEVELAND

LORAIN
ELYRA

CANTON
STEUBENVILLE
WEIRTON

COLUMBUS

WHEELING

PARKERSBURG
MARIETTA

HUNTINGTON
ASHFIELD

CHARLESTOWN

KINGSPORT BRISTOL

GREENSBORO

WINSTON

SALEM
HIGH POINT

YOUNGSTOWN
WARREN

PITTSBURGH

BUFFALO ELMIRA

N.E.PENNSYLVANIA

WILLIAMSPORT

JOHNSTOWN LANCASTER

YORK

WASHINGTON

RICHMOND

LYNCHBURG

ROANOKE

PETERSBURG
COLONIAL HEIGHTS
HOPEWELL

BURLINGTON

RALEIGH-DURHAM

NEWPORT NEWS
HAMPTON

NORFOLK
VIRGINIA BEACH
PORTSMOUTH

ROCHESTER

SYRACUSE

UTICA-ROME

MANCHESTER

LEWISTON
AUBURN

PORTLAND

LAWRENCE-HAVERHILL

BOSTON
BROCKTON
NEW BEDFORD

ALLENTOWN
BINGHAMTON BETHLEHEM
EASTON

FALL RIVER
PROVIDENCE-WARWICK-
NEW LONDON-   PAWTUCKET
NORWICH
MERIDEN
NEW HAVEN-WEST HAVEN
BRIDGEPORT-NORWALK-STAMFORD
NASSAU-SUFFOLK

NEW YORK
JERSEY CITY
NEWARK
NEW BRUNSWICK-PERTH AMBOY-SAYREVILLE
LONG BRANCH-ASBURY PARK
TRENTON
PHILADELPHIA
ATLANTIC CITY
VINELAND-MILLVILLE-BRIDGETON
WILMINGTON

KNOXVILLE

NASHVILLE
DAVIDSON

CHATANOOGA

ASHVILLE

HUNTSVILLE

MEMPHIS

FLORENCE
GADSDEN

TUSCALOOSA

BIRMINGHAM

COLUMBUS

CHARLOTTE
GASTONIA

GREENVILLE
SPARTANBURG

COLUMBIA

AUGUSTA

FAYETTEVILLE

WILMINGTON

CHARLESTON

SAVANNAH

ATLANTA

JACKSONVILLE

GAINSVILLE

ORLANDO

DAYTONA BEACH

MELBOURNE-TITUSVILLE
COCOA

TAMPA
ST. PETERSBURG

LAKELAND
WINTER HAVEN

SARASOTA

FORT
MYERS

WEST PALM BEACH
BOCA RATON

FORT LAUDERDALE
HOLLYWOOD

MIAMI

0   200   400   600   800 km.

SAN JUAN

MAYAGUEZ

PONCE

CAGUAS

0   200km

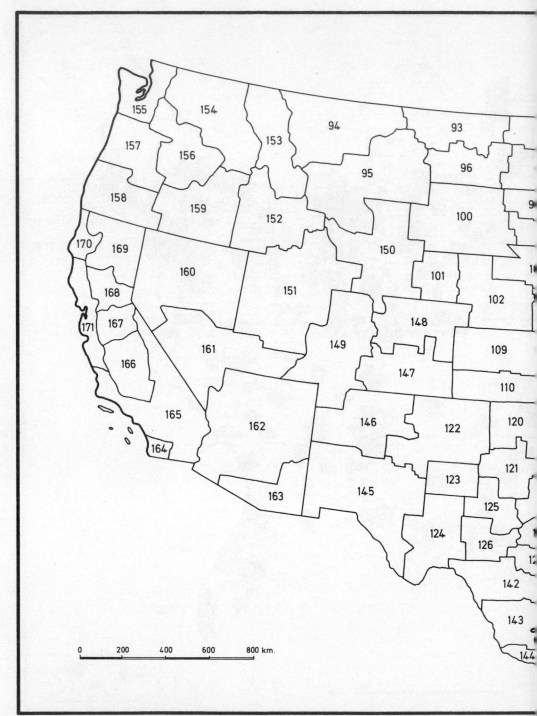

Fig. 1.2   USA: BEA economic areas

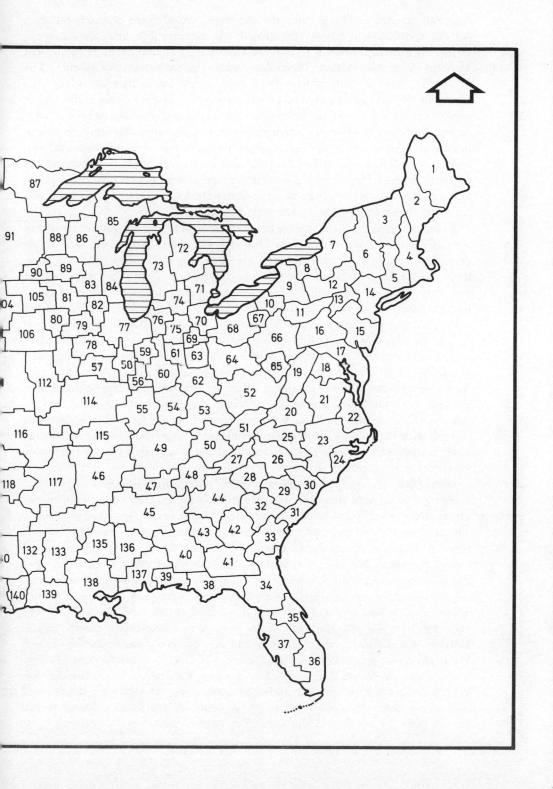

economic structure. The greater the earnings derived from primary activities such as agriculture, the lower the growth. As earnings from manufacturing increase, the growth rate tends to stabilise around the national average – consistent with the economist Wilbur Thompson's notion of an urban size ratchet. The greater the share of earnings from the tertiary sector, involving residentiary activities, the greater the population growth rate. One reason for this is the higher growth rate of many tertiary industries such as research and development, education, and other intellectual activities; another is migration for retirement, supporting a tertiary sector through transfer payments. In general, increased size and increased economic diversification tend to stabilise growth at around the national average. Small size plus primary specialisation usually means population decline. Conversely, the faster-growing DUS's in the 1–2.5 million range tended to depend on massive government spending.

As important as these differences between areas, though, are differences within them. Growth in the contemporary United States, Berry points out, is now self-generating within large metropolitan regions. Migration takes place between these regions, and also within them through dispersion towards the metropolitan periphery. Average population densities are dropping; many of the great cities, that grew in a previous era of industrial urbanism, are now losing people: of the twenty-one cities with more than half a million people in 1960, fifteen lost people in the following decade. New growth – industrial, commercial and residential – is now concentrated not here, but in the suburban and exurban parts of Daily Urban Systems. The reasons, Berry suggests, are social rather than economic; they arise from the mobility of Americans, from their desire to express themselves through work and status, especially through the quality of the home and its surrounding environment. Thus suburbia develops in the form of 'homogeneous niches', with high-status zones in environmentally superior areas, middle-status zones nestling near them, and low-status residents relegated to the least desirable areas (Berry 1973, pp. 17–40).

Since 1970, the concluding point of Berry's 1973 analysis, there is powerful evidence that some of these trends – particularly the centrifugal outward movement – have actually intensified, to introduce a new era in American urbanism. The analyses by Sternlieb and Hughes (1975, 1977) are based on the more traditional SMSA boundaries, using specially processed Census data for the period 1970–4 (or 1975). Sternlieb and Hughes conclude that there are now three central features of American urban change: an accelerating regional shift, an emerging metropolitan–non-metropolitan dynamic and expanding intra-metropolitan differentials. A new regional momentum, which has developed over the period 1960–75, is taking growth away from the older metropolitan centres of the North-east and North-central states to the new growth areas of the South and West. The great industrial belt from Boston to St Louis – which Wilbur Thompson calls the 'American Ruhr' – has begun a long-term period of relative decline. Within this zone, between 1960 and 1975 there was a growth in employment of only 26 per cent – as against nearly 47 per cent nationally and close on 70 per cent in both the South and the West. Part of the reason here was the sluggish growth in manufacturing jobs over this period – which turned into an actual decline, nationally, in the period 1970–5; another was that this loss was concentrated in the older industrial areas, while the South and West actually recorded modest gains. But behind this, as Berry also earlier stressed, are powerful forces impelling people from the older, higher density environments of the East towards a more liberated, congenial life-style in pristine or high-amentiy areas.

Reinforcing these great regional shifts was another remarkable change: the flight from the older central cities was in turn becoming a flight from larger industrial urban areas. After 1970, the twenty largest metropolitan areas of the United States remained almost stagnant in population (with a 0.3 per cent annual growth), while smaller metropolitan areas came to dominate the growth pattern (with 1.5 per cent annually), challenged in turn by non-metropolitan America which was growing by no less than 1.3 per cent per year. The large metropolitan areas were by then areas of massive out-migration, while the non-metropolitan areas were receiving an equally massive inflow. The losses from the bigger urban areas are concentrated in the North-east and North-central states; here, the non-metropolitan areas were growing fastest. In the South and West, in contrast, the major gainers were the smaller metropolitan areas. The halt to large metropolitan growth is particularly drastic for the North-west, because 60 per cent of its people live in only four such areas. Every one of the major metropolises in the North-east and North-central regions lost through migration after 1970; yet elsewhere, Houston, Miami and Atlanta continued to make substantial migrant gains. In this regard, oddly, the West behaved like the East; Los Angeles and Seattle experienced out-migration, San Francisco only modest in-migration.

Sternlieb and Hughes conclude that several forces combine to explain the new phenomenon of non-metropolitan growth. Suburban growth has now rippled out beyond metropolitan boundaries. The historic industrial metropolis may now be on the point of decline. But new foci of post-industrial urban growth may be taking their place – especially in the dynamic 'sunbelt' of the South and West. In the older areas, the infrastructure itself may be becoming redundant; we may be starting to witness the dismantling of the traditional industrial base.

This second trend relates closely to the third: that of the increasing differentials within metropolitan areas. From 1970, for the first time, the central cities of SMSA's lost population – but all this decline was concentrated in the largest metropolitan areas. The suburban rings, in contrast, were everywhere still growing. Blacks are taking the place of whites in the cities as the latter move out, but they do not make up in numbers for the loss. High-income residents tend to leave and their place is taken – if at all – by lower-income in-migrants, with a resultant massive loss in purchasing power: $29.6bn in the years 1970–4 alone. Small wonder that the authors conclude: 'The sheer magnitude of regional and metropolitan shifts clearly renders obsolete much of our political wisdom and folkway.' (Sternlieb and Hughes 1977, p. 240.)

The broad trends revealed in the Sternlieb–Hughes analysis are amply confirmed in other studies using similar data (Berry and Gillard 1977; Berry in Berry

1976; Berry and Dahmann 1977; Beale 1977; Alonso 1978; McCarthy and Morrison 1977, 1979). Between 1970 and 1975, movers out of metropolitan areas exceeded movers into them for the first time, reversing previous trends. Generally, despite this, metropolitan growth has continued due to natural increase plus foreign immigration; but natural increase was falling sharply, and in some areas, there was an actual population decline. Between 1970 and 1975, for the first time in this century, non-metropolitan growth in America exceeded metropolitan growth. Out of 259 metropolitan areas 42 suffered net decline – and they included some of the bigger ones, including New York, Philadelphia, Pittsburgh, Cleveland, Chicago, St Louis, Los Angeles–Long Beach and Seattle–Everett. Berry concludes: 'Thus, the process of population concentration that was the essence of urbanisation in the previous century of national growth appears to have ended' (Berry and Gillard 1977, p. 109). Popular preferences have been overwhelmingly for smaller places and lower densities, with richer environmental amenities; and they have won out. This has happened because of four new driving forces: the emergence of a nationally integrated society, in which movement is relatively easy; the emergence of a post-industrial economy; the rising cultural pluralism of the American public; and the increasing role of communications rather than transportation in locational choice. 'Many of the constraints that have limited locators to choices among metropolitan areas and places within them', Berry concludes, 'continue to be relaxed. The consequences can only be still further dispersion, still more widespread commuting fields, and still further changes in the nature of settlement in the United States.' (Berry and Gillard 1977, p. 126.)

This phenomenon forms one of the major demographic puzzles in the contemporary United States. For though some of the non-metropolitan increase represents a continuation of the 'wave' phenomenon – whereby metropolitan growth moves out first from central city to suburbs within SMSA's, and then out of SMSA's altogether, to adjacent non-metropolitan counties – some certainly does not (Table 1.2). Truly remote non-metropolitan areas, outside SMSA commuter range and containing no big cities, are among the fastest growers. Thus it is not even possible to ascribe the growth to 'population centralisation', observable in the 1960s, whereby migration from the metropolitan areas passed into free-standing non-metropolitan cities. Careful statistical work, by Beale (1977) and by McCarthy and Morrison (1977, 1979), fails to pinpoint any one factor, or group of factors, as a principal explanation of non-metropolitan increase.

Traditionally important explanations, like the presence of urban centres or reliance on manufacturing or government, are less important for growth in the 1970s than in the 1960s. Reliance on recreation and retirement is more important; so are southern location, lack of towns – and, in general, low *per capita* income. So people were failing to follow the rules: they were migrating down the income gradient towards the least urbanised, most remote, poorest places. Perhaps they were looking for jobs at any cost. Perhaps they were retreating from the economic problems of life in the big city during a recession. Perhaps they were seeking psychic income in the form of scenery and low pollution levels, even

Table 1.2   United States population growth

	Annual population change rate		Annual migration change rate	
	1960–70	1970–5	1960–70	1970–5
Standard Metropolitan Statistical Areas (SMSA's)	1.6	0.8	0.5	0.1
Over 1 million	1.6	0.5	0.6	−0.2
500 000–1 million	1.5	1.0	0.4	0.3
250 000–500 000	1.4	1.3	0.2	0.5
Under 250 000	1.4	1.5	0.2	0.7
Non-metropolitan counties percentage commuting to SMSA's	0.4	1.2	−0.5	0.6
More than 20	0.9	1.8	0.1	1.3
10–19	0.7	1.3	−0.1	0.8
3–9	0.5	1.2	−0.4	0.6
Fewer than 3	0.2	1.1	−0.8	0.5
Adjacent to SMSA's	0.7	1.3	−0.3	0.8
Non-adjacent to SMSA's	0.1	1.1	−0.9	0.5
Purely rural[a]	−0.4	1.3	−1.2	0.9
United States total	1.3	0.9	0.2	0.2

Note: [a]   Containing no town of 2500 or more people.
Sources: Beale (1977), Gordon in Kawashima (1980).

at the expense of low *per capita* income; perhaps, then, jobs are created in the wake of their arrival. But, as McCarthy and Morrison (1979, pp. 46–7) conclude:

> the striking changes in the geography of development in the 1970s outpace our understanding of their nature, causes, and current or impending problems. . . . We must admit to a great deal more honest uncertainty about what is happening in different localities, why and how it is happening, and the proper role of regional development programs from the perspective of local well-being and the national interest.

Meanwhile, the out-movement from the cities – an out-movement dominated by the rich, the white, the better educated and the more highly skilled – continues. There is one sign of a counter-trend: a process of inner city 'gentrification' associated with the remarkable growth, since 1970, of what the American Census calls primary individual households – that is, households consisting of people living alone or with other non-related people (Berry and Dahmann 1977; Kirwan 1979). But these same observers seem agreed that the process is a very limited one, restricted to a few places where the central city economy offers high-paying white-collar jobs to young workers (Morrison 1978). In other words, it may help revitalise Washington, Boston or San Francisco, but it is unlikely to do much for the bulk of America's stricken cities. And even in the favoured few, it can lead to the phenomenon of regeneration in some tracts and dereliction a few miles or blocks away.

We can sum up what can be called the American hypotheses on contemporary urbanisation in the following way: the process of deconcentration has taken on a new dimension since 1970. People (and presumably also jobs) are continuing to move in a wave-like motion from central cities to suburbs; to adjacent non-metropolitan counties; but in addition, there is now a movement to remote, sparsely populated and even poor rural areas. The South and West are particular beneficiaries of this process, but there even metropolitan areas – and in the West, even some central cities – show continued vitality, while in the older industrial areas of the North-east many metropolitan areas are in decline and central city out-migration is general. Subject to that regional qualification, in general, larger metropolitan areas and central cities are showing a greater propensity to decline than smaller ones (see Table 1.2). It appears then that the pattern of movement is from city to suburb, from urban to rural, from large to small city, and from North and East to South and West. No one knows for sure what is causing all this, but many experts seem to agree that at least some of it represents a movement in search of amenity and easy living, even at the expense of an obvious economic base and a good money income: truly, a post-industrial phenomenon.

Urban Change in Canada and Australia

No other nation has produced systematic analysis of urban growth and change on quite the American scale. For this there are a number of obvious reasons: fewer urban analysts, a less rich and manipulable data base, and probably also less consciousness of impending urban problems. Nevertheless, in some other advanced countries the scale and quality of work are quite remarkable. Canada is especially interesting, because its urban system is logically an extension northwards of the American one, and because many of the forces operating to shape it – particularly the individually-motivated society and the high level of communications technology – are almost identical. Yet there are differences: the greater stress on collective action and control, the relative lack of a racial problem in Canada's central cities, the bi-polar bases of Canadian nationhood.

In Canada as in the United States and other advanced industrial countries, there is a rapidly declining rate of national population growth – a product first of the decline of the birth-rate, second of a lower rate of in-migration. Especially because of the latter, 'the period of rapid urban growth in Canada appears to be nearing an end' (Bourne 1978, p. 13). And, associated with this, 'recent trends represent new and different paths of urbanization and thus provide the outline of an emerging urban reality which departs substantially from that in the past' (Bourne 1978, p. 5). Though Bourne admits that as yet Canadian data provide no firm evidence of widespread 'de-urbanization' on the American model, nevertheless he concludes that they do suggest important structural and social changes.

Among the twenty-four *Census Metropolitan Areas* (CMA's) with populations over 100 000 – themselves very similar to American SMSA's – almost one half were growing more slowly than the national average by the period 1971–6; two, Windsor and Sudbury, registered absolute though slight population declines. Of the eleven centres that grew most rapidly, eight were political capitals: the others were Calgary (based on oil), Kitchener–Waterloo (representing suburbanisation) and Vancouver (a regional centre of an amenity-rich region, but not the provincial capital because of an accident of history). The proportion of people living in the three biggest metropolitan areas was static – though in the Toronto case, this represents spreading over CMA boundaries. In terms of another framework for statistical analysis – the 125 urban-centred regions originally defined by Simmons (1974), which exhaust almost the whole territory and thus correspond to the Berry–BEA regions of the United States – it is clear that there is no simple association between size and growth either of a positive or a negative kind. Growth rates over 1971–6 were higher for the smallest such areas (50 000–100 000) and for the larger medium-sized ones (300 000–500 000) than for the smaller medium-sized centres or for the very largest centres (Table 1.3). Bourne concludes: 'In Canada at least regional and economic diversity produces highly variable growth rates . . . between cities of different sizes.' (Bourne 1978, p. 17.) Certainly, from his evidence, it would be unfair to conclude that de-urbanisation of an American kind has yet affected Canada. And some of the faster growing places – such as Oshawa, Guelph, Barrie and Kitchener – are around Toronto and seem to owe this growth to metropolitan expansion and de-concentration. Though the phenomenon recalls the American experience of the 1960s, it arises not so much from the deterioration and abandonment of the core metropolitan city, as from the opposite phenomenon of high costs and congestion within it. Indeed the largest centres – Toronto and Montreal – may well have been ex-

Table 1.3   Canada population growth

Total population (percentage) in	*1951*	*1961*	*1971*	*1976*
3 national metropolises	23.2	25.9	29.7	29.5
23 metropolitan areas	44.9	48.3	55.4	55.5
Growth rates		*1971–6*		
3 national metropolises		4.9		
8 major regional centres		8.4		
14 regional centres		3.7		
36 small regional centres		8.1		
64 local centres		5.1		
Total, urban regions		6.4		

Source: Bourne (1978).

tending their spheres of influence to envelop these sub-dominant centres (Bourne and Logan in Berry 1976, pp. 120–2).

These trends may reflect – but in turn reinforce – some persistent spatial inequalities in the Canadian economy (Bourne 1975, pp. 164–7). One of these is regional: the contrast between the urbanised regions and the rural peripheries (the Maritimes, eastern Quebec, the agricultural fringe of mid-Canada and the North). Another is between French- and English-speaking Canada; and, in terms of migration, it is evident that the two form largely self-contained systems (Bourne and Logan in Berry 1976, p. 128). Income levels may vary by as much as 100 per cent between provinces and regions; they are 50 per cent higher in larger metropolitan areas than in rural areas, and 30 per cent higher in larger than in smaller metropolitan areas. However, the rapid growth of the Toronto fringe may well be causing this differential to narrow.

In some critical respects, the Australian urban system resembles the Canadian. Both were set down in a negative physical environment, with large obstacles to settlement. Both were imposed colonially by an outside power, initially through a series of port cities. Both continued to have a dependent relationship with Britain for a long period, exporting primary produce to pay for imports of manufactured goods. But in Australia these features all tend to have been quite extreme, and to have persisted for longer periods. Indeed, as is generally known, the Australian urban system is still dominated by the great initial port cities that came to serve as regional centres and thus to inhibit the development of strong rival cities within their hinterlands (Bourne and Logan in Berry 1976, pp. 115–16). Political divisions helped this until the achievement of the Commonwealth in 1910, and probably even afterwards. When manufacturing industry began to develop, it logically did so in these same big cities. There is evidence that settlement systems with a high degree of concentration or primacy tend to remain, and in the Austrialian case the inertia is probably helped by the hierarchical structure of modern multinational enterprises (Bourne and Logan in Berry 1976, pp. 115–19).

As a result, in 1971 no less than 86 per cent of the population lived in urban centres (defined rather generously as places with over 1000 people); over 58 per cent lived in the six state capitals, 40 per cent in Sydney and Melbourne alone. During the 1950s and early 1960s the state capitals had grown persistently faster than the population as a whole, and the differential widened during the period. However, just as in Canada one of the most significant developments has been the heavy population growth in suburban and exurban extensions of the major urban areas, albeit usually outside the present metropolitan area boundaries. Thus in the area around Sydney, Gosford (50 miles north) and Blue Mountains (50 miles west) showed rapid growth during 1966–71; similarly with the Gold Coast area north of Brisbane, Wollongong near Sydney and Geelong near Melbourne. In Australia as in Canada, and in contradistinction to the United States, the reason for out-migration seems to be not deterioration of the large central core city, but rather congestion and high costs within it (Bourne and Logan in Berry 1976, pp. 120–1).

There is one other similarity with the Canadian urban system: Australian growth in the post-World War II period has been dominated by heavy in-migration, accounting for about three-quarters of the growth around Sydney (from 1947 to 1971) and in Melbourne for about four-fifths. Internal migration to these places, in comparison, was negligible. But both exported people to other, smaller state capitals – as well as to urban places just beyond their boundaries. Again as in Canada, Australian cities grew also through high natural growth – but this, again, has diminished in the late 1970s to around zero.

Australia and Canada, in summary, seem to share some features of the American growth pattern. Both are tending to export populations from larger to smaller urban places – albeit, especially in the Australian case, nearby. In Canada there is also a regional effect, with the more rapid growth of the prairie and western cities paralleling that of the cities of the American sunbelt. But neither yet manifests the problem of the stagnation and probable decline of large older urban areas. This undoubtedly reflects the relatively later development of the space-economy of the two countries and its still less mature evolution.

Recent Urban Developments in Japan

Until the late 1970s, though many interesting analyses were available of Japanese urban growth, there was no comprehensive and rigorous account comparable with those made in the United States. This has now been remedied, through detailed work by Norman Glickman in association with Tatsuhiko Kawashima (and, as already explained in the introduction to this report, in parallel with the European study described here). For this purpose, Glickman had to devise regions which were as far as possible comparable with those already developed in the United States and in course of being developed for the European study. Data difficulties prevent an exact correspondence, but Glickman's basic units of analysis – *Regional Economic Clusters* and *Standard Consolidated Areas* – correspond reasonably well to the American Standard Metropolitan Statistical Areas and Standard Consolidated Statistical Areas, respectively. There are eighty Regional Economic Clusters and thirty-three of them are grouped into eight Standard Consolidated Areas. They do not by any means exhaust the Japanese national territory, and they are not even contiguous in the so-called Tokaido megalopolis between Tokyo and Kobe (Fig. 1.3).

Glickman's main analysis (Glickman 1978, Chapter 2) covers the period of rapid Japanese growth, 1950–70. He shows that in this period the Japanese population has been highly concentrated into a limited number of city regions occupying a relatively small part of the total land area. In 1970 two-thirds of the population lived in the eighty REC's and a full 50 per cent lived in the eight SCA's. Further, this system of cities tended to centralise between 1950 and 1970 as the larger population centres, especially in the Tokyo and Osaka regions, grew faster than average. And many of these important growth centres were actually based on manufacturing. Within metropolitan areas, the 1950s saw a notable tendency to centralise in the central cities, though by the 1960s this had given way to relative decentralisation in which suburbs grew more rapidly than core

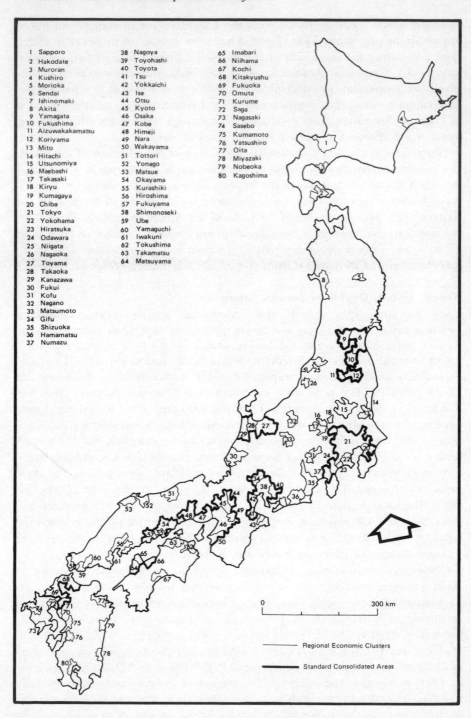

1	Sapporo	38	Nagoya	65	Imabari
2	Hakodate	39	Toyohashi	66	Niihama
3	Muroran	40	Toyota	67	Kochi
4	Kushiro	41	Tsu	68	Kitakyushu
5	Morioka	42	Yokkaichi	69	Fukuoka
6	Sendai	43	Ise	70	Omuta
7	Ishinomaki	44	Otsu	71	Kurume
8	Akita	45	Kyoto	72	Saga
9	Yamagata	46	Osaka	73	Nagasaki
10	Fukushima	47	Kobe	74	Sasebo
11	Aizuwakakamatsu	48	Himeji	75	Kumamoto
12	Koriyama	49	Nara	76	Yatsushiro
13	Mito	50	Wakayama	77	Oita
14	Hitachi	51	Tottori	78	Miyazaki
15	Utsunomiya	52	Yonago	79	Nobeoka
16	Maebashi	53	Matsue	80	Kagoshima
17	Takasaki	54	Okayama		
18	Kiryu	55	Kurashiki		
19	Kumagaya	56	Hiroshima		
20	Chiba	57	Fukuyama		
21	Tokyo	58	Shimonoseki		
22	Yokohama	59	Ube		
23	Hiratsuka	60	Yamaguchi		
24	Odawara	61	Iwakuni		
25	Niigata	62	Tokushima		
26	Nagaoka	63	Takamatsu		
27	Toyama	64	Matsuyama		
28	Takaoka				
29	Kanazawa				
30	Fukui				
31	Kofu				
32	Nagano				
33	Matsumoto				
34	Gifu				
35	Shizuoka				
36	Hamamatsu				
37	Numazu				

0 ————————————— 300 km

———— Regional Economic Clusters

━━━━ Standard Consolidated Areas

Fig. 1.3   Japan: regional economic clusters and standard consolidated areas

cities. Throughout, employment was found to be more strongly centralised in the core cities than were residences.

Glickman concluded that up until 1970, Japanese urban development was, in important respects, quite different from that occurring in other industrialised nations. Urban growth was much more rapid than in the United States or Britain, for instance. More of it was going into the largest city regions, each with several million people. Thus the dominance of Tokyo was increasing while that of New York or London was decreasing. Japan's urban regions were more spatially centralised than those of North America or Britain, and this degree of centralisation was actually increasing – or, at any rate, was before 1960 (Glickman 1978, Chapter 2). And the tendency for the big regions to grow was in spite of government policies aimed at dispersal (Glickman 1978, Chapter 6).

In a supplementary analysis (Glickman 1978, Chapter 3), Glickman uses the same spatial framework to study changes after 1970. Between 1970 and 1975 the Japanese urban system continued to centralise, with increasing concentration into a relatively small number of metropolitan areas. The REC's actually increased their share of the total national population, if only marginally, from 67.3 to 68.4 per cent. And the three biggest metropolitan areas – Tokyo, Osaka and Nagoya – experienced a combined growth rate in excess of the national rate. However, within the metropolitan areas there was by this time quite marked decentralisation: suburban growth was faster than central city growth, and so the central cities' share of the total REC population fell. Yet smaller metropolitan areas – with fewer than 800 000 people – were still centralising as a group, even in the 1970s.

A significant feature was that some of the fastest-growing REC's were in the fringes of major metropolitan regions – as in the Tokyo suburbs of Chiba and Yokohama, the Nagoya suburb of Toyota and the Kyoto suburban areas of Otsu and Nara. The rapid growth was restricted to a relatively few areas of the country, where SCA's were found. And within these consolidated areas, it was notable that the bigger central REC's (Tokyo and Osaka) grew more slowly than the suburban 'middle' ring. In fact the central cities of Tokyo and Osaka lost population in absolute terms during this period. For the first time, medium-sized metropolitan areas as a whole had higher growth rates than large ones – a striking change from the 1960s. There was an evening-out of growth rates between larger and smaller regions, and more growth outside the metropolitan core regions. Yet the most peripheral REC's still tended to demonstrate the slower growth rates, and non-metropolitan Japan continued to decline relatively to the metropolitan areas – a striking contrast with the contemporary USA (Glickman 1978, Chapter 3).

Nevertheless, Glickman found some limited evidence of convergence during this period between Japan and the nations of the industrialised west (Glickman 1978, Chapter 3). The slowing-down of the rate of increase in the largest centres, the absolute losses from the largest central cities, the growth of medium-sized cities near to major centres and even of medium-sized cities in more rural areas – all these trends suggest that increasingly, Japan will come to resemble North

America and Europe. It appears that in comparison with these other areas, Japan's urban evolution has simply been later. In the post-World War II period, it has gone through phases which were characteristic of other industrial nations in earlier decades of this century.

Using the same data base, Kawashima has shown that the regions that grew fastest during the decade 1960–70 expanded less rapidly during the overlapping period 1965–75. In particular, the Tokaido–Sanyo megalopolis area lost momentum, with a 30 per cent growth rate in the first period and a 26 per cent rate in the second. The lower-growing regions in the former period – such as the area of Honshu outside the Tokaido–Sanyo megalopolis, the Shikoku and Kyushu regions – increased their growth rates, even though in these last two cases they still tended to remain below the national average. Thus it can be

1	Aldershot	44	Halifax	84	St Albans
2	Ashford	45	Harlow	85	St Helens
3	Aylesbury	46	Harrogate	86	Salisbury
		47	Hartlepool	87	Scunthorpe
		48	Hastings	88	Sheffield
4	Barnsley	49	Hemel Hempstead	89	Shrewsbury
5	Barrow-in-Furness	50	Hereford	90	Slough
6	Basildon	51	High Wycombe	91	Southampton
7	Basingstoke	52	Huddersfield	92	Southend
8	Bath	53	Hull	93	Southport
9	Bedford			94	Stafford
10	Birmingham	54	Ipswich	95	Stevenage
11	Blackburn			96	Stoke
12	Blackpool	55	Kidderminster	97	Sunderland
13	Bolton	56	King's Lynn	98	Swansea
14	Bournemouth			99	Swindon
15	Brighton	57	Lancaster		
16	Bristol	58	Leeds	100	Taunton
17	Burnley	59	Leicester	101	Teesside
18	Burton on Trent	60	Leigh	102	Thurrock
19	Bury	61	Letchworth	103	Torquay
		62	Lincoln	104	Tunbridge Wells
20	Cambridge	63	Liverpool		
21	Canterbury	64	London	105	Wakefield
22	Cardiff	65	Luton	106	Walton & Weybridge
23	Carlisle			107	Warrington
24	Chatham	66	Maidstone	108	Watford
25	Chelmsford	67	Manchester	109	Wigan
26	Cheltenham	68	Mansfield	110	Woking
27	Chester	69	Milton Keynes	111	Worcester
28	Colchester			112	Workington
29	Corby	70	Newcastle	113	Worthing
30	Coventry	71	Newport		
31	Crawley	72	Northampton	114	Yeovil
32	Crewe	73	Norwich	115	York
		74	Nottingham		
33	Darlington			116	Aberdeen
34	Derby	75	Oxford	117	Ayr
35	Dewsbury			118	Dundee
36	Doncaster	76	Peterborough	119	Dunfermline
		77	Plymouth	120	Edinburgh
37	Eastbourne	78	Portsmouth	121	Falkirk
38	Ellesmere Port	79	Port Talbot	122	Glasgow
39	Exeter	80	Preston	123	Greenock
				124	Kilmarnock
40	Gloucester	81	Reading	125	Motherwell
41	Great Yarmouth	82	Rhondda	126	Perth
42	Grimsby	83	Rochdale		
43	Guildford				

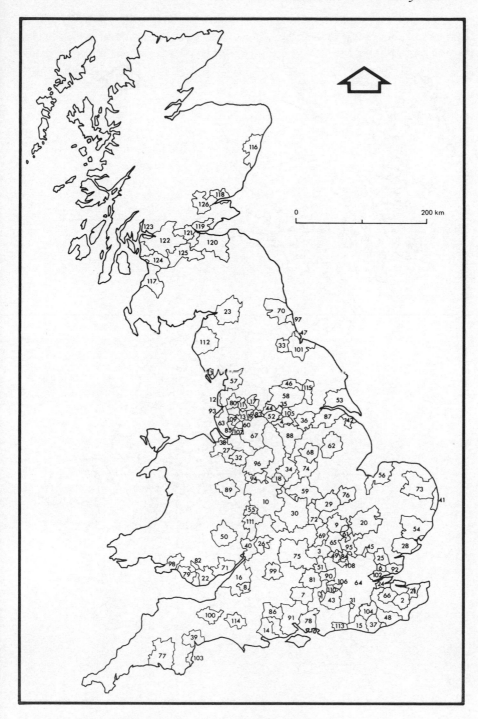

Fig. 1.4 Great Britain: standard metropolitan labour areas

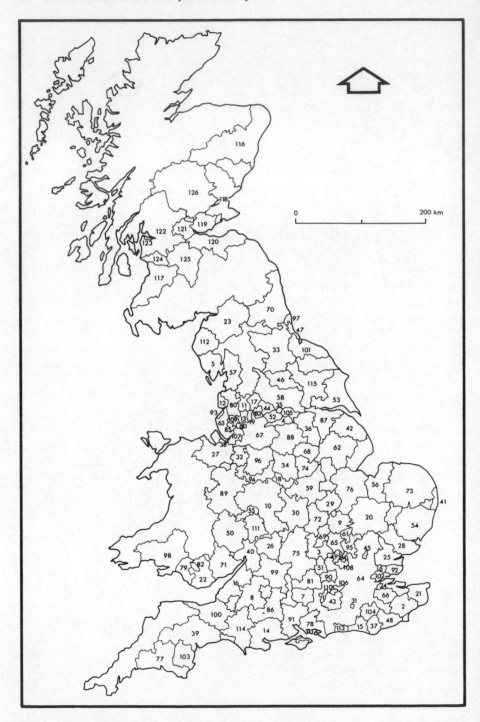

Fig. 1.5   Great Britain: metropolitan economic labour areas

concluded that the momentum of the major shifts in Japanese urban populations – from non-metropolitan to metropolitan areas, and from the Shikoku and Kyushu regions to the Honshu region – has gradually weakened during the period 1960–75 (Kawashima 1977, p. 30).

The European Experience: the Special Case of Britain

Within Europe, as will soon become evident, similar analyses present special problems. From what was said at the outset of this chapter, Europe's cities and urban regions need to be considered as a continent-wide system, comparable with those of North America. Yet the statistical base for this analysis is nationally fragmented, with very different geographical data collection units, with data that vary in amount and range and quality, and even with different Census dates. Therefore the task of analysis is a daunting one, and until this study – with the exception of Kingsley Davis's population statistics for the 1950s – it has not been attempted.

The studies that have so far been made, therefore, relate to individual countries. Perhaps the most important, if only because it provided a direct precursor to the present study, is that started in Britain at Political and Economic Planning from 1966 to 1971 – published in Hall *et al.* (1973) – and then continued at the London School of Economics (Drewett, Goddard and Spence in Berry 1976; Department of the Environment 1976). The significance is that a specific attempt was made to devise two sets of standard urban regions: one analogous with (and comparable with) the American Standard Metropolitan Statistical Areas, the other with the Daily Urban Systems of Brian Berry. Though problems of data availability and cost of analysis made it impossible to devise DUS's in quite the sophisticated way that Berry did, nevertheless the results are broadly comparable. Figs. 1.4 and 1.5 show the resulting systems of *Standard Metropolitan Labour Areas* (SMLA's) and *Metropolitan Economic Labour Areas* (MELA's) as re-defined by the LSE team on the basis of 1966 Census data. Like their American equivalents, the SMLA's do not exhaust the national territory while the MELA's (virtually) do.

There is however one important point of difference: the two sets of British regions have a one-to-one equivalence, in that they share common cores. This in turn reflects the fact that the cores were defined not simply in terms of whole central cities (though in most cases they are so defined) but rather in terms of employment concentration. Thus they are areas with a minimum number of 20 000 workers, or (in the case of urban agglomerations) groupings of areas each of which has at least five workers per acre (3200 workers per square mile). This, it is hoped, avoids one problem that seemed to arise in Kingsley Davis's earlier regionalisation: that the definitions of the larger central core cities were often arbitrary and inconsistent.

The broad conclusions reached by the PEP team from their analysis of the data (Hall *et al.* 1973) have been confirmed, enriched and updated in the ongoing LSE work: the summary here is based on that later work (Drewett, Goddard and Spence in Berry 1976). Of the 126 SMLA's, there are seven with over one million people (and one, London, with 8.8 million in 1971); there are 32 with over a quarter of a million; but the majority are small or medium-sized, with a median SMLA size of only 142 000. Overall, the 126 SMLA's apparently present a stable system of cities when presented in a rank-size graph; the shape of the curve alters very little between 1951 and 1971; yet within this apparently stable picture, many individual SMLA's changed their fortunes and their rankings. Drewett, Goddard and Spence show that SMLA's with a persistently low growth rate have been concentrated mainly in northern and northwest England, Yorkshire and Scotland. The broad mass of central and southern SMLA's have enjoyed higher than the national average rate during the period. Those SMLA's that have reversed their fortunes during the whole twenty-year period have a varied distribution; but one notable group, in Lancashire, moved from relatively slow to relatively fast growth, mainly due to local out-migration from the regional centres of Liverpool and Manchester.

Within the metropolitan areas, the dominant trend was one of accelerating population decentralisation initially (in the 1950s) into the rings of the SMLA's but then (in the 1960s) farther out into the outer rings of the MELA's. Thus the main thrust of population growth has been progressively farther from the major employment cores. During the 1950s the populations of the cores still increased, albeit more slowly than those of the suburban rings; but by the 1960s, this relative decline had been turned into an absolute loss. By this latter period, growth in the outermost MELA ring had jumped from 3 to 10 per cent – a rate nearly double the national average.

The picture for employment is more complicated. During the 1950s, it was actually concentrating in the urban core areas. The metropolitan rings also increased their shares, but very marginally; the outermost rings, and the non-metropolitan areas, lost jobs (but again, only marginally). By the 1960s, with relatively low national growth of employment compared with the 1950s, the core areas were tending to lose jobs while there was more growth in the metropolitan rings and more modest growth in the outermost rings. Overall, therefore, during the twenty-year period a process of centralisation of employment was reversed; jobs began to follow people in the outward suburbanising trend. Still, in 1971, jobs were much more concentrated in the cores than were residential populations (58.6 versus 47.4 per cent of national totals). But what may well be happening is a lagged phenomenon. Despite the recent decentralisation of jobs, the urban cores have become increasingly dependent for labour on the rest of the urban system.

The LSE researchers conclude that metropolitan growth is still characteristic: new metropolitan cores are emerging, older ones are expanding their hinterlands. The urban system is in a continual state of flux, with individual members gaining or losing places: medium and small cities tending to grow fastest, especially those based on new towns or otherwise influenced by planning. Within the metropolitan areas, population decentralisation has spilled out from suburban rings to the more distant exurban rings, which have only weak allegiances to central core areas. During the 1960s, employment too reversed its relative movement, and began to decentralise outward – thus following the population trend, with a certain time-lag effect (Drewett, Goddard and Spence in Berry 1976, p. 55).

The European Mainland

Necessarily, studies on the European continent tend to have been restricted to individual national frameworks. To this, there are few exceptions. Kingsley Davis's work has already been mentioned; it produced a framework of metropolitan areas, albeit based on concepts that were not always comparable, but it gave population figures only for the 1950/51 Census date and (from official estimates) for a date in the mid-1950s (usually 1955), so that no proper analysis of trends could be made from it. The PEP–LSE work in Britain, done after consultation with Davis, indicated that more detailed and rigorously applied criteria would in practice give rather different results. Another international comparison, by German scholars (Neundörfer 1964) uses regions that are much larger than either SMSA's or DUS's and are in no way comparable with them.

The national studies tend to have been based on concepts similar to the traditional American SMSA. This is true for instance of the official Netherlands agglomerations based on socio-economic criteria (Schmitz 1966) and also for the city regions (Stadtregionen) in the Federal Republic of Germany (Boustedt 1960, 1968). The Dutch work used a 15 per cent commuting cut-off level (as a percentage of the resident workforce of an area commuting to a central city or cities) while the German studies used a 20 per cent level. However, in practice the differences in definition make it impossible to use these studies as they stand as the basis for international comparison. And, in many cases, they are based on conditions in the early 1960s – whereas, for comparison with American and Japanese studies, more recent definitions are desirable.

Reviews of urban trends in Europe, although not based on any rigorous comparable areal units, have been made by Elisabeth Lichtenberger and by Vining and Kontuly – Vining having been also an active observer of trends in the recent (post-1970) American urban system (Lichtenberger in Berry 1976; Vining and Kontuly 1977, 1978). They suggest that a decentralisation process from city to suburb has been setting in, marked by declines in the populations of larger central cities. The major cities of northern Europe, such as London and the cities of the Dutch Randstad (Amsterdam, Rotterdam, The Hague) were all reporting heavy population losses by the mid-1970s, and there was even evidence of a radical slowing down in growth rates of southern European cities (Hall 1977; Vining and Kontuly 1977, 1978). In contrast, medium-sized cities tended to be showing the most rapid growth almost everywhere. This was probably in accord with the expressed preferences of most citizens, whether for plant location or for residential choice (Lichtenberger in Berry 1976, p. 82); but it was also in line with some government policies. Thus Britain, France and the Netherlands had all tried to persuade both public and private employment to move from the larger cities, using a combination of direct orders for government ministries and incentives to private employers; in Britain this was supplemented by a system of permits for new industrial and office construction (Hall 1974, Chapters 7, 9).

Conclusions

The first conclusion that emerges from this review is that there is no substitute for carefully designed, rigorous statistical analyses of urban trends based on well-understood (and comparable) definitions. This is the lesson of the rich American experience, and more recently of the Japanese and British studies using similar spatial frameworks of analysis. Such a framework has been lacking in Europe until now, and it has seriously inhibited the understanding of urban growth processes.

The second conclusion is that the industrialised urbanised world is by no means homogenous. In particular, recent trends in Japan seem to have been in many ways the reverse of those in the United States – though with some limited evidence of convergence from the 1970s. A tentative hypothesis is that all indus-trialised nations fit somewhere on to a path of urban evolution, but at very different points along it. The Japanese urban system in the 1950s and 1960s seems to have been behaving rather like the American (and probably the British) systems in earlier decades – perhaps the 1920s and 1930s. Thus, as the PEP team in Britain suggested (Hall *et al.* 1973, I, pp. 251–3), there may be distinct stages of urban development. First, population concentrates into metropolitan areas and centralises within them. Second, the concentration continues, but decen-tralisation of people begins within the larger metropolitan area boundaries, while jobs too begin to move out with a time-lag effect. In the final stage, metropolitan areas (particularly the larger and older ones) tend as a whole to stagnate and to decay, as people and jobs move out to the inter-metropolitan peripheries at the boundaries of Daily Urban Systems. Within such a simple model, post-1945 Japan would appear to be in Stage One while the America of the 1970s has already entered Stage Four. We need to know whether this model stands up to testing, and in particular whether European experience accords with it.

Chapter 2
Hypotheses and Objectives

We can best approach the present study by recapitulating, from the previous chapter, some of the main hypotheses that powerfully emerge from the recent spate of American work on urban change (Alonso 1978; Beale 1977; Berry and Dahmann 1977; McCarthy and Morrison 1977, 1979; Morrison 1978; Sternlieb and Hughes 1975, 1977). They may be summarised succinctly by stating that urban growth is passing:

(a) *downwards* through the urban hierarchy from larger to smaller urban systems;
(b) *outwards* within metropolitan areas from cores to rings;
(c) *outwards* from metropolitan to non-metropolitan areas – that is, from urban to rural areas;
(d) *across* from older industrialised and urbanised regions dominated by manufacturing (the Northeast, the Midwest), to newly industrialising and urbanising regions, dominated by service industry (the South, the West).

Another way of putting this is that the process of urban change in the United States has taken on a new dimension since 1970. Though people (and presumably also jobs) are continuing to move in a wavelike motion from central cities to suburbs to adjacent non-metropolitan areas – as was already evident in the 1950s and 1960s – there is now also a movement to remote, sparsely populated rural areas. Superimposed on this is a regional effect: in the North and the East some metropolitan areas are declining and most central cities are losing people and jobs, while in the South and West most metropolitan areas and even a number of central cities are still gaining. But in addition, the South and West are disproportionately the beneficiaries of the urban–rural (or metropolitan–non-metropolitan) shift.

There has certainly been a new dimension to the process of urban deconcentration in the United States since 1970; and it has led some observers to postulate the theory of a 'clean break' (Vining and Kontuly 1978; Gordon in

Kawashima 1980). The central notion is that the long-continued pattern of rural-to-urban migration, characteristic of all developing and developed countries since the first Industrial Revolution, is in process of being reversed – or at least dramatically slowed down. Vining and Kontuly even argue that the same process can be detected in other advanced industrial countries – above all in Europe. Others have argued that the American data do not conclusively support this conclusion: that, arrayed in terms of decreasing metropolitan influence, non-metropolitan counties prove to have diminishing growth rates (Gordon in Kawashima 1980, Table 1). Table 1.2 – based in part on Gordon's evidence – certainly lends support to these doubts. Gordon further argues that during 1970–5 most non-metropolitan growth was still in counties adjacent to SMSA's and that these adjacent counties continued to grow faster than non-adjacent ones. Gordon concludes: 'the small or lightly populated non-metropolitan counties and the smaller SMSA's are the major gainers; looking at *where* the major non-metropolitan growth is taking place, we are back to spillover effects' (Gordon in Kawashima 1980).

This related work was just beginning to be formulated, and its conclusions presented, as the present study began. As our study ended, at the Laxenburg conference of October 1978, much of the discussion turned on the point of how far our results helped prove – or disprove – the clean break hypothesis. However, from the start the present study was intended to try to examine the facts; it began without any predetermined hypotheses to prove or disprove. It was during the course of the work, as the American literature began to focus on the theme, that it came to appear as one central question to be answered. Do the European data show any recent tendency for a clean break? Have the long-continued paths of movement, from rural areas into European cities, actually been reversed? Or do they at least show some evidence of slowing down? If they did, that might suggest an additional hypothesis: that urban trends in advanced industrial countries were showing a process of convergence.

The Objectives of the Study

Stage One objectives
From the start, the study was conceived in two stages. Stage One would be basic and definitional. It would involve drawing up a scheme of comparable Daily Urban Systems units, and providing for each of them a set of basic data about area, population and (where available) aggregate employment by place of work at Census dates. This stage was designed to be self-contained, as far as possible, in the event that further stages of the research had to be abandoned or postponed. Thus its purpose was not purely definitional; through analysis of the very simple aggregate data that would be available, it could begin to try to answer two groups of questions.

The first group was about *comparative growth*. What had been the pattern of recent growth (or decline) of individual DUS's and groups of DUS's? Do growth patterns relate to position in European geographical space? How far are they related to size of urban systems, and if so, how? Is it true that larger DUS's are growing most rapidly (as in Japan) or that medium-sized ones tend to show the greatest dynamism (as in the United States or Britain)? Is there any relationship between growth and other variables available at this stage – for instance density? Are population growth and employment growth systematically and closely related, as seems to have been the case elsewhere?

The second group was about *internal change.* How far has decentralisation of residential population and of employment been taking place? Or is the pattern anywhere one of continued centralisation, as appears to have been the case (at any rate until the 1970s) in Japan? Are the movements of people, and of jobs, taking place in similar directions – or in opposite ones? Can patterns of centralisation or decentralisation be systematically related to available indices – such as geographical position, size, or density? What appears to be the sequence of movement: does population lead employment, or vice versa?

Under both these headings, it was the intention that data should be available for individual areas, for national groupings, for regional groupings (groups of countries) and for all western and central Europe. This is the pattern of the analyses in Chapters 4 and 5.

Stage Two objectives

In Stage Two of the study, which would follow immediately on the end of Stage One, a much wider range of questions would be addressed.

First, *the analyses of Stage One could be deepened and enriched.* In particular, differential patterns of growth and of internal shift could be further examined in terms of *disaggregated data about employment and/or income support,* as Berry has already done in his American study. (It will be remembered from Chapter 1 that Berry concluded that there was a systematic relationship, whereby urban systems depending on primary industries had a lower-than-average growth rate, while those depending on tertiary industry and/or government funding had a higher-than-average growth rate). Shift-share analysis would permit a systematic analysis of the relationship of urban growth to changes in the European economic structure.

Second, there could be a further enrichment of the data base, permitting analysis of variations in *quality of life* between one Daily Urban System and another. Up to now, work in this area has been done either at a coarse national aggregate level or for metropolitan areas within one country, particularly in the United States (Hoch 1973; Smith 1973, 1977). At present, comparison is vitiated by lack of precisely comparable areal definitions; for instance, comparisons among Paris, London, New York, Tokyo and Moscow are greatly affected by the precise geographical units chosen for comparison. One important output from this work would be to test a hypothesis already developed by Berry for his American study: that increasingly, employment is drawn to amenity-rich locations reflecting the spatial preferences of a sophisticated and highly mobile labour force. Within the linguistic and cultural constraints of Europe, and in the recession-struck world of the late 1970s, such free expression of preference might not be so evident; but it seemed desirable to test the notion.

Third, the Daily Urban System would provide an exceptionally convenient framework for the measurement of *resource and energy stocks and flows*. Models of this type had been developed in recent work for systems that are reasonably closed, but to develop them for urban areas – apart from special cases like Hong Kong (Boyden, 1979) clearly present problems of data capture. Much of the information is not disaggregated in the right way, and flows in particular might be difficult to monitor. This part of the study would focus on the comparative efficiency of different urban systems in terms of resource use. One aspect, land use, would relate particularly to the themes of population growth and change already discussed.

Fourth, and centrally, the data would permit a better understanding of the capacity and limitations of *national public policies*. During the thirty years following the end of World War II, virtually every European nation embarked on some scheme of regional development. All sought to promote the development and the welfare of lagging, often peripheral regions; some even deliberately tried to inhibit the growth of their most dynamic areas. Not a few embarked on attempts at a national urban growth strategy. Most aided the establishment or relocation of industry in regions deemed worthy of development. Some deliberately restricted the location of new industry, or extension of existing industry, in more prosperous areas to this end. Most European countries have introduced restrictions on the freedom of landowners to develop. These land-use planning policies, which have differed in emphasis and force from one country to another, seem to have operated against a backcloth which is to some extent common: one of increasing concentration of industry and people into super-megalopolitan regions, and of growing dispersion within those regions. (At least, pending more definitive evidence, that was the general impression.) A comparative urban systems study, it was argued, would permit a series of verdicts on just how effective these policies had been at different scales, in particular: first, *macro* or *national–regional* – the attempt to steer development into backward or depressed regions and to re-make the national urban settlement hierarchy; second, *micro* or *regional–local* – the attempt to steer development in certain directions, through land-use planning and associated measures in housing and transportation policies. The anomaly is that despite much urban public policy analysis in recent years, often of a comparative nature (Rodwin 1970; Hall 1974, 1977; Bourne 1975), it is impossible to get reasonably hard answers without a rigorous study of the present kind.

Fifth and last, the study could lead into a further stage of work: on the development of *models of the entire national or continental urban system* (cf. Pred 1977). Though much work has been done on the development of models of urban development at the intra-urban (or intra-metropolitan) scale (Wilson 1972; Batty 1976) comparatively little has been done at this more extended scale. If work on this level could be developed, it would hopefully provide decision-makers with a prospective picture of likely trends in the European urban system over the immediately coming decades. This would surely be of value not only to government planners but also to decison-makers in the fields of industry, housing, transportation and communications, and wholesale and retail distribution.

In the event, by no means all this ambitious programme had been completed – or even started – in the years 1975–8. The first-stage definitional work has been completed approximately according to plan, and is reported here. Of the second stage, the first theme – industrial analysis – has been treated, and is reported in Chapter 6. The fifth – policy analysis – and the other themes still await analysis – though the researchers at IIASA will begin the construction of models of national urban systems during 1979, as reported in Chapter 7.

Chapter 3
The Technical Building Blocks

This chapter is necessarily technical, specialised and rather long. It is a synthesis of the working papers produced by the University of Reading and IIASA research groups and gives a generalised account of the problems of areal definition and data collection for each of the countries analysed in the study. It will be mainly useful for the academic researcher who wants to check on the methods used, and on the source materials. Further details, including a full listing of the administrative units used to make up each of the Urban Systems Regions, are given in the working papers, and reference should be made to them if additional information is required.

The more general reader, who may be unconcerned with such matters, may skip the chapter altogether. Or, if he wants a general review, he can read the immediate next section and then skip to the final conclusions.

The Major Problems

The objective here is first to devise a system of *Urban Systems Regions* or *Daily Urban Systems* that as far as possible are comparable with each other, are defined on the basis of identical criteria uniformly applied, and are also broadly comparable with other units being used by researchers elsewhere (for instance, the United States and Japan). Second, it is to provide a uniform set of basic area, population and employment data for each of these units. As soon as this is stated, however, it is evident that in the European context the objectives will be uniquely difficult to realise.

The first problem concerns the basic building blocks: the units for which statistical data are collected and presented. Most national Censuses collect and store data by very small basic units, consisting of a few hundred neighbouring households. But the data are not readily available in this form, and to obtain them would either be prohibitively expensive or (in the case of the 1950/51 Census round that was completed before the general use of the computer) virtually impossible. Published data are presented for administrative units; even within one country these may vary greatly in size for purely historic or contingent reasons, and for comparisons among countries the variations are even greater. Thus, within Europe there is a striking contrast between countries such as Britain and Sweden, where local government is organised on the basis of rather large units, and on the other hand countries such as Belgium, Spain and Italy, that still use a system based on many small municipalities. All countries have basic population data for the smallest kind of administrative area, while restricting data on other matters to bigger units. This presented serious difficulties especially where employment and commuting data were concerned. In the first place, many of the larger European cities are administratively overbounded (i.e. the physical built-up area is smaller than the administrative boundary enclosing it, thus containing tracts of non-urban land); a situation for which no compensatory method could be devised. As a result it was found to be impossible to adhere to a totally consistent urban area definition, based as it was on employment statistics, thus leading to problems of inter-urban density comparisons. Underbounded cities, fortunately, posed no such difficulties – an employment density criterion having previously been introduced so that contiguous urban administrative areas could be aggregated with the central building-block. Second, large administrative units restrict the accuracy in the definition of the regional boundaries as commuting statistics, which were used in the majority of the regionalisations to identify an urban core's functionally related hinterland, are normally only presented for the whole unit. Consequently, it is impossible to discern the spatial distribution of the residences of commuters within any administrative area, and often a peripheral area may have significant connections with another region. Where relatively smaller units are in evidence, the degree of accuracy of the regional boundaries is increased, although, ironically, the countries with the smallest units (Spain, Italy) have no published commuting data at all. And, if there is a major administrative reform between Censuses, time-series comparison may be difficult – a point to which we return below.

The second, related problem concerns the variability of the data between countries. Though, of course, all national Censuses present basic population data, they vary greatly in their coverage of such topics as employment (especially employment structure), commuting, and migration. The biggest problem concerns commuting, because the very concept of the daily urban system depends on it. As we shall see in detail, not all European Censuses publish data on commuting. When there is a lack, it is necessary to use a clearly imperfect substitute. Some socio-economic indicators are available, but their application poses great difficulties of comparability.

One aspect of this problem is the question of definitions. Though some concepts in Censuses are unambiguous (a person is a person) most are capable of varied interpretation. The definitions of legal residence (or presence on the Census day); of employment (especially in the case of people with part-time jobs or more than one job or unpaid jobs); and even of land areas (for instance, the treatment of water and of foreshore) all present pitfalls. Commuting definitions are another case in question. Most Censuses ask for place of usual residence and place of employment thus providing, in many instances, no distinct differentiation between daily or weekly commuting. This is highlighted in the workplace tables of the 1971 Census of England and Wales where, for example thirty-six persons (theoretically 360 persons as it is a 10 per cent sample), enumerated as usually resident in Lancashire, state the City of London as their workplace. This has little effect upon the regionalisation method in a country where employment centres are numerous because the pull of a local centre in terms of volume of commuters would almost always be greater than that of a distant centre. In a country such as Portugal, however, where the settlement pattern reveals but a few major cities, the repercussions are more serious. Here the volume of 'commuting' to Lisbon is so high from the eastern areas that even with a cut-off threshold it was found to be impossible to distinguish between the daily urban system and the weekly urban system. Given that the objective was comparability, we were forced to work according to the statistics as we had not involved any radical subjective judgements for this situation in other countries. Very often, in practice, it is necessary to take the definitions that are available in each national Census; it is not always possible or, indeed, desirable to make arbitrary corrections for the sake of standardisation.

The third problem, again related to this last, is that of time comparisons. Definitions, both of areas and of concepts used in Censuses, may change from time to time. And not all European Censuses are taken at the same point in time. Though most were taken (following the United Nations recommended practice) in the years 1950/51, 1960/61 and 1970/71 (and generally within a short period between New Year and June), several countries had a Census in 1947, for instance. And France, which links its Census-taking to the demands of its economic planning machine, has uniquely made its counts at between six- and eight-year intervals: thus 1954, 1962, 1968 and 1975. In such cases, the only remedy is interpolation or extrapolation of the data, to render it in standard form.

These problems, and others, were discussed in the Laxenburg workshop that launched the research project, in October 1975. Armed with a review of available Census and other information, and supplemented by information from participants, the conferees addressed the main problem: how to define Daily Urban Systems units? The participants agreed that these units should have clearly defined cores with a certain minimum level of population and/or employment. (A population threshold of 50 000 was suggested.) Additionally, a hinterland would need to be defined around this core, based on commuting and/or central place information. But it had to be recognised that the core–hinterland division would not be everywhere appropriate. In thinly populated areas, urban centres were too small and too few to provide cores; here, undifferentiated non-metropolitan regions might be more realistic. Conversely, in very heavily urbanised megalopolitan zones, it might be possible to define multiple cores but the simple core–hinterland distinction might break down. And in rapidly growing urban regions, decentralisation of activities from cores to hinterlands tended to blur the distinction further – as Berry has stressed for the United States.

Above all, it was important to keep in mind the need for comparability with other parts of the industrialised world and with parallel research. The workshop was particularly impressed by the similarity between the 173 Bureau of Economic Analysis Daily Urban System units in the United States (Berry 1973) and the official seventy *A-regions* of Sweden (Pred and Törnqvist 1973), both of which completely exhausted their respective national territories. Because of the abundant evidence that urban growth and decentralisation were appearing to bind more and more of national territories into Daily Urban Systems, the decision was taken to base the European study on such exhaustive regionalisations (Hall, Hansen and Swain 1975b).

This admittedly was questionable. Berry's Daily Urban Systems – the BEA units – were then thought likely to replace the SMSA concept as the basic unit of urban analysis in the United States; but that expectation proved wrong. In fact the US Census Bureau has not adopted such a radical step – mainly for political reasons – because the SMSA's were already being widely used to define the pattern of Federal and State assistance to local areas (Berry and Gillard 1977, pp. 17–18). Again, Glickman's and Kawashima's analysis of the Japanese urban system proved in the event to be based firmly on the SMSA concept. However, it can confidently be said that as the concept of the DUS has been employed in the European context, the difference between it and the SMSA concept is merely a marginal one of degree. Cores have been defined, as they were in the PEP–LSE British Study, on a standard basis using a threshold of employment concentration. (The lower limit, 20 000 jobs, is close to the 50 000 population threshold used in the delimitation of American SMSA's.) The difference between the SMSA and the DUS boundaries is therefore merely one of attenuation of commuting patterns. Ideally, the application of both concepts to each European regionalisation would have been preferable with an inner ring, conforming to the SMSA 15 per cent commuter ring, nesting within the DUS. Again, however, the absence of journey-to-work information in several countries precludes this finer intra-regional breakdown. In practice, whichever concept is used there will still be a substantial part of the national territory of most countries that cannot be included within the sphere of influence of a major employment centre; these non-metropolitan regions will be common to any system of analysis. The main difference concerns the inclusion in the DUS rings of a wide belt of rural territory, which in some European countries might still be experiencing agricultural out-migration until fairly late in the 1950–70 period.

It must remembered throughout that each regionalisation is a 'fixed' rather than a 'floating' definition. In other words regions are delimited which relate to the 1970/71 situation, with 1950/51, 1960/61 and 1975/76 statistics conforming to unchanging spatial units to allow consistent comparisons over time. To have chosen a regionalisation date nearer the mid-point of the twenty-five-year period under observation would have been a more logical solution (Hall in Chisholm and Manners 1971; Kennett 1978) but again overall data availability and quality had to be considered.

A Country-by-Country Analysis: Great Britain

It seemed logical to start with Britain because this was the country best known to the researchers – and had indeed been the subject of detailed urban systems research by one of them (Hall *et al.* 1973). That research, based on analysis of commuting flows in the 1961 Census, had produced a set of regions (Metropolitan Economic Labour Areas, or MELA's) similar in concept to Berry's Daily Urban Systems regions. Researchers at the London School of Economics (Drewett, Goddard and Spence in Berry 1976) had updated this schema using 1966 Census data, adding some regions in England, altering boundaries as appropriate, and extending the analysis to Scotland.

Neither of these analyses, however, included areas which were essentially rural in character and which did not satisfy a rather restrictive criterion as to minimum size of employment concentration in the central core (approximately 20 000 workers). This made them inconsistent both with the Berry–BEA regions and with the Swedish A-regions (see below), whose delimitation method was considered as the basis for European regionalisation at the 1975 Laxenburg conference. However, though Sweden is certainly comparable with the thinly populated periphery of Britain – especially with the Scottish Highlands – it is hardly typical of the densely-populated English megalopolis that stretches from Lancashire and Yorkshire down to the south coast. Here, rigid application of the A-region principle could easily produce a fragmented pattern of very many – perhaps several hundred – regions based on minor towns, which were themselves tributary to larger cities in terms of service provision or labour catchment areas (Hay and Hall 1976b). The Swedish system might then still be applied to the non-urbanised peripheral regions, but there would then be a danger of non-comparability with the urban regions.

After much debate and after detailed examination of commuting flows in different contrasting regions of Britain, the decision was taken to produce two rather different kinds of region. First, in those parts of the country where urban influence was more or less complete, *Metropolitan Areas* were produced which were essentially derived from the PEP–LSE concept of the *Metropolitan Economic Labour Area* (MELA). In these areas of the country, the system of MELA's exhausted the territory. The MELA's all have a clear core and inner–outer ring structure, in which the core and inner ring (SMLA) combined are similar in character to that of an American *Standard Metropolitan Statistical Area* (SMSA); because the great majority of Berry's Daily Urban Systems units were similarly based, these areas are thus consistent with his American analysis. Second, in the non-urbanised parts of the country, a system of *Non-Metropolitan Areas* was developed. These were defined following the very useful detailed analysis by M. W. Smart (Smart 1974), which argued – from analysis of 1961 commuting data – that in many parts of the country, there was no clear single centre which attracted commuters. This argument was accepted for the rural areas of the country, where urban centres clearly exert less of a daily pull than the larger centres characteristic of the more heavily urbanised regions.

The resulting metropolitan areas derive closely from the 1966 updating by the LSE researchers (Drewett, Goddard and Spence in Berry 1976); they have however been further updated by reference to 1971 commuting data to make them compatible with the rest of the study. The basic building block is the *local authority* area; this is bigger than its equivalent in many other European countries, though smaller than the reorganised areas introduced through the Local Government Act 1972 (on which the 1981 and subsequent Censuses will necessarily be based). Each metropolitan area consists of an urban core with a total of at least 20 000 jobs, a metropolitan ring of authorities contiguous to the core (or, in the case of agglomerations, a group of contiguous authorities with at least one having 20 000 jobs plus other authorities meeting a criterion of a minimum employment density of five workers per acre*) plus a ring of contiguous authorities sending commuters to the core, so long as more travel to that core than to any other. Certain difficult marginal cases were examined individually in detail: thus Yeovil was included because it was a fast-growing centre with just under 20 000 jobs; two new towns, Milton Keynes and Telford, were admitted as multiple-core areas on similar grounds; and three areas (Workington–Whitehaven, Great Yarmouth–Lowestoft and Corby–Kettering) were admitted as multiple-core areas although the double cores were not contiguous (Hay and Hall 1976a, p. 4). A further constraint was that the entire population of the MELA (core plus ring) must be at least 60 000 in 1971; this was less than the 70 000 lower limit used in the PEP–LSE studies, but was justified in comparison with other European countries where, for instance, thirty-four out of the seventy Swedish A-regions were under 70 000, with the smallest having only 26 000 people (Hay and Hall 1976a, p. 5).

Similar adjustments and compromises inevitably arose in adding individual local authorities to the rings. Certain areas were included with cores different from the one to which they sent the greatest number of commuters, because they did not satisfy a contiguity constraint. Any local authority totally surrounded by a metropolitan area was included, whether it sent commuters to its core or not. Isolated authorities on the peripheries of urban regions, which did not send commuters to any defined core, were allocated on the basis of indirect workforce movements to the region with which they showed the greatest connectivity. It must be stressed that in such areas, errors will necessarily arise due to the use of a 10 per cent sample and the exclusion of flows of fewer than fifty persons from the Census workplace tables. Finally, five authorities in the outer ring of the London region (Aldershot, Guildford, Harlow, Walton and Weybridge, Woking) were separately identified as cores, though they were completely engulfed in the London region.

As Fig. 3.1 shows the resulting system consisted of 138 metropolitan areas in Great Britain (125 in England and Wales and 13 in Scotland). This, it will be noted, compares with 126 in the LSE team's schema which was based on 1966 data.

The non-metropolitan areas were derived using the non-centralised labour market principle of Smart; this involves calculation of levels of self-containment in employment for each local authority, followed by the aggregation of contiguous authorities with weak self-containment but with the strongest commuting

* 12.35 jobs per hectare.

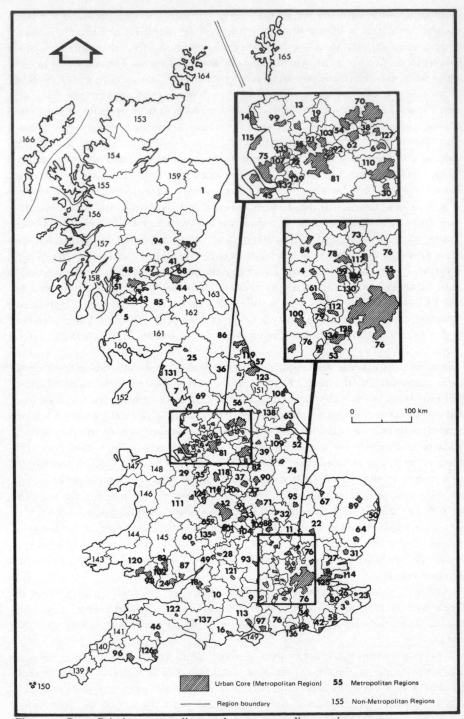

Fig. 3.1   Great Britain: metropolitan and non-metropolitan regions, 1971

METROPOLITAN REGIONS

1	ABERDEEN	47	FALKIRK	93	OXFORD
2	ALDERSHOT	48	GLASGOW	94	PERTH
3	ASHFORD	49	GLOUCESTER	95	PETERBOROUGH
4	AYLESBURY	50	GREAT YARMOUTH	96	PLYMOUTH
5	AYR	51	GREENOCK	97	PORTSMOUTH
6	BARNSLEY	52	GRIMSBY	98	PORT TALBOT
7	BARROW-IN-FURNESS	53	GUILDFORD	99	PRESTON
8	BASILDON	54	HALIFAX	100	READING
9	BASINGSTOKE	55	HARLOW	101	REDDITCH
10	BATH	56	HARROGATE	102	RHONDDA
11	BEDFORD	57	HARTLEPOOL	103	ROCHDALE
12	BIRMINGHAM	58	HASTINGS	104	ROYAL LEAMINGTON SPA
13	BLACKBURN	59	HEMEL HEMPSTEAD	105	RUGBY
14	BLACKPOOL	60	HEREFORD	106	ST ALBANS
15	BOLTON	61	HIGH WYCOMBE	107	ST HELENS
16	BOURNEMOUTH	62	HUDDERSFIELD	108	SCARBOROUGH
17	BRIGHTON	63	HULL	109	SCUNTHORPE
18	BRISTOL	64	IPSWICH	110	SHEFFIELD
19	BURNLEY	65	KIDDERMINSTER	111	SHREWSBURY
20	BURTON UPON TRENT	66	KILMARNOCK	112	SLOUGH
21	BURY	67	KING'S LYNN	113	SOUTHAMPTON
22	CAMBRIDGE	68	KIRKCALDY	114	SOUTHEND-ON-SEA
23	CANTERBURY	69	LANCASTER	115	SOUTHPORT
24	CARDIFF	70	LEEDS	116	STAFFORD
25	CARLISLE	71	LEICESTER	117	STEVENAGE
26	CHATHAM	72	LEIGH	118	STOKE-ON-TRENT
27	CHELMSFORD	73	LETCHWORTH	119	SUNDERLAND
28	CHELTENHAM	74	LINCOLN	120	SWANSEA
29	CHESTER	75	LIVERPOOL	121	SWINDON
30	CHESTERFIELD	76	LONDON	122	TAUNTON
31	COLCHESTER	77	LOUGHBOROUGH	123	TEESSIDE
32	CORBY	78	LUTON	124	TELFORD
33	COVENTRY	79	MAIDENHEAD	125	THURROCK
34	CRAWLEY	80	MAIDSTONE	126	TORBAY
35	CREWE	81	MANCHESTER	127	WAKEFIELD
36	DARLINGTON	82	MANSFIELD	128	WALTON AND WEYBRIDGE
37	DERBY	83	MERTHYR TYDFIL	129	WARRINGTON
38	DEWSBURY	84	MILTON KEYNES	130	WATFORD
39	DONCASTER	85	MOTHERWELL AND WISHAW	131	WHITEHAVEN
40	DUNDEE	86	NEWCASTLE UPON TYNE	132	WIDNES
41	DUNFERMLINE	87	NEWPORT	133	WIGAN
42	EASTBOURNE	88	NORTHAMPTON	134	WOKING
43	EAST KILBRIDE	89	NORWICH	135	WORCESTER
44	EDINBURGH	90	NOTTINGHAM	136	WORTHING
45	ELLESMERE PORT	91	NUNEATON	137	YEOVIL
46	EXETER	92	OLDHAM	138	YORK

Non-Metropolitan Regions

139	Camborne-Redruth/Truro	149	Isle of Wight	159	Elgin
140	Bodmin	150	Scilly Isles	160	Stranraer
141	Launceston	151	Kirkbymoorside/Helmsley	161	Dumfries
142	Barnstaple	152	Isle of Man	162	Galashiels/Hawick
143	Haverfordwest	153	Thurso/Wick	163	Berwick-upon-Tweed
144	Aberystwyth/Cardigan	154	Dingwall	164	Orkney
145	Brecon	155	Inverness	165	Shetland
146	Merioneth	156	Fort William	166	Outer Hebrides
147	Bangor/Caernarvon	157	Oban		
148	Colwyn Bay/Rhyl	158	Dunoon/Kintyre		

inter-relationships, until a level of 75 per cent self-containment is achieved (Smart 1974). In thinly-populated areas, because of the less pronounced work-place movements, this technique could in practice be modified through the use of proportionate flow-line diagrams (Fig. 3.2) to indicate self-contained labour markets. Where this did not give an immediate visual picture for purposes of definition, the precise movements were calculated from any local authority area into each adjoining area, the authority was then assigned to the region with which it had the greatest connectivity. In general there was no justification for the creation of non-metropolitan areas in England apart from the extreme south-west peninsula of Devon and Cornwall, because elsewhere all rural areas showed greater connectivity with existing metropolitan areas than with each other. But in Wales and above all Scotland, non-metropolitan areas occupy substantial areas of the territory. In all, twenty-eight non-metropolitan areas were defined in this way, giving a final total for Great Britain of 166 regions.

Ireland: Northern Ireland and the Republic

As is generally known, Ireland consists of one independent republic (the Re-public of Ireland) plus one province which is a unit of the United Kingdom – albeit with a considerable degree of administrative autonomy in matters such as the collection of statistics. The two statistical offices are quite independent of each other and follow different procedures in their Censuses, though both seek to follow United Nations recommendations and in addition both take their Cen-suses in the same year. Because Northern Ireland is part of the United Kingdom economy, it was a moot point whether it should not have been included in the analysis of Britain (Hay and Hall 1976a). But, after discussion within the team, it was decided instead to analyse it together with the Republic on the grounds of the discrete quality of the entire island, fortified by the many links that do exist across the border between the two states.

The statistical position is however quite different on the two sides. Northern Ireland, in common with other parts of the United Kingdom, asked a question on commuting in the 1971 Census and has published the results. The Republic asked a similar question but the results were not available in either published or another form at the time of completion of Stage One of the project in summer 1977. Commuting patterns and employment by place of work are therefore avail-able for the Province but not for the Republic. For earlier Census dates, 1961 and 1951, neither the Republic nor the Province have any such data.

The first step in analysing the Irish data, therefore, was to devise journey-to-work regions for Northern Ireland, using the standard criteria employed else-where in the International Urban Systems Study. First, major employment centres were defined in terms of concentrations or levels of employment above certain defined thresholds (20 000 at the workplace). Because there were no major urban agglomerations, this proved a simple matter. Only Belfast County Borough and Londonderry County Borough were defined as urban cores on the ground of their employment levels (and Londonderry had to be included as a

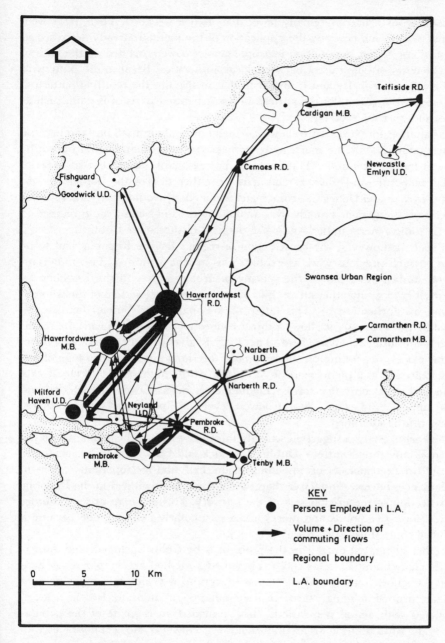

KEY

● Persons Employed in L.A.

➤ Volume + Direction of commuting flows

— Regional boundary

— L.A. boundary

Fig. 3.2 Great Britain: non-metropolitan area regionalisation, 1971 – commuter flow-line diagram of S.W. Wales

special case, as it had marginally fewer than 20 000 workers). Then, rings were defined round each core, by the application of the method already described in the previous section. Again, non-metropolitan areas were defined on the basis of internal flows of commuters between local authorities. Because the pattern of local government in Ireland is similar to that in Britain, the resulting pattern of areas somewhat resembles the pattern in less urbanised parts of Britain, such as Wales and parts of Scotland.

The analysis for Northern Ireland was useful not only in itself but also because it gave guidelines for the much more impressionistic procedures that had to be followed for the Republic. Thus it could be reasonably assumed that areas of similar economic and physical character on either side of the border (for instance, Tyrone and Donegal; Armagh and Monaghan) would have rather similar patterns of interaction. Equally, the commuting field of Belfast could be used to provide some general understanding of the field of the larger Dublin.

In general, however, the construction of regions for the Republic had to be based on such previous work as existed. This in fact is limited. Two important general studies exist: one of the spacing of urban centres in the Republic by O'Farrell (1970), the other an analysis of the central place system of the whole of Ireland by Forbes (1970). This latter work is particularly useful because, by including the Province, it allows a direct connection to be made with the results of the commuting analysis there. The analysis gives six alternative systems of central places, depending on the minimum threshold (in terms of range of services, expressed as a points score) that is used. At the highest level (score of sixty points and over) only five towns (Londonderry, Belfast, Dublin, Limerick and Cork) appear (Fig. 3.3a). At the lowest level (one point and over) over 200 centres can be identified.

The Forbes analysis suggested strongly therefore that, on the analogy with the Province, only three centres – Dublin, Limerick and Cork – could be justified as cores of urban regions. Corresponding to the four non-metropolitan regions in the Province, however, no fewer than twelve could be identified in the Republic – a reflection of the greater size of the territory. Forbes's map of second-order centres (forty-five points and more) was a particularly helpful guide because it identified some thirty such towns (Fig. 3.3b).

Another general approach to the problem is by Colin Buchanan and Associates (Buchanan and Partners 1968). They used a method first employed by Economic Associates in their study for a new town in Mid-Wales, by employing data on retail turnover to gauge 'theoretical shopping populations' for leading centres. Compared with actual populations, these provided an estimate of the populations of the rural hinterlands around each town. However they cannot be used to map the location and extent of such hinterlands. A map in the Buchanan report (reproduced here as Fig. 3.3c) shows arbitrary spheres of influence around seventeen towns. In many cases they correspond roughly to counties or groups of counties. And in general they do not overlap (though the spheres of Drogheda and of Bray are entirely contained within that of Dublin). However, they do not exhaust the territory of the Republic. Though the coastal areas are fairly well

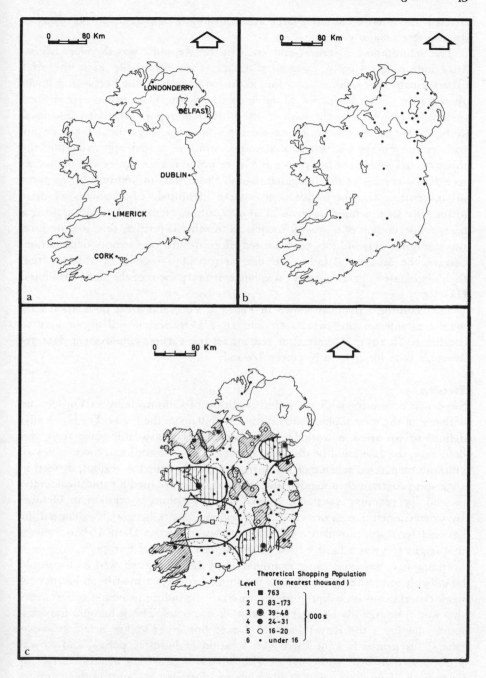

Fig. 3.3a   Ireland: first-order central places
Fig. 3.3b   Ireland: second-order central places
Fig. 3.3c   Ireland: hierarchy of towns as retail centres

covered, the interior has fairly large areas outside the apparent spheres of any of the seventeen major centres.

The delimitation of centres and areas in the Republic was therefore necessarily done judgementally, using such studies as were available. First, the three urban centres were defined according to the evidence from the Forbes and Buchanan studies – that happened to agree on this point. Their areas were defined mainly by reference to the map in the Buchanan report translated into local authority areas. The centres of non-metropolitan areas were then chosen on the basis of the Forbes and Buchanan studies, using as a first approximation the thirty centres with forty-five points and more in the Forbes survey and the seventeen major centres of the Buchanan study. From this, in addition to the three urban centres, another twelve centres were identified. The 'spheres' of these towns were then defined in terms of whole counties or parts of counties, using a fairly crude version of a gravity model. As in other countries, the basic decision was taken not to spend too much wasted effort on such problems of delimitation, because the analysis of individual non-metropolitan regions (as distinct from their aggregate in each country) was not a primary focus of the study (Hall and Hay 1977).

The resulting scheme is shown in Fig. 3.4. For each area, population data were available for the 1951, 1961 and 1971 Censuses as well as the area as constituted in 1971. However, for reasons set out earlier, employment data are available only for 1971 in Northern Ireland.

Sweden

Sweden is a country with the oldest tradition of Census-taking in Europe and with one of the most sophisticated statistical systems in the world. For physically-defined urban areas, a workable definition has been available since 1950; this definition, the *tätort*, will be discussed further below. In addition, Sweden has an officially recognised scheme of nodal regions: the so-called A-regions, devised in 1958 and progressively amended and updated since, are used for statistical analysis and for planning purposes. Indeed, the Laxenburg workshop in October 1975 determined that in principle the A-regions system, because it exhausted the national territory, provided a suitable analogy to Berry's Daily Urban Systems that might serve as a basis for the urban regionalisation of Europe.

In practice, however, closer examination of the concept showed that it would be difficult to extend. It was based, not simply or even primarily on journey-to-work criteria, but on a multitude of criteria – including provision of services – that would not readily be available for other countries. This is because the originating agency – the Royal Labour Market Bureau (*Kunglige Arbetsmarknadstyrelsen*) – is primarily concerned with location of industry policy, and so was interested to identify those places with adequate provision of services for the needs both of employers and their employees. Detailed accounts of the delimitation procedure by the Bureau (Sweden: Kungl Arbetsnadstyrelsen 1958, 1960, 1961) show that it was based on population and service data. A register of urban areas, maintained by the Stockholm Building School, classifies them

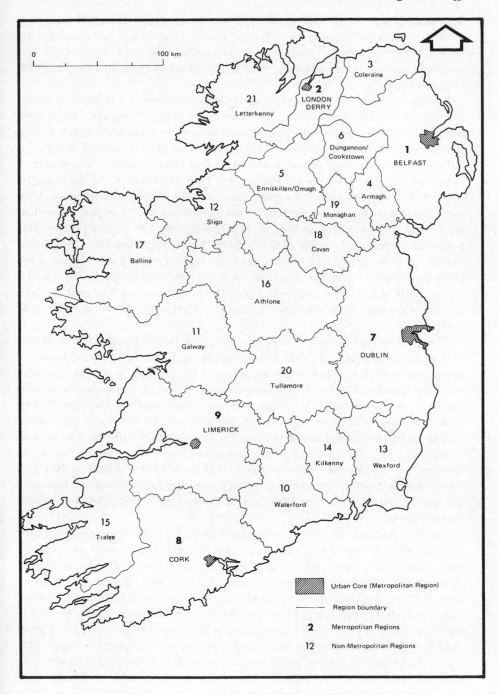

Fig. 3.4 Ireland: metropolitan and non-metropolitan regions, 1971

according to their retail trade facilities; it also shows their retail trade influence. Where detailed information on influence was lacking, it was supplemented by data about newspaper circulation areas, recruitment areas for high schools, recording areas for cottage hospitals, road traffic data and (in some cases) patterns of telephone calls.

Because of the sparse population over much of Sweden, it is difficult to derive a system of central places providing an adequate range of shopping and public services. Generally, a minimum population of about 30 000 is necessary to support a grammar school, specialised vocational education, a general hospital, a daily newspaper, a court of law, and a main line railway station. The system of A-regions was based on centres having this level of provision. In the sparsely-populated parts of northern Sweden, therefore, the minimum population level can go down as low as 26 000; of the ninety-one original A-regions, nine had fewer than 30 000 while the biggest, Stockholm, had 1.6 million people. This makes the A-regions basically different from the metropolitan areas defined for Britain, or from Berry's Daily Urban Systems, both of which have a higher minimum threshold. Though the A-regions were later reduced in number to seventy, as the result of the recommendations of an Expert Group on Regional Analysis in 1966, this made little difference to the size distribution (Sweden: SCB 1966, 1968).

The decision was therefore taken to construct a new regionalisation, comparable as far as possible with that already made for Great Britain, and based on journey-to-work data. There was some difficulty in this, because the basic Swedish statistical building block – the commune (*kommun*), which is the smallest reporting unit for journey-to-work – is on average rather large. At the 1970 Census there were 464 with an average size of 887 km^2 and an average population of 17 400: in Britain in 1971 in comparison, the average local authority had an area of only 123 km^2 but an average population of 28 950. The average density in Sweden was therefore less than one-tenth that in Britain: 19.6/km^2 against 235/km^2. Since that time, reorganisation in both countries has substantially increased the average size of unit; but that does not affect the majority of comparisons reported here.

The real problem that results is the overbounding of Swedish core communes: in 1970, the average size of communes meeting the employment criterion for core delimitation was 842 km^2, with a mean employment density of 78/km^2. (Comparable British figures were 40.1/km^2 and 1625/km^2.) Fortunately the concept of Physical Urban Areas, or *tätorter*, dating from the 1960 Swedish Census, provides a closer approximation to the British core definition, because – unlike the commune – it refers to a closely bounded built-up area with no gaps of more than 200 metres between houses, urban open space excepted (Sweden: SCB 1972). Therefore *tätorter*, not communes, were used to delimit Swedish cores. In one case, Malmö and Lund, *tätorter* were combined to form a multi-core because their respective commuter fields were almost identical.

To define rings around these cores, the procedure was the same as in Britain, with one exception: communes sending fewer than 1 per cent of their resident workforce to a core were not considered to belong to that ring in order to maintain some kind of consistency with the British analysis where flows of fewer than fifty people were not recorded. The twenty-two metropolitan regions, thus defined, included 313 out of the total 464 communes of 1970; these accounted for only 47.1 per cent of the land area but for no less than 78.5 per cent of the population. The remaining 151 communes were classified as non-metropolitan; they were regionalised according

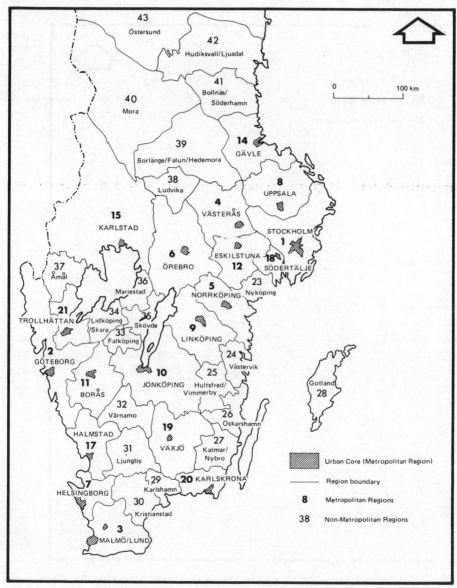

Fig. 3.5a   Sweden (south): metropolitan and non-metropolitan regions, 1970

to the non-centralised labour market principle, earlier employed in the British study. Twenty-five non-metropolitan regions were defined in this way, giving a final total of forty-seven regions (Hay and Hall 1976b).

The regions thus produced (Figs. 3.5a and 3.5b) are in general larger than the A-regions. Of the seventy A-regions resulting from the 1966 revision, no fewer than forty-seven had fewer than 100 000 people, while only two of our metropolitan regions were below this level (and these were both in the 75 000–100 000 range).

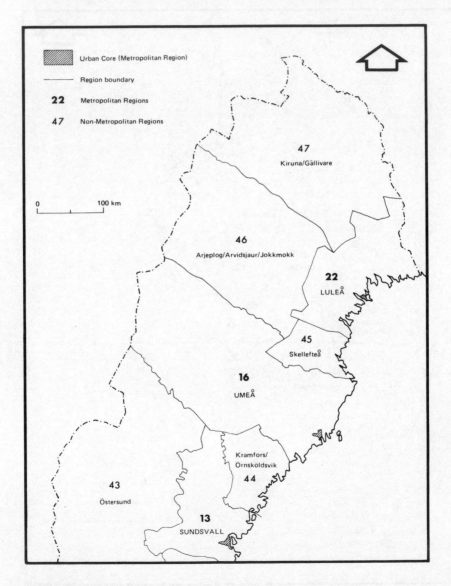

Fig. 3.5b   Sweden (north): metropolitan and non-metropolitan regions, 1970

Twenty-one of the twenty-five non-metropolitan regions did fall below this level, but twelve of these were above the 50 000 mark.

Norway

The regionalisation of Norway logically followed in many ways from that of Sweden because the geography and also the administrative structure are so similar. The country is large and sparsely populated, with the bulk of the people concentrated in relatively small areas in the southern one-third of the land area. The commune (*kommune*) is – as in Sweden – the smallest unit for which journey-to-work data are recorded, and as in Sweden it is large: in 1970 there were 451 with an average area of 483 km² and an average population of 8590.

Because of the sparse population and scattered urban pattern, it was decided to relax the minimum threshold for core employment (20 000 workers) in the case of Ålesund and Tromsø, which evidently performed a central urban function for their surrounding areas. Underbounding of cores did not occur, but overbounding is a serious problem, as in Sweden. Further, it could not be corrected – as it was in Sweden – by the use of the *tätort* concept, because employment figures are not reported in this way in Norway, (although an urban area definition is available, it is based only on population data). It has generally been assumed, however, that there are few jobs in the commune outside the physical urban area, because the nature of the terrain (and the fact of urban centrality itself) generally precludes this.

The procedure gave ten urban cores only – nine single, and one multi-core, Porsgrunn–Skien, where the cores had overlapping fields. Communes were then allocated to cores in the same way as in Britain or Sweden, using the same 1 per cent cut-off point earlier adopted for Sweden to give rough comparability with the British conventions. Extension to include any and every workplace movement would in some cases have produced regions astride major physical boundaries. The ten metropolitan areas, thus defined, accounted for 253 out of 451 communes, including 45.9 per cent of the land area and 72.3 per cent of the population: proportions very closely comparable with those in Sweden.

The remaining 198 communes were then allocated to non-metropolitan regions, using the labour market principle earlier described for Great Britain. In all, twenty-four non-urban regions were delineated, giving a final total of thirty-four regions for all Norway (Hay and Hall 1977b). As in other countries, these totally exhausted the national territory (Figs. 3.6a and b).

Denmark

Again, in many respects the regionalisation problem and its solution was similar for Denmark as for the other two Scandinavian states. Though the country is smaller than either Sweden or Norway and is by no means so sparsely populated, for the most part it has a rural character. Further, the basic unit of local government, for which journey-to-work flows are reported – the commune (*kommune*) – is on average fairly large: at the 1970 Census there were 278 having a mean area of 155 km², larger than the average (123 km²) for Britain's local authorities. As

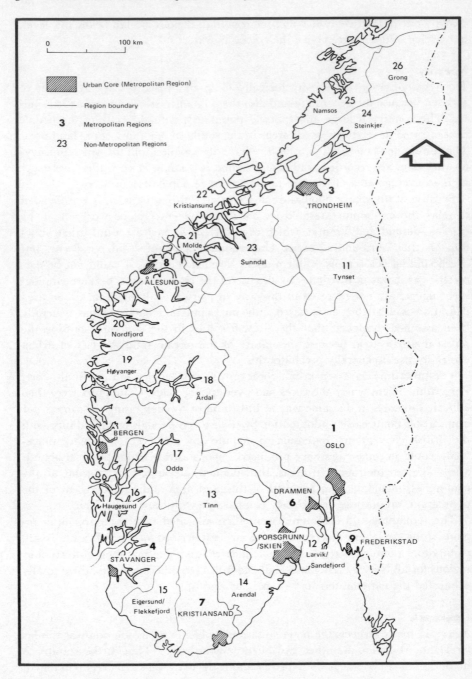

Fig. 3.6a   Norway (south): metropolitan and non-metropolitan regions, 1970

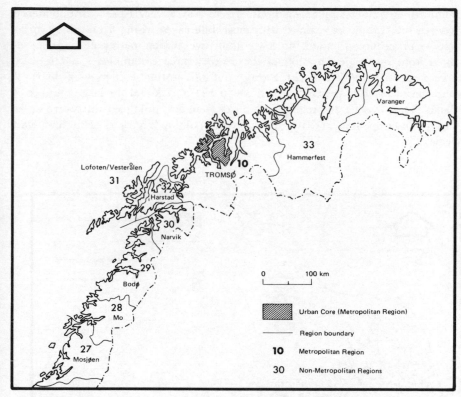

Fig. 3.6b   Norway (north): metropolitan and non-metropolitan regions, 1970

in Norway and Sweden, communes tend to be overbounded, giving again a problem of core definition; as in Norway, this cannot be corrected through the substitution of the Swedish *tätort* concept, but it has been assumed that there are insignificantly few jobs in the commune outside the physically built-up core.

In total, the procedure gave twelve urban cores: eleven single and one (Copenhagen) multiple, comprising several contiguous communes. The procedure for allocating communes to the rings around the cores was the same as for all the other countries so far considered; as in the case of the British Census, the Danish workplace tables do not record flows of fewer than fifty persons so that all recorded flows were analysed. The twelve metropolitan areas, thus defined, accounted for 205 of the 278 communes including 73 per cent of the area and no less than 85.3 per cent of the population.

The remaining seventy-three communes were regionalised into non-metropolitan areas, using the same labour market principle employed in the British and other studies. The resulting areas were compared with the 'employment hinterlands' (*Arbejdskraftoplande*), defined by the Regional Plan Development Secretariat (Denmark: Landsplanudvalgets Sekretariat 1974), that are labour markets delimited by rather similar methods. There was a very close correspondence between the two sets of regions, with most differences arising from minor variations in procedure. In total, no fewer than twenty non-metropolitan areas resulted from our regionalisation of the seventy-three communes – a relatively large proportion compared with Britain, but fully justifiable in view of the rural character of much of the central and western Denmark and the large number of islands. Thus overall, the regionalisation of Denmark produced thirty-two areas – twelve metropolitan and twenty non-metropolitan (Fig. 3.7) (Hay and Hall 1976c).

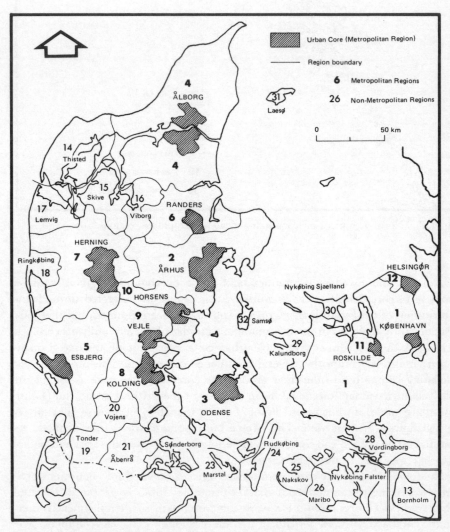

Fig. 3.7   Denmark: metropolitan and non-metropolitan regions, 1970

The Netherlands

In comparison with Britain and Scandinavia, the regionalisation of the Netherlands surprisingly presented problems of a fundamental kind. Though the country has a well-developed and sophisticated statistical service, it had not produced journey-to-work data for municipalities (*gemeente*) from the 1971 Census at the time of our study. Therefore, we based our regionalisation instead on the results of a joint research project conducted by Dr F. Schuurmans of the University of Groningen and the Dutch Central Bureau of Statistics (*Centraal Bureau voor de Statistiek*) that, we are satisfied, provides an extremely close approximation to the work completed for other western European countries. It would have been possible to derive journey-to-work regions directly from 1960 data, but the fundamental changes that have taken place in the Dutch economic–spatial structure in the period since then – particularly, the promotion of regional development outside the heavily populated western region, and the general process of suburbanisation – made this highly inadvisable. Much of the remainder of this section, therefore, is based on the results of the Schuurmans–CBS study (Schuurmans 1974).

This work was begun on behalf of the National Council for Labour Markets (*Nationaal Raad voor de Arbeidsmarkt*) – a part of the Social Economic Council which advises the central government – and its constituent regional councils. For the purpose of regional labour market policy, it was important that any division should delimit areas with socio-economic coherence and relative homogeneity in terms of labour catchment areas.

The concentration of employment and dispersal of population in the Netherlands led to an initial definition of centres by Schuurmans on the criterion of the size of employment in manufacturing industry, and urban areas with more than 7500 jobs in this category were selected. These nodes revealed a marked similarity to centres used by Buursink and Keuning (Buursink and Keuning 1972) in a previous study of service centres and their respective service areas in the late 1960s. Buursink and Keuning defined centres empirically according to the degree of provision of twenty-five selected 'service elements of an institutional nature' and the retail importance of centres in relation to other centres, resulting in a classic classification of centres into three categories – primary, secondary and tertiary – although centres indicating a predominant retail function only were classified separately. Schuurmans therefore adopted the Buursink–Keuning primary and secondary centres as the basis of his regionalisation, including some tertiary centres in areas where primary and secondary centres were absent. In total fifty-three centres were originally defined of which only seven were in the tertiary category.

In the absence of journey-to-work statistics, the definition of the labour catchment areas of the selected centres was based on analysis of the communications infrastructure surrounding each centre, in order to indicate the potential accessibility to the centres from the neighbouring municipalities. By use of bus and train timetables, as well as an estimation of travel times by cars at different speeds according to road categories, Schuurmans included with each centre all those municipalities potentially within forty-five minutes' travel time. Municipalities divided between two or more centres were reconciled by reference to the frequency of bus and train connections to each centre within the allotted time period and checked by use of 1960 commuting data.

The result was described by Schuurmans as a system of 'spatial units developed on nodal principles'. These 'spatial units' were then subsequently aggregated into twenty-six 'zonal' regions in order to provide a more accurate representation of labour market areas with the aim of maximising within-area migration flows and minimising between-area flows. This was feasible because of the preponderance of relatively short distance migration in the Netherlands. In cases where it was possible to draw a clear boundary around a region, this region was kept separate. In cases where this was not possible, because there were too many interrelationships in terms of migration and/or commuting, the relevant regions were combined. Schuurmans writes: 'It will be clear that such a combination always implies a compromise. According to his own specific purpose the user can choose the spatial unit which was developed on either zonal or nodal principles together with its characteristics and possibilities for use.' (Schuurmans 1974.)

Most official governmental statistics in the Netherlands are the responsibility of the Central Bureau for Statistics. In order to improve the quality of regional statistics, the CBS has undertaken a number of regionalisations. One such, into eighty school catchment areas, was completed in the late 1960s by the CBS educational statistics department. Its objective was not only to provide an adequate description of current patterns, but also to provide a framework for future regional educational capacity planning. And for this latter purpose, the division into no fewer than eighty regions was not very useful; it gave too many small regions with limited catchment populations. The CBS therefore wished to find a logical way of amalgamating their eighty units into larger regions.

It was then realised that there were significant similarities between the needs of the regional educational system and the system of labour markets – thus providing the opportunity for collaboration between CBS statisticians and the Schuurmans research group in Groningen. The CBS had already proposed aggregating their eighty school areas into twenty-four; this proved to be almost identical to the twenty-six region scheme of the Schuurmans group. A number of possible regionalisations were tested, and the result was the adoption of a CBS–Schuurmans 'compromise' plan with twenty-six regions. This was accordingly accepted by CBS for the presentation of 1971 Census data on a regional basis (Netherlands: CBS 1977).

After careful consideration, it was decided to adopt a slightly modified version of this schema for the Dutch component of the European urban systems project. Its two advantages are first, a great range of already-aggregated data are available from the CBS; second, it is closely comparable with the regionalisations already produced for other European countries. The only inconsistency is that it does include a few areas with twin (non-contiguous) cores and though they occur also in other countries, here the cores are sometimes far apart. However, it is clear that Dutch researchers themselves consider this to be a peculiarity of the

settlement system of their country: in some places, the facilities that would normally be present in one centre are instead divided between two or even three –
none of which is dominant (Buursink 1971). The twin-centred areas are Maastricht–Heerlen and Deventer–Apeldoorn. After further consideration, to maintain consistency with the principles used to delimit metropolitan areas in other
densely-populated and complex regions in Europe, we aggregated seven other
CBS–Schuurmans areas into three; thus, Haarlem with Amsterdam, Dordrecht
with Rotterdam and Leiden and Delft with The Hague.

Beyond this, we made some other small amendments to the CBS–Schuurmans
scheme in order to obtain maximum comparability with the criteria we had
already used elsewhere. Thus Alkmaar was amalgamated with Amsterdam, and
Gorinchem with Rotterdam, following a suggestion in Schuurmans's earlier
work that functional links existed between these two pairs of cities. Regions
containing a core city that did not meet our usual employment threshold have
been treated as non-metropolitan; there are five of these: Winschotem, Doetin-
chem, Tiel, Breda and Roermond. Thus in all, as compared with twenty-six
areas of the CBS–Schuurmans regionalisation, we have twenty-four: five multi-
core and fourteen single-core metropolitan regions as well as five non-metropolitan regions (Hay and Hall 1977d). There are exceptionally few in this last category in comparison with most other European countries – a reflection of the
highly-urbanised character of the country. Further details are shown in Fig.
3.8.

Belgium and Luxembourg

Belgium – with which is included the essentially single commuting area of the
Grand Duchy of Luxembourg – presented in many ways an easier problem of
regionalisation. Here, in contrast with the countries so far considered, the average size of building-block is relatively small: in 1970 there were 2379 *communes*
with an average area of only 12.82 km² and an average population of 4057.
Evidently, then, a finer-grained division is possible in Belgium.

Unfortunately, in the case of the largest core – Brussels – employment data by
place of work are not available for individual communes within the agglomeration.
Rather than resort to inconsistent definitions, it was decided to estimate employment figures for Brussels from other Census dates at which detailed figures were
available. The method is far from satisfactory in view of the establishment of new
factory and other employment zones in the intervening period, but it is considered the least unsatisfactory alternative.

Further difficulties of accurate urban area definition are also encountered in
several cases when the core commune is overbounded; notably Antwerpen,
Brugge and Gand, where amalgamations of communes have created uncom-
monly large areas. Identification of the actual employment zones proved impossible and would have been unjustified because both employment and journey-
to-work data relate to the whole commune. Therefore we again had to adopt the
assumption that the proportion of jobs outside the urban area but within the

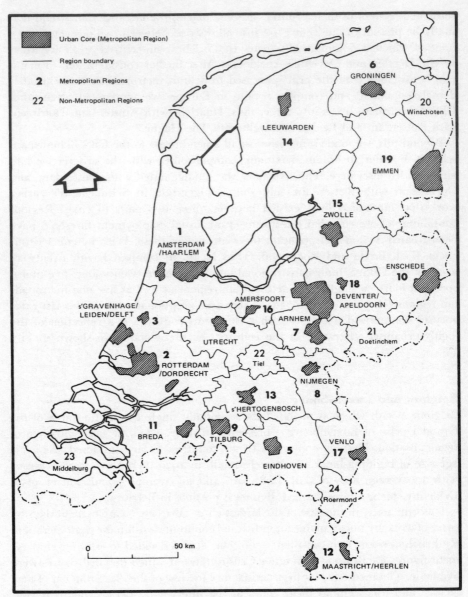

Fig. 3.8   The Netherlands: metropolitan and non-metropolitan regions, 1971

overbounded core commune is negligible due to the proximity of the labour centre.

Fifteen urban areas met the criteria for core status (including Luxembourg) of which five had additions of contiguous communes to represent extensions of the employment area. Verviers was included despite a total of only 18 000 jobs because of its location on the Liège–Aachen axis and its high density of employment. Around the cores thus defined, rings were delineated on the basis of journey-to-work movements, using unpublished data available from the *Institut National de Statistique* in Brussels.

Like the Netherlands, Belgium proved to be a highly urbanised country. Only 156 of its 2379 communes, all located in the rural upland areas of south-east Belgium, failed to meet the criteria for inclusion in a metropolitan region. By using the same methods as already described for Britain and Scandinavia, we allocated them to five non-metropolitan regions showing a high degree of closure in terms of commuting patterns. Their average area, interestingly, was much smaller than that of the metropolitan areas: 620 km² against 2200 km² (Hay and Hall 1977a). One reason for this is the great extent of the Brussels metropolitan area – a product of a great expansion of its commuting field between 1961 and 1970, especially to the south and south-east, and the decline of the southern coalfield area leading to the submergence of Mons into this region. By the latter date, indeed, no fewer than 97 per cent of all the country's communes supplied workers to Brussels (Van der Haegen and Van Waelvelde 1974). The full scheme of fifteen metropolitan and five non-metropolitan areas is set out in Fig. 3.9.

Recent work, completed since our Belgium regionalisation was first published, provides an interesting comparison. Elaborated by a research group at the University of Leuven, city regions (*régions urbaines**) conforming to SMSA rather than metropolitan region concepts (as we have applied them), were defined around the sixteen major Belgian cities (although, as one region is dual-centred, fifteen city regions resulted). Meticulous work, based on data for commune subdivisions (Belgium: INS 1975) permitted the identification of no fewer than six intra-regional zones: the city-centre (*noyau urbain*); the central city (*ville centrale*); the urban area (*agglomération morphologique*); the agglomeration (*agglomération opérationelle*), that is the urban area in terms of whole communes; the city region (*région urbaine*); and finally the commuter area (*zone des migrants alternants*) (Van der Haegen and Pattyn 1979).

For precise definitions of the regional zones we refer the reader to the original publication, but two points merit further discussion. First, there is virtually full agreement between the two regionalisations as to which cities qualified as cores in 1970, despite the methodological differences in definition (levels of service provision against a minimum employment threshold). We omitted Mons and La Louvière because neither attained the minimum thresholds standard to the study. Genk also failed to qualify according to our fairly rigorously applied criteria, and the Leuven group also did not include it as a single core but in conjunction with Hasselt. Only one core, St Niklaas, met our criteria but was not identified by the Leuven Group, suggesting that, overall, agreement is being reached as to the minimum requirements for metropolitan region core status. Second, in a country as complex as Belgium, in terms of place of work–place of residence relationships, it is surprising that the extent of the commuter hinterlands of both studies bear a remarkable resemblance to each other in areas where the spacing

* For reasons of space economy, the French terms only are given.

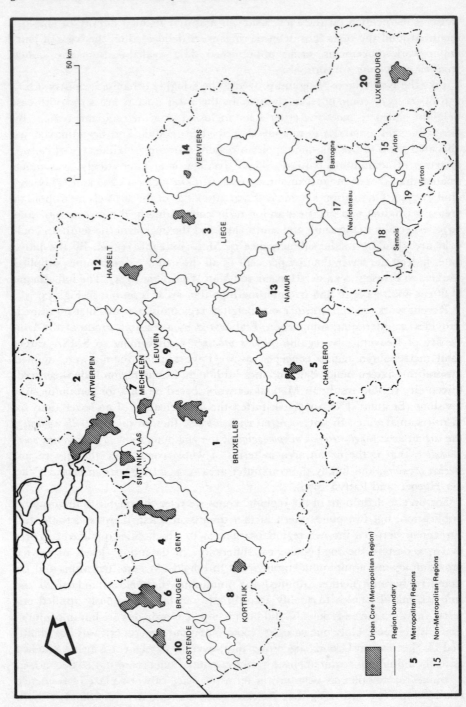

Fig. 3.9   Belgium and Luxembourg: metropolitan and non-metropolitan regions, 1970

between centres is relatively low. Elsewhere, the different commuter thresholds adopted (SMSA versus metropolitan region concepts) results in the smaller regions of the Leuven group, although there is no reason why the two systems could not be merged into one to give a seven or eightfold division of the territory, according to physical and functional criteria, for more detailed analysis.

France

The definition of urban-system regions for France presents problems which are rather different than for any other European country. Generally, European countries either possess full journey-to-work data (Great Britain, Sweden, Norway, Denmark, Belgium for instance) or they do not (Italy, Spain, Republic of Ireland). But in France the data are partial in their coverage. The Census asked a journey-to-work question in 1962 and in 1968, but neither was completely processed and it does not seem to have been repeated in 1975. Employment data for 1962 (by place of work) exist, and were used for larger towns in the valuable publication *Les Villes Françaises* (Charré and Coyaud 1969–73). But, though the 1968 data were recorded on tapes, they were never fully processed – and the cost of now doing so would be prohibitive. Workplace data exist at the National Statistical Institute (INSEE) in Paris for the 960 urban *communes* with more than 10 000 workers but not for the remaining 35 000 communes.

Consequently the French themselves have had some difficulty in defining urban spheres of influence. The most ambitious is that made by INSEE for the Censuses of 1962, 1968 and 1975; it is called the *ZPIU*: (*Zone de Peuplement Industriel et Urbain*). The ZPIU's are functional, not physical, urban regions centred on an urban unit (a *unité urbaine* or *agglomération urbaine* that is a continuous built-up area covering one or more communes). In practice the 'ring' around such a 'core' is defined on the basis of various characteristics – commuting, industrial employment and rapid population increase. If two catchments are contiguous, they are usually fused into one unless this would result in the combined unit becoming too large (France: INSEE 1970).

In 1968, INSEE defined no fewer than 812 ZPIU's. They covered about one-fifth the area of France, but included some 79 per cent of the population. The problem for the purpose of this study is that they are very unlike the standard urban systems definition adopted for the rest of Europe. Not only do they leave four-fifths of the territory untouched; but also over one-quarter consist of a single commune, and a large proportion of them have fewer than 50 000 people. In fact a significant number have fewer than 2 000 because they are centred on very small towns. Moreover, because they are delimited according to an SMSA-type commuter cut-off point, they do not provide a very useful basis for the definition of wider urban systems. Therefore, though this present study took note of the location and extent of ZPIU's, in practice it had to adopt its own methodology.

The foundations for this was the fact that many of the regional offices of INSEE have made special extractions and analyses of 1968 journey-to-work data. In all, nineteen out of the twenty-one regions of mainland France appear to have information in some form, which they supplied directly to us. In two of these cases, the data cover only certain selected towns; in the others there is a uniform coverage, at any rate for the most important centres of employment. Unfortunately, the method of analysis differs somewhat from region to region, and so does the method of presentation. Thus, though in most cases both a map (or maps) and statistical tables are available, in some cases there is only a map. Further, in some of these cases it is not clear how precisely the journey-to-work regions were defined. While most regions have used *cantons* as the basic unit of analysis, some use the much finer grained communal basis. (France has over 36 000 communes, the majority of which have fewer than 2000 people.) Again, in some cases commuting patterns are recorded to the central commune, in others to the wider agglomeration (a rigorously defined technical expression in the French Census) of which it forms a part.

In summary, of the twenty-one economic planning regions into which INSEE is divided, some kind of commuting information was available for all but two (Aquitaine and Bourgogne). In the majority of cases the information was fairly complete and permitted an accurate regionalisation to be made. In some others (Auvergne, Picardie, Nord-Pas de Calais, Bretagne) the information was of rather limited use for our purpose.

On this basis it was at least possible to begin the construction of urban systems regions. The starting-point was to identify major employment centres, defined as places with more than 20 000 workers at place of work. Commuting fields were then delimited around these centres, extending to the farthest limits of commuting (or alternatively to the break-point where more workers travelled to another centre). Unfortunately, the precise definition of the cores, in terms of the status of the building-blocks, could not be standardised in every case, as employment statistics were reported sometimes by *agglomération*, sometimes by *canton* and sometimes by commune. For reasons of consistency in presentation, however, the core areas shown for all metropolitan regions (for which data are presented) is the agglomeration as defined in the year 1968.

Two problems then remained. First, it was necessary to find equivalent areas for the regions where commuting data were not available. Here information from the French education planning process, known as *La Carte Scolaire* (or Educational List) proved an invaluable aid. For the second cycle of secondary education covering the ages 14–18, all France is divided into education districts, which are groupings of the education sectors used for the first cycle. They are invariably based on communes but deliberately ignore all other divisions, even in some cases Departments, because they are essentially based on the location of educational establishments and also on social, economic and demographic considerations – and especially on patterns of movement. Thus they form the natural 'journey-to-work' regions of all senior school pupils in France (France: La Documentation Française 1973).

But in practice the districts cannot be used as they stand. They have in theory a maximum population of 200 000 and in thinly populated rural areas they may have as few as 50 000. And, because the location of establishments is heeded, they may in places have rather artificial boundaries. Thus many of them seem to be based on rather small towns, and to cover areas that pass that close to major agglomerations. In regions where there are both good commuting data and the school districts, they may not by any means agree. In practice therefore we had to use considerable judgement in adapting the education districts to serve as the basis for urban systems.

The second and related problem was to regionalise the remaining thinly populated rural areas of France, which did not appear to fall into the commuting field of a major employment centre. For a very few regions – such as Franche–Comté and Provence–Côte d'Azur – detailed data could be used to build up a picture of commuting to small towns and also the cross-commuting patterns from one such small town to another, that could then be used to construct non-metropolitan regions similar to those developed for other parts of Europe. For most regions, however, such data are completely lacking. Here it is again necessary to employ the educational district data – and for this purpose, they may in fact be more relevant.

The result of this process is a scheme of 158 regions, of which eighty-six were metropolitan and seventy-two were non-metropolitan (Hall and Hall 1977). In addition two urban cores in Switzerland, Basle and Geneva, extended their hinterlands into France, accounting for about 5300 km² of French territory and 387 311 people in 1968. These regions are shown in Fig. 3.10.

As the map shows, the metropolitan regions are concentrated in the northern coalfield, the Paris basin and the lower Seine, Alsace–Lorraine, the Loire valley, the Rhône–Saône valley extending eastwards to Grenoble and Geneva, Aquitaine, and Languedoc–Provence (the Mediterranean coast). The non-metropolitan regions in the northern half of France in effect form 'watersheds' dividing the main groups of metropolitan regions. An almost continuous belt of non-metropolitan areas divides the Paris basin from Alsace–Lorraine and from the Rhône–Saône and Loire valleys; another divides the middle Loire from the upper Loire–Dordogne valleys. In southern France, the Massif Central and the Alps form a much more complete system of non-metropolitan areas, which dominates the map.

Data for these regions were obtained from the French Censuses of 1954, 1962, 1968 and 1975; these dates, corresponding to the requirements of the French national four-year plans, are of course quite out of line with the rest of Europe, requiring interpolation in the first three cases to standardise the data to the usual 19x0/19x1 dates. A Census was additionally taken in 1946; but this date was too far from 1950 to provide useful data. The 1975 figures were however used (with corrections as necessary) for areas of cantons because this information is nowhere else available in the French Censuses. Additionally, area data for *arrondissements* were obtained from the *Bottin* directory, an invaluable source for this purpose (France: Bottin 1976).

Population data are readily available for all four Census dates, making allowance for boundary changes and amalgamations where appropriate. (Compared with the rest of Europe, these have been very few in number except in the

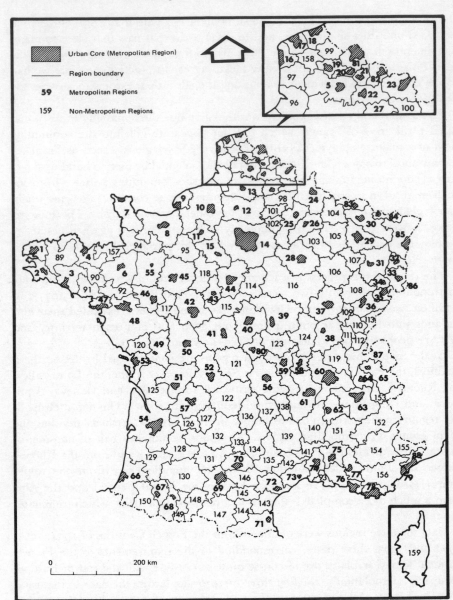

Fig. 3.10   France: metropolitan and non-metropolitan regions, 1968

Lorraine region and around Lyon). For the three most recent Censuses, the best population data refer to *population sans doubles comptes*, a concept that eliminates double counting of the people who were enumerated away from their usual area of residence. This measure has not been developed for the 1954 Census; therefore, these figures were corrected arbitrarily, using a factor derived from the 1962

METROPOLITAN REGIONS

1	BREST	31	ÉPINAL	61	ST ETIENNE
2	QUIMPER	32	COLMAR	62	VALENCE
3	LORIENT	33	MULHOUSE	63	GRENOBLE
4	SAINT BRIEUC	34	BELFORT	64	CHAMBÉRY
5	ARRAS	35	MONTBELIARD	65	ANNECY
6	RENNES	36	BESANÇON	66	BAYONNE/BIARRITZ
7	CHERBOURG	37	DIJON	67	PAU
8	CAEN	38	CHALON-SUR-SAÔNE	68	TARBES
9	LE HAVRE	39	NEVERS	69	TOULOUSE
10	ROUEN	40	BOURGES	70	ALBI
11	EVREUX	41	CHÂTEAUROUX	71	PERPIGNAN
12	BEAUVAIS	42	TOURS	72	BÉZIERS
13	AMIENS	43	BLOIS	73	MONTPELLIER
14	PARIS	44	ORLÉANS	74	NÎMES
15	CHARTRES	45	LE MANS	75	AVIGNON
16	BOULOGNE-SUR-MER	46	ANGERS	76	MARSEILLE
17	CALAIS	47	ST NAZAIRE	77	AIX-EN-PROVENCE
18	DUNKERQUE	48	NANTES	78	TOULON
19	BRUAY-EN-ARTOIS	49	NIORT	79	CANNES
20	LENS	50	POITIERS	80	MONTLUÇON
21	DOUAI	51	ANGOULÊME	81	LILLE
22	CAMBRAI	52	LIMOGES	82	VALENCIENNES
23	MAUBEUGE	53	LA ROCHELLE	83	THIONVILLE/LONGWY
24	CHARLEVILLE/MÉZIÈRES	54	BORDEAUX	84	FORBACH
25	REIMS	55	LAVAL	85	STRASBOURG
26	CHÂLONS-SUR-MARNE	56	CLERMONT-FERRAND	86	BASLE
27	ST QUENTIN	57	PÉRIGUEUX	87	GENEVE
28	TROYES	58	ROANNE	88	NICE
29	NANCY	59	VICHY		
30	METZ	60	LYON		

Non-Metropolitan Regions

				135	Millau
89	Morlaix	112	St Claude	136	Aurillac
90	Mauron	113	Pontarlier	137	St Flour
91	Vannes	114	Montargis	138	Brioude
92	Châteaubriant	115	Romorantin Lanthenay	139	Mende
93	Stes Maries	116	Auxerre	140	Privas
94	Avranches	117	Saumur	141	Alés
95	Alençon	118	Vendôme	142	Le Vigan
96	Abbeville	119	Bourg en Bresse	143	Narbonne
97	Montreuil	120	Fontenay le Comte	144	Limoux
98	Laon	121	Guéret	145	Carcassonne
99	Hazebrouck	122	Brive	146	Castres
100	Vervins	123	Moulins	147	Foix
101	Soissons	124	Autun	148	St Gaudens
102	Château Thierry	125	Charentes	149	Galan
103	St Dizier	126	Bergerac	150	Oloron St Marie
104	Verdun sur Meuse	127	Sarlat la Caneda	151	Nyons
105	Bar le Duc	128	Agen	152	Gap
106	Chaumont/Langres	129	Mont de Marsan	153	St Jean de Maurienne
107	Neufchâteau	130	Auch	154	Digne
108	Vesoul	131	Castelsarrasin	155	Guillaumes
109	Dole	132	Cahors	156	Draguignan
110	Arbois	133	Villefranche de Rouergue	157	St Malo
111	Lons le Saunier	134	Rodez	158	St Omer
				159	Corse

figures. The maximum possible error involved in this is very small, invariably less than 1 per cent.

Employment data by place of work are available only for 1962. There, they are presented for the rural part of each canton and additionally for individual towns and urban agglomerations. This involves a considerable task of aggregation because many of the towns are very small. For other dates, employment figures are available by place of residence. These may be useful in analysing change in an entire urban system because each system can be regarded as reasonably closed in terms of home–work movements; but it can give no accurate picture of the movements to and from the workplace within each system. A question on workplace was included in the 1968 Census, but was never processed because of the civil disturbances in France at that time.

Spain

When we pass into southern Europe, in general a quite different situation obtains. Journey-to-work data are few or non-existent, and if this part of Europe is to be included in the analysis at all then alternatives must be found. Such is the case with Spain.

Spain lacks both Census journey-to-work data, and Census employment by place-of-work data. Fortunately, after negotiation we were fortunate enough to be granted access, by the *Ministerio de Planificación de Desarrollo*, to a regionalisation made for the Fourth National Plan (which, in the event, was never published due to political changes which took place in the mid-1970s). Elaborated by the SIE (*Sociedad de Investigación Económica*) under the direction of Dr Pierluigi Raule, it is based on concepts used earlier to define commercial areas for the 1963 *Atlas Comercial de España* (Spain: Cámaras de Comercio, Industria y Navegación 1963); but it has been updated to 1970 (Spain: SIE 1976). The regions are delineated on two distinct levels: first the commercial hinterlands of local centres, second a grouping of these to represent the wider spheres of influence of major cities.

The question therefore was how to adapt these regions to the criteria we had employed elsewhere in the study. The first problem was to delimit urban cores, given the lack of Census data for employment at place of work. Two possible alternatives were found to exist: the first are data from the *Instituto Nacional de Previsión* (INP), published by the Ministry of Housing in an attempt to delimit Spanish metropolitan areas (Spain: Ministerio de la Vivienda 1974). However these omit certain major categories of employment, including the civil service and the self-employed; further, employees in many large firms were presented for the head office location only. Second, the SIE have used data from the unpublished 1970 workplace Census (*Censo de Locales*); but unfortunately they are again incomplete, because of the absence of agricultural statistics.

Thus we had to proceed cautiously in our use of these statistics for purposes of definition. More reliance was placed than elsewhere on a population criterion: centres were generally defined as those with at least 50 000 people living in the core *municipio* (Spanish municipalities are small: there were 9200 of them compared with 464 Swedish communes in 1970, for example). In general, because there is here as elsewhere an approximate 2 : 5 relationship between employment and total population, this is a very rough approximation to a workforce of 20 000. However, corrections were also made by inspection of the employment data – especially when considering the extension of the bigger cores beyond the boundaries of the municipalities of Barcelona, Valencia and Bilbao.

In constructing regions around these cores, the SIE system provided an acceptable alternative to the missing journey-to-work data because it used a related concept: the attractive power of commercial centres. These centres (fifty-six in total) were identified according to the intensity of provision of various goods and services. As regional building-blocks, the smallest local commercial areas earlier identified for the Commercial Atlas of 1963, were given a gravitational value to indicate their degree of connectivity in 1970 with these fifty-six major centres, using indices such as migratory flows, goods flows by road, traffic intensity, an analysis of physical structure as a determinant of the communications network and, in a few cases, simple application of a gravity formula based on mass and distance. Thus fifty-six major systems, sub-divided into 271 new sub-areas according to the 1970 situation, resulted.

These fifty-six systems were somewhat inconsistent with the areas we had devised for other countries. Forty-one of the fifty-six centres did appear to meet our criteria for urban core status as far as the limited employment data did allow us to judge. The main problem was that the hinterlands clearly represented some kind of maximum extent of the spheres of influence of the cores: they embraced large rural tracts with low population density and presumably very weak links with the cores in terms of daily interactions. In association with Spanish experts who had been responsible for the original study, we eliminated some sub-areas from the fifty-six systems by a careful process of judgement, using as a basis maps of communications networks and traffic flows (Spain: Ministerio de Obras Públicas 1970). In this way we obtained regions that included 49.6 per cent of the land area and 77.7 per cent of the population – results close to other European countries. The residual areas, including the whole of fifteen of the SIE areas, were classified as non-metropolitan in consistency with the scheme adopted previously.

As a result it was possible to derive a set of regions at least roughly comparable with those developed elsewhere (Hay and Hall 1977f). But it proved an equally large problem to fit data to these regions. No employment data of any quality are available before 1965, so a time-series analysis for Spain must be restricted to population trends. The final scheme of regions is illustrated in Fig. 3.11.

Portugal

Portugal in many ways presented special problems because of its weakly developed urban pattern. The basic building block is the *concelho*, as it is the smallest administrative unit for which commuting information is available. At the time of the 1970 Census of Portugal there were 274 *concelhos* having an average area of 323 km² as compared with 123 km² for the average British local authority. Mean figures, however, disguise inequalities of population distribution; the eight littoral *distritos* contain 71 per cent of the total population in 33 per cent of the land area at a density of 188 persons/km², whereas the remaining ten *distritos* are settled at a density of only 40/km².

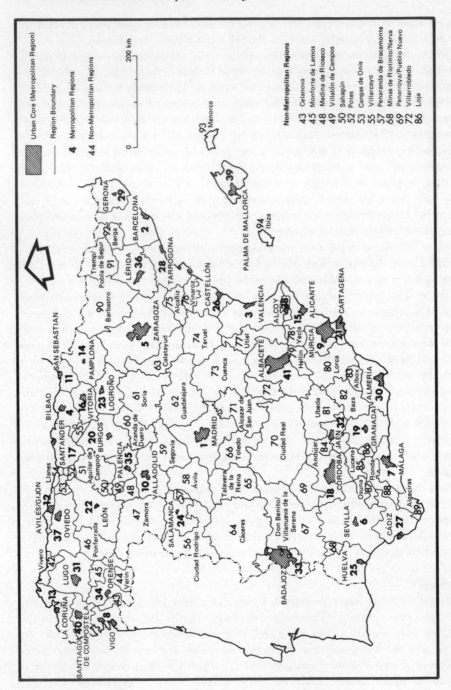

Fig. 3.11   Spain: metropolitan and non-metropolitan regions, 1970

In the definition of cores, the main problem was overbounding of administrative areas. This, it will be recalled, also occurred in Norway, Denmark and Belgium; but there, it could be assumed that little employment was located outside the physically built-up heart of the core commune. In Portugal, however, the greater dispersal of employment made this highly questionable.

The Portuguese Statistical Institute (*Instituto Nacional de Estadistica*) did, however, make available a table, based on a 20 per cent sample, of the population of urban centres defined as continuous built-up areas with a minimum population of 10 000, although corresponding employment data were not supplied. This enabled urban cores to be selected on a criterion of a minimum of 50 000 population. Three cities in Portugal (Lisbon, Porto and Coimbra) actually contained more than 50 000 people in 1970 while Setúbal and Braga had over 48 000 each and were included as urban centres as they were only marginally below the 50 000 criterion. In addition Oeiras and Vila Nova de Gaia were incorporated in the cores of Lisbon and Porto respectively because local advisers confirmed that had employment data for physical urban areas been available, these two areas would almost certainly have met the criterion of 12.35 jobs per hectare (five per acre) applied elsewhere. A similar case was put for the inclusion of Matozinhos with the Porto core, but maps showing the extent of the built-up area in this region indicated that Matozinhos could not be considered as a continuation of that built-up area. Finally, examination of *concelho* employment figures for Guimarãis suggested that it is an important employment centre with 47 000 jobs in 1970 compared with only 33 000 jobs in the *concelho* of Braga, that had already qualified for core status. Despite having an urban area population of only 25 000, Guimarãis was added to the core of Braga with the assumption that the population–employment discrepancy could not be explained by urban area population figures alone. Thus five metropolitan cores were defined, four single and one multiple, broadly comparable with those defined for other countries included in the study.

Functional hinterlands, represented by the maximum extent of commuting, were drawn for each urban centre after reference to 1970 journey-to-work tables. The unpublished tables, which were provided by INE, showed all *concelho* commuter interrelationships based on a 20 per cent sample of Census return forms, although they do not differentiate between daily and weekly commuting. The same is true, however, of similar tables used in the regionalisations of most other countries in this series. To compensate for weekly commuting a *concelho* was only considered for inclusion in a functional region if it supplied more than 1 per cent of its resident workforce to a defined core.

By this method 165 out of the 274 (60.2 per cent) Portuguese *concelhos* were defined as constituent parts of the five metropolitan areas, accounting for 74.7 per cent of the population and 51.9 per cent of the area. The remaining 114 *concelhos* that failed to meet the criteria for metropolitan status were classified as non-metropolitan and regionalised into non-centralised labour market areas (Fig. 3.12). The resultant ten regions have a minimum of commuting across their boundaries and although they were defined on the basis of non-predetermination of nodes, all but one of them contain sizeable towns.

Various territorial sub-divisions were elaborated at the time of the 3rd Plan (1969) by the *Secretariado Técnico* of the *Presidência do Conselho*. Their approach was hierarchical and regions were defined according to traffic intensity and volume of telephone calls. Their primary centres were Lisbon, Porto and Coimbra, although Faro was included as a major centre for the southern part of Portugal in the *Hipóteses de Reestruturacão do Rede Urbana* describing one option for a planning sub-division. It is interesting to note that the Lisbon level one region has almost the same extent as the region defined for the study (Portugal: Secretariado Técnico 1969, p. 43). Our final scheme, however, was considered by some Portuguese experts to exaggerate the size of several of the urban regions if they were to be considered as daily urban systems. Perhaps an over-preponderence of workers in the weekly commuting category is the reason behind this phenomenon. Alternatively, bias in the sample data or the absence of large employment centres may be contributory factors (Hay and Hall 1977c).

Italy

The situation in Italy was as starkly difficult as in Spain. Basically, very little relevant data existed. Though population data were available at successive Censuses for a small-grained system of communes (*comuni*), aggregated into districts and provinces, there were no data for commuting. Some employment data were presented in the Census of Industry and Commerce for 1961 and for 1971, but were available only for the private sector. Missing sectors (agriculture, public services and public administration) were aggregated from the population Census tables of employment by place of residence for 1961 and 1971 in the hope that not too much in- and out-commuting in these occupations took place. Consequently the figures for Italian employment must be treated cautiously, but as they were the only data at our disposal we felt that they might be useful to include to illustrate general trends.

The corrected employment figures were subsequently utilised in the isolation of urban centres. We adhered to the procedure, standard to the project, of selecting the central communes of cities according to a fixed threshold of 20 000 jobs; with additions, where necessary, of contiguous communes exhibiting high employment densities to represent extensions of the central employment zone. Employment centre underbounding only occurs in three cases – Milan, Turin and Naples – although, given the small average size of the Italian commune (37 km²), more would be expected. In fact, the majority of the urban cores appear to be overbounded – communes meeting the criteria for core status have an average area of 183 km² and a population density of 1575/km² whereas equivalent figures for Great Britain are 58 km² and 2715 persons/km² – thus highlighting the difficulties involved in making accurate, comparable definitions of urban areas with administrative area statistics.

Metropolitan areas were defined by SVIMEZ for 1951, 1961 and 1965 and up-dated by TECNECO to 1971 (Cafiero and Busca 1970; Italy: TECNECO

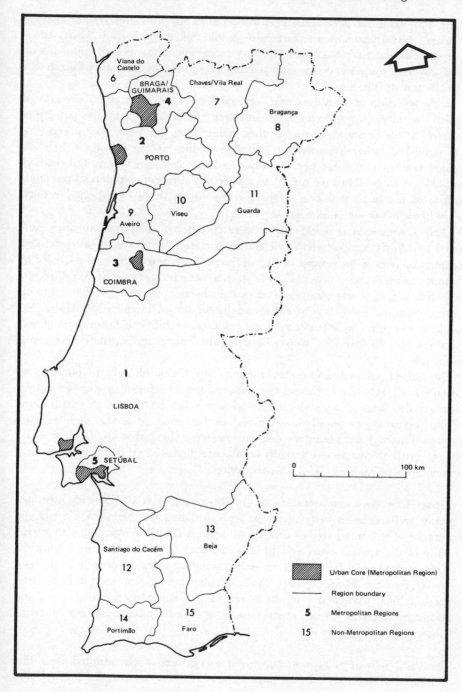

Fig. 3.12   Portugal: metropolitan and non-metropolitan regions, 1970

1973). This definition is also based on the demographic and employment characteristics of the Italian commune, but the thresholds differ significantly. Thirty-three
metropolitan areas were defined for 1971 (some·including two or more major
cities) covering some 25 000 km² compared with 15 000 km² for eighty-four urban
areas by our definition.

In the selection of an alternative regional framework – forced by the lack of
data – we attemped to remain as consistent as possible with the principles
common to the regionalisations of other countries in the series. The absence of
any published urban–regional integrative variables at the commune level to
define labour market areas meant that we had to look for a different, but readily-
available, solution. Thus we turned to a selection of recent commercial regionalisations in the hope that one might correspond, in terms of expected results,
to a scheme of labour market areas.

Three commercial regionalisations were considered. The first, an atlas produced by SOMEA, appeared to be the most comprehensive work as it defined
commercial regions for centres of five different levels according to the degree of
commercial and service provision at each successive level (Italy: SOMEA 1973).
Unfortunately, as it was based on a hierarchical system of centres, it proved to be
unsuitable as our method is based essentially on non-hierarchical principles. No
one level of centres indicated any degree of comparability with our pre-defined
cores and its use, therefore, would have required arbitrary revisions of regional
boundaries.

The second regionalisation, elaborated by the Union of Italian Chambers of
Commerce (UICCIAA), divided the national territory into 343 socio-economic
areas on the basis of a gravity model (Italy: UICCIAA 1975). Centres were
selected according to population size and to the supply of certain facilities and
services. The regional boundary delineations were checked in the field by sampling in order to compare the results with actual behavioural patterns. However,
in a note to the authors, Dr S. Cafiero writes:

'Apart from any consideration on methodology, UICCIAA areas are too
many and too small in comparison with, for instance, Berry's DUS mainly
because of the small size of centres considered. Furthermore, the size variability of the areas is great and their boundaries have been forced to coincide
with regional boundaries. It is my impression that whereas some areas around
the largest cities (Rome, Milan, Turin, Naples) are in effect metropolitan sub-
areas, others, particularly in the inner part of the Mezzogiorno, miss both
significant internal urban centres and significant influences from external
urban centres.'

The third scheme, which in the event was subsequently adopted with the
minimum of adaptation, is the second edition of *La Carta Commerciale d'Italia* (Commercial Map of Italy) which was drawn under the direction of G. Tagliacarne
and also published by the UICCAA (Italy: UICCIAA 1968). The map is reproduced in the *Atlante delle Aree Commericale d'Italia* (Atlas of Italian Commercial

Areas) which, having published in 1973, has the advantage of presenting 1971 statistical information relating to the commercial areas (Tagliacarne 1973). More important in our decision were two additional factors. First, the commercial areas are defined by a method similar to that used by the *Atlas Comercio de España* (Commercial Atlas of Spain) (Spain: Cámaras de Comercio, Industria y Navegación 1963). Second, the methodology places more emphasis on the analysis of actual journey patterns, albeit journeys-to-shop, than on theoretical gravity models which, although useful as a comparison, cannot represent human behaviour to the same degree of accuracy.

The starting-point of the *Carta Commerciale d'Italia* was a questionnaire survey of the purchasing habits of the residents in each Italian commune. The survey concentrated on middle-order goods whose purchase was not of everyday necessity thereby requiring medium-range shopping trips to centres with a wider range of provision than local centres. Region cores, again, were identified on the basis of minimum thresholds of provision of various goods and services, although population size and the location of centres relative to other centres were taken into account during the process of core designation. The result, after the first survey, was the definition of 218 major centres and 196 sub-area centres. Updating in the second edition identified 212 major and 230 sub-centres.

Regional boundaries were drawn directly as a result of the questionnaire and checked for accuracy by the analysis of public transport patterns, traffic surveys and by the application of a gravity model. The final system presents a two-level division of the territory with sub-areas nested within the 212 commercial areas.

As we had already defined centres according to standard criteria, it was a relatively simple task to adapt the commercial areas to our requirements – regional boundaries remained unchanged, commercial areas containing a defined core became classified as urban regions – those without as non-metropolitan (Fig. 3.13). Thus eighty-four metropolitan regions – of which two, Busto Arsizio and Legnano in Lombardia, were represented by sub-areas due to their cores meeting the criteria for urban region centre status – and 128 non-metropolitan regions resulted.

Two questions remained: how consistent were the commercial areas with daily urban systems and did the Italian situation require any further aggregation of commercial areas and sub-areas such as that which had proved necessary in the regionalisation of Spain? The first question could only be resolved by reference to some independently processed 1971 commuting statistics obtained for the Province of Venezia.* The commuter hinterland of Venice comprised fifteen communes, total 1097 km², whereas the commercial area contained twelve communes (837 km²) although only seven communes were common to both areas – the journey-to-work hinterland extending further to the north-east and south of the commercial area while the commercial area had five communes situated to the west of the journey-to-work hinterland. Thus, although no conclusions can be drawn from such a small sample, the differences between the two methods

---

* 1971 commuting statistics for Venezia Province were processed by a research group at the University of Venice.

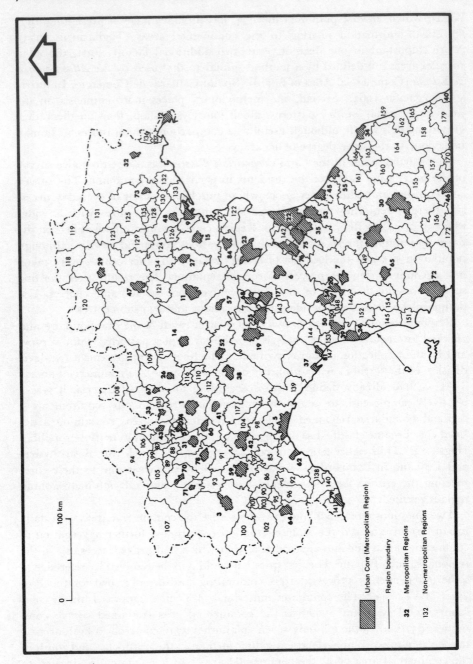

Fig. 3.13a   Italy (north): metropolitan and non-metropolitan regions, 1971

METROPOLITAN REGIONS

1 MILANO	25 RÉGGIO NELL'EMILIA
3 TORINO	26 BERGAMO
5 GÉNOVA	27 VICENZA
6 BOLOGNA	29 BOLZANO
7 FIRENZE	30 PERÚGIA
9 VENÉZIA	31 NOVARA
11 VERONA	32 UDINE
12 TRIESTE	33 COMO
14 BRESCIA	34 ANCONA
15 PÁDOVA	35 FORLÌ
17 MODENA	37 LA SPÉZIA
19 PARMA	38 PIACENZA
20 PRATO	39 PISA
22 RAVENNA	40 PESCARA
23 FERRARA	41 PAVIA
24 LIVORNO	42 ALESSANDRIA

43 VARÉSE	64 CÚNEO
45 RIMINI	65 SIENA
46 TERNI	67 LECCO
47 TRENTO	68 CARPI
48 TREVISO	70 BIELLA
49 AREZZO	71 IVREA
50 LUCCA	72 GROSSETO
51 BUSTO ARSIZIO	73 PORDENONE
52 CREMONA	74 LEGNANO
53 CESENA	75 FAENZA
54 PISTOIA	76 IMOLA
55 PÉSARO	77 GALLARATE
57 MANTOVA	78 VERCELLI
59 ASTI	79 SAN REMO
60 VIGÉVANO	81 CARRARA
62 SAVONA	84 ROVIGO

Non-Metropolitan Regions

85 Acqui Terme	107 Aosta
86 Alba	108 Chiavenna
87 Arona	109 Clusone
88 Borgomanero	110 Crema
89 Borgosésia	111 Erba
90 Bra	112 Lodi
91 Casale Monferrato	113 Lóvere
92 Ceva	114 Luino
93 Chivasso	115 Sóndrio
94 Domodossola	116 Tréviglio
95 Fossano	117 Voghera
96 Mondovì	118 Bressanone
97 Nizza Monferrato	119 Brunico
98 Novi Liguri	120 Merano
99 Omegna	121 Rovereto
100 Pinerolo	122 Adria
101 Racconigi	123 Agordo
102 Saluzzo	124 Bassano del Grappa
103 Savigliano	125 Belluno
104 Tortona	126 Castelfranco Veneto
105 Varallo	127 Chióggia
106 Verbania	128 Conegliano

129 Feltre	150 Péscia
130 Oderzo	151 Piombino
131 Pieve di Cadore	152 Pontedera
132 Portogruaro	153 Viaréggio
133 San Doná di Piavé	154 Volterra
134 Thiene	155 Foligno
135 Vittória Veneto	156 Orvieto
136 Gorizia	157 Spoleto
137 Monfalcone	158 Ascoli Piceno
138 Albenga	159 Civitanova Marche
139 Chiàvari	160 Fabriano
140 Impéria	161 Fano
141 Ventimiglia	162 Fermo
142 Lugo	163 Jesi
143 Sassuolo	164 Marcerata
144 Castelnuovo di Garfagnana	165 San Benedetto del Tronto
145 Cécina	166 Senigállia
146 Émpoli	170 Rieti
147 Massa	172 Viterbo
148 Montecatini Terne	177 L'Aquila
149 Montevarchi/San Giovanni Valdarno	179 Teramo

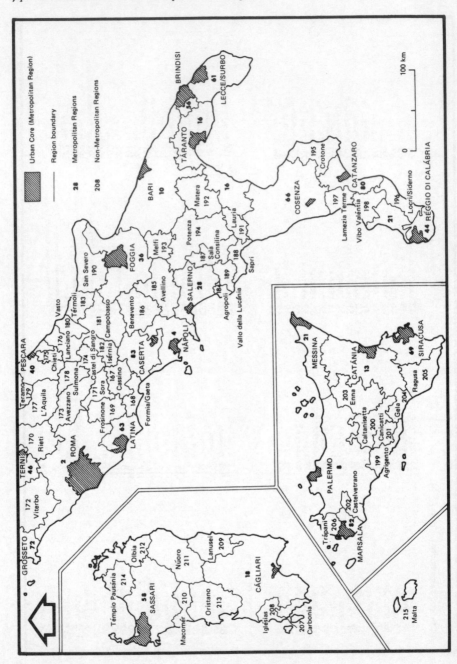

Fig. 3.13b   Italy (south): metropolitan and non-metropolitan regions, 1971

appear to be relatively minor and therefore in no way invalidate the adoption of commercial regions as a substitute.

The second question appeared relevant because, although the Spanish and Italian commercial regionalisations had been fundamentally approached from the same direction, we had decided to adapt the Spanish scheme according to aggregations of areas performed by the SIE (*Sociedad de Investigación Económica*) whereas no aggregations were deemed necessary in the Italian case (Spain: SIE 1976). The SIE maintained that the commercial areas in Spain were inconsistent with their Italian counterparts due to the lower population thresholds of each area. Our only solution was to compare the results of the final regionalisations for the project in terms of statistical averages. Mean areas diverged greatly from 6100 km² (Spain) to 2190 km² (Italy), but the smaller number of centres in a larger territorial area would tend to explain this discrepancy. Mean populations of urban regions were much closer: 643 000 (Spain) and 504 000 (Italy) which, although not suggesting totally comparable regionalisations, would appear to reject the need for any aggregation of the Italian areas (Hay and Hall 1977e).

Federal Republic of Germany
The regionalisation of Federal Germany was the first of three, now to be described, that were made by Niles Hansen and Koren Sherrill at IIASA (Sherrill 1977). It started from a review of existing central-place and labour-market regionalisations in Germany, which are especially abundant and of high technical quality. Particularly notable here is the system of sixty-three higher-order central place regions (*Oberbereiche*) devised for regional planning purposes by the German *Länder* in association with the Federal government (Kroner 1970; Germany: BROB 1975). Seventy-nine such centres were originally defined and although the criteria were not always consistent or even clear, the great majority have at least 50 000 residents and 20 000 jobs. These were then aggregated into the sixty-three higher-order central place regions, by including middle-order central places and their hinterlands within the areas of higher-order places. The resulting areas do give a good approximation both to commuting areas and to functional economic areas, but they are not precise equivalents because of the subjective element involved in the original choice of places. However, they were used by Sherrill in areas of the country where 1970 commuting data were not available.

The other important source is the system of 184 regional labour markets (Klemmer *et al.* 1975) based on analysis of 1970 commuting flows to centres of at least 30 000 population, and taking into account also factors such as employment density, commuting balance, journey-to-work times, distances to other centres and the network of federal highways and railways. The boundaries of the Klemmer regions could often be used to establish hinterland boundaries, especially where the patterns of flows were complex. They could not be used as they stood as the basis for metropolitan areas, because many of the urban cores contain considerably fewer than the 20 000 jobs used elsewhere in the European urban systems project.

The study by Sherrill started with a list of 118 cities in Federal Germany having (at the 1970 Census) the required minimum level of 20 000 jobs, together with the highest-order central places already described; these were the candidates for designation as cores. Those finally selected had to satisfy three other criteria: minimum population of 50 000, positive commuting balance and strong commuting ties with at least one contiguous medium-sized administrative unit (*Kreis*). Of 139 cities considered, eighty-seven met these criteria (or were allowed as special cases). Four of these are multi-core cities; thirteen have fewer than 50 000 people, but were included because they satisfied the remaining criteria and were major local employment centres. Eighty-seven cores thus became the basis of seventy-eight functional urban regions.

Hinterland *Kreise* were allocated to urban cores by using commuting flows at county level (in Germany commuting data are available at a finer-grained level, but the problem of analysis would have been insuperable; additionally, detailed employment data are available only at *Kreise* level. The 542 *Kreise* of the Federal Republic offer a good approximation to the units used for delimitation in Britain, Scandinavia and France. The method used to allocate Kreise to cores was the same as that used elsewhere in the European urban systems study; the resultant scheme of regions is thus broadly comparable with those developed for other countries where commuting data are available.

The only anomalous point about the German regions is that none of them is regarded as non-metropolitan; the whole contiguous territory of the Federal Republic has been exhausted in a set of urban regions, possibly because of the above-average levels of commuting. It must also be remembered, however, that some of the cores were admitted despite having fewer than 50 000 people. Most of these had 20 000 jobs or more, and so would have been admitted as cores in other countries. The ones below this threshold are only four in number: Bad Hersfeld, Friedberg and Limburg in *Land* Hessen, and Moers in *Land* Nordrhein-Westfalen. The first and last of these had more than 18 000 workers in 1970, and might have been admitted as special cases. It does appear therefore that in general, most of the Federal Republic can be regarded as falling within the sphere of influence of a true urban core. The seventy-eight urban regions are mapped in Fig. 3.14.

Population data for these regions are readily available for 1950, 1961 and 1970. Fortunately, within this period there were relatively few boundary changes and they can readily be corrected for. By 1975, however, massive reorganisation of local government areas meant that no consistent core definition could be retained, where these had been affected. Employment data from the Population Census, by place of work, are available for 1961; the data for 1970 exclude the unemployed, those for 1961 include them in the industry for which they last worked. (In 1961, in any case, the numbers of unemployed were very few.) No such data for place of work were published in the 1950 Census; however they were collected and even though they are available at the offices of the *Länder*, it proved impossible to obtain full coverage. Consequently a set of data was assembled from the Census of Non-Agricultural Employment of 1950, plus the Agri-

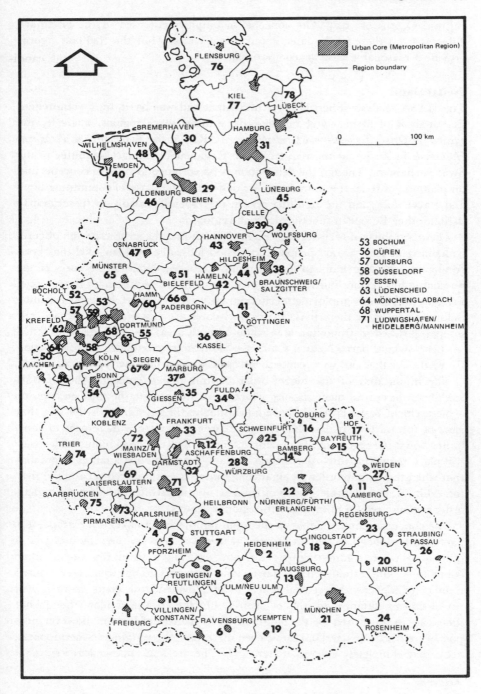

Fig. 3.14 Federal Republic of Germany: metropolitan regions, 1970

cultural Census of 1949. The concepts of employment used in the latter are different from those in the later Population Censuses, but the resultant figures provide a reasonable base for comparison.

Switzerland

The IIASA analysis (Sherrill 1977) of Switzerland was based on a comprehensive analysis of higher- and middle-order central place regions, made by the *Institut für Orts-, Regional- und Landesplanung* (ORL) at the *Eidgenössische Technische Hochschule* in Zürich at the request of the Regional Planning Committee of the Swiss parliament. Though the delineation is based on central place concepts and on planning criteria, the hinterlands are defined on the basis of commuting flows and travel time, and the resulting system corresponds broadly to those used to delimit other European functional urban regions.

There are thirteen such regions. Eight of them met the strict criterion of cores containing at least 50 000 people and 20 000 jobs; one of them, Biel, has been combined with Neuchâtel to form a multi-core area. None of the cores of the remaining five regions individually met the population requirement though one, Fribourg, meets the employment criterion. However, Aarau–Olten and Lugano–Bellinzona do meet the criteria if the twin cores are aggregated. This, we considered, justified metropolitan area status as both areas are quite densely settled in their lowland parts. Neither Chur nor Sion–Sierre combined, however, qualify by these rules, and were consequently classified as non-metropolitan.

The hinterlands of the higher-order central places comprise the sixty-six middle-order central place regions, which were allocated to the thirteen cores on a hierarchical basis. Particularly significant, Sherrill points out, is the fact that each of the thirteen regions has a high degree of closure with respect to commuter flows: the vast majority of commuters work in the same higher-order central place region in which they reside. In fact, more detailed analysis shows also that when the middle-order regional components are considered separately, they too exhibit a considerable degree of closure; in other words, the thirteen higher-order regions contain numerous sub-regional centres.

The conclusion must be that in the mountainous heart of central Europe, it is particularly difficult to delimit functional urban regions on the same basis as in other areas where commuting flows are more easy and more evenly spread. Some commuters will certainly travel fairly long distances to the relatively limited number of higher-order central places of employment; the great majority will travel shorter distances to smaller centres. On the criteria similar (though not identical) to those used for the delimitation in the rest of Europe, however, it is possible to divide Switzerland into eleven metropolitan and two non-metropolitan areas that completely exhaust its territory. The areas are mapped in Fig. 3.15.

Austria

The analysis made at IIASA for Austria (Sherrill 1976) was based fairly strictly on commuting data similar to those used to produce metropolitan and non-metropolitan regions in much of northern, western and central Europe. Such

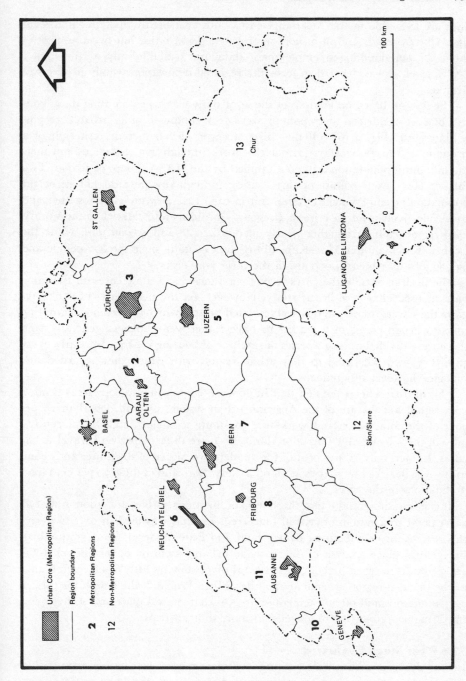

Fig. 3.15   Switzerland: metropolitan and non-metropolitan regions, 1971

data are available in the Austrian Census both at a highly disaggregated local basis (the *Gemeinde*) and at a more aggregated *Bezirk* basis; but because most of the basic population and employment data are available only at the higher Bezirk level, it was decided to form the regional delineation wholly in terms of Bezirke.

The system, based on analysis of the 1971 daily Census commuting data, consists of a set of thirteen metropolitan areas each composed of an urban core plus a hinterland (Fig. 3.16). Of the thirteen cores, eleven met the criterion of a minimum of 20 000 workers (at place of work) though five of these do not meet the minimum population criterion, applied by the IIASA group, of 50 000. Two further cores each consist of three cities; individually they do not meet the population or employment criteria, but in each case they are close together and they collectively meet the criteria; Bregenz, Dornbirn and Feldkrich in the Vorarlberg region contain together nearly 78 000 people and 40 000 jobs, while the Leoben–Bruck am der Mur–Kapfenburg area contains over 159 000 people and 63 000 jobs, of which 41 000 are in the three core cities.

The Bezirke outside the cores were then allocated to those cores on the same basis as used elsewhere in the study. However, on the peripheries of urban regions there were numerous relatively isolated Bezirke which showed no commuting links to urban cores; they tended to have rather weak linkages generally, and these were divided among a series of small neighbouring centres. In nearly every case they were allocated to that urban region with which they recorded any linkages, however insignificant.

This in turn reflects the fact that in general, commuting to core areas is not a very significant feature of the Austrian urban system. Overall, less than 15 per cent of the total hinterland workforce commute to major employment centres; only in the Vienna and Linz hinterlands do more than 15 per cent travel to the cores. In fact, only 16 per cent of the resident workforce of the hinterlands commute over Bezirke boundaries at all on a daily basis, and of these 70 per cent have destinations in the cores.

It is interesting to note that the system of functional urban areas does not at all correspond to a system of central place regions, that was used in part to derive the systems for neighbouring Switzerland and Federal Germany. A comprehensive central place analysis of the Austrian urban system by Bobek (Bobek 1966, 1975) results in seven higher-order central places having little or no resemblance to the thirteen-region scheme already described. Probably the reason for this, in a mountainous and often fragmented area, is that central place travel involves a much higher proportion of longer and more difficult trips.

The First Stage Evaluated

Inevitably, from such a wide-ranging study few general conclusions are possible. The European urban systems study started with a set of highly uniform, even rigid, criteria which were to be employed as far as possible throughout Europe. Given the great range of physical and economic conditions, and the equally great range in the amount and quality of data, divergences and compromises

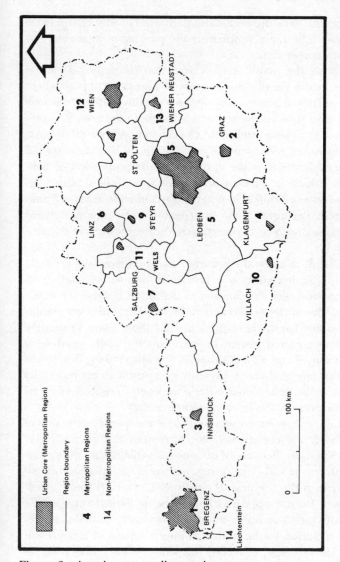

Fig. 3.16   Austria: metropolitan regions, 1971

resulted. Nevertheless, it is notable that over most of western, northern and central Europe it was possible to devise a set of regions based principally on the standard criteria. Partial exceptions occur in Ireland, the Netherlands, some of France and parts of Germany; but in all these, sufficient commuting data exist at least to check the broad outline of the results.

The real problems occur in the Mediterranean south. It cannot be pretended that the information here, and the resulting regionalisations, are in any way fully comparable with those parts of Europe where data are more comprehensive.

Nevertheless it is fairly certain that the regionalisations are broadly comparable with the scheme elsewhere. The main problem is the paucity of available employment-by-workplace data over time.

Already, from a glance at the maps, it is evident that the regional–spatial structure is very different in the various major parts of Europe. Although there may have been differences in detail between the methods employed by different researchers on this collaborative project, the contacts throughout the research were sufficient to guarantee that they were minimal. The differences that do appear, therefore, are in large measures reflections of true variations in urban spatial structure. Particularly notable, here, is the variation in the proportion of non-metropolitan territory. It is high in parts of Scandinavia, in Ireland and Scotland and Wales, in south-western France, in upland Italy, in wide areas of Spain and in southern and eastern Portugal. These in general are the relic peripheral areas of Europe, and it is hardly to be expected that they exhibit great dynamism.

It is, of course, very difficult to assess the accuracy and consistency of the final product without recourse to further analysis or fieldwork. No one regionalisation or even individual region can ever be considered definitive because of many reasons, not least the inability of the researchers to be familiar with every situation in Europe. On the other hand, the argument that those more intimately acquainted with the urban–regional system in each country could produce a more realistic representation of the actual situation is indisputable; but to co-ordinate such an operation across Europe presents great difficulties, especially where data limitations leave the definitional criteria too open to subjective interpretations and hence reductions in the levels of comparability.

At the outset of the study, the intention was to include comparable schemes of regions from countries inside the communist bloc of eastern Europe and, perhaps, from the Soviet Union itself. Because of the unobtainable nature of the raw data, particularly of employment and commuting, the work was 'sub-contracted' out by IIASA to researchers in the countries themselves. The results were varied. Only the regionalisation of Poland appeared before the analytical stage of the project was completed, although five other countries eventually contributed, regrettably all too late for inclusion in the statistical interpretation of this present volume. It is important, nevertheless, to record this valuable documentation, as extensions to comparisons with urban systems, whose recent stages of evolution are based on entirely different economic and political forces, must be a logical continuation of this research.

Thus, Korcelli's work on Poland is important as the regionalisation adheres in general to the principles applied elsewhere (Korcelli 1977). Enache and Holtier's paper on Romanian functional regions introduces some supplementary criteria to the delimitation method, which, by no means invalidate all comparisons, but, contrary to the definition used previously, they employ a 'floating' definition whereby cores and regions are delimited at discrete intervals: 1956, 1966 and 1977. The number (50) of regions remains the same throughout and, as the territory is exhausted, each time, so too does the total area covered. However, the territorial distribution between core and hinterland varies between dates (Enache and Holtier in Kawashima 1979).

The precise approaches to regionalisation involved in the presentations of Hungary (Lackó *et al.* in Kawashima 1980), the DDR (Heinzmann in Kawashima 1980), the Czech Socialist Republic (Hampl *et al.* in Kawashima, 1980) and Bulgaria (Grigorov in Kawashima 1980) are unclear. However, spatial systems according to the fundamental notion of city and hinterland are defined in every case, albeit each with a different *modus operandi*. Again, much useful analysis of change is included for Hungary and Bulgaria.

For the record, also, a functional urban regionalisation has recently been made for Finland (Hirvonen in Kawashima 1980). Although this too appeared after the research in the second stage of the study had been completed, it is important to note that the principal criteria applied elsewhere are repeated by Hirvonen thus permitting future researchers to compare some of his analysis with the section on northern Europe in Chapter 4.

It is promising, none the less, to see that the functional urban region approach to regional analysis is becoming more widely accepted. The pioneering studies by Berry and others have provided a basis for our work and, indeed, for research by academics in Europe – some of whose results have been reported in this chapter. More emphasis, we believe, should now be given to the conceptual problems of definition so that many of the intuitive decisions we were forced to make are eliminated. To this end, for example, research is currently in progress by a group at the University of Newcastle-upon-Tyne who are testing a multiplicity of algorithms in order to arrive at an acceptable re-definition of SMLA's for use as 1981 Census of Great Britain statistical reporting units. (Coombs *et al.* 1978, 1979).

On the other hand, a regionalisation is only as good as the data used to define it. Obviously, it would be prohibitively expensive to cater for every research need in each country, but even the two most fundamental requirements of our work – data on employment at the workplace, and on commuting – must surely be a basic necessity to policy-makers, as well as academics, in our increasingly more mobile and complex urban societies. In addition we believe that more consideration should be given to the potential effects upon the statistical base when local government reorganisation is proposed, or, if no compromises are feasible, care should be taken after the event to rationalise the system of statistical presentation in order to perpetuate areal continuity between Census dates. The initiative taken by the EEC of issuing directives to each member country to collect and present a certain minimum of information according to standard conventions at the 1981 Censuses is a positive step in the right direction. We hope that more will follow.

Chapter 4
Urban Systems in Flux: An Overview

This chapter is the first of three that present the substantive findings of the study. For the fifteen countries of western and central Europe – embracing no fewer than 539 separate urban systems (metropolitan areas) as defined in Chapter 3, plus 351 non-metropolitan residual areas – it presents a very broad overview of urban development and urban change in the period 1950–75. The main focus is on metropolitan area aggregates, subdivided into *metropolitan cores* and *metropolitan rings*, but analysis of *non-metropolitan remainders* is given where pertinent. For these areas, population data and (wherever available) employment data are presented for the Census dates 1950/51, 1960/61 and 1970/71 (or their nearest equivalents, standardised by interpolation and extrapolation to correspond to the standard dates) and for 1975, where the population figures (save for Sweden and France which had Censuses) are official estimates.* Additionally, a series of maps based on these data shows the broad patterns of growth and change, disaggregated to the level of individual metropolitan systems.

In order to provide the overview for such a complex mass of data, some simplification is necessary. The data are presented first for the *whole of* Europe – that is for the fifteen countries together. Then, they are disaggregated into major groups of countries; these groupings are admittedly arbitrary because they are not based on any rigorous statistical analysis, but they have the merit of being conventional. *Atlantic Europe* comprises Great Britain and Ireland (Northern Ireland plus the Republic). *Northern Europe* comprises the Scandinavian group of Sweden, Norway and Denmark. *Western Europe* comprises the Netherlands, Belgium, with Luxembourg, and France. *Southern Europe* includes Spain, Portugal and Italy. Lastly *Central Europe* comprises the Federal Republic of Germany, Switzerland and Austria. The main statistical tables refer to these groups, but reference is also made in the text to variations within them (and summaries for individual countries are included in the Appendix). And the maps are produced for each of these groups, so that it is possible to study the behaviour of urban

* Henceforth in this chapter, these dates are described conventionally as 1950, 1960, 1970 and 1975.

systems across international frontiers. Ideally, perhaps, there should have been maps relating to all the fifteen countries on one sheet; but, within the limits of scale of a conventional book, and given the detail that had to be shown, that was not possible.

A further problem arises with the 1975 population estimates. First, they were not available at all for five countries – Ireland, Luxembourg, Portugal, Switzerland and Austria. The fifteen-country analysis, made for the 1950–60 and 1960–70 periods, is therefore reduced to a ten-country analysis. Additionally, the Federal Republic of Germany had extensive boundary changes during the 1970–5 period – involving major extensions to the areas of about half the cities – and neither the Federal nor *Land* authorities were able to supply comparable corrected figures. It is therefore impossible to produce a core-ring analysis for Germany, though a limited analysis of some areas is made in this chapter. Accordingly, the main tables show alternative comparisons for 1970–5 and for previous inter-censal decades: one, a *ten-country analysis* excluding Ireland, Luxembourg, Portugal, Switzerland and Austria; the other, a *nine-country analysis*, also excluding Germany.

In what follows, all references are to the fifteen-country analysis unless specifically stated.

The Overall Picture: European Urban Concentration and Change

Table 4.1 presents the aggregate overview – Table 4.1a for population, Table 4.1b for employment. Consistently over the period, the great majority of the people of Europe – 86.0 per cent in 1950, rising to 87.0 per cent in 1960 and 88.3 per cent in 1970 – lived in metropolitan areas, or daily urban systems in the American sense. The nine-country analysis shows a further rise in this share between 1970 and 1975; the non-metropolitan areas continued to lose population. Because metropolitan areas have been quite rigorously defined as far as possible and because no attempt has been made to include territory that does not properly belong, this is a remarkable testimony to the urbanisation of Europe.

Perhaps the most significant aspect, however, is the concentration in *cores* of these areas, which steadily increased over the period: from 35.9 per cent of the population in 1950 to 38.2 per cent in 1970. The nine-country comparison then shows, for the first time, an overall fall in core populations: from 40.9 per cent in 1970 to 40.2 per cent in 1975. The share of the metropolitan *rings* had a chequered course: it actually decreased from 1950 to 1960 (from 50.1 per cent to 49.0 per cent) but then rose to 50.0 per cent again by 1970. Thence, the nine-country analysis shows a further rise from 44.7 per cent in 1970 to 46.1 per cent in 1975. The gains in cores over the first twenty years were largely at the expense of the non-metropolitan areas.

The rate of change figures bring this out clearly. During 1950–60 for the fifteen-country comparison the cores were gaining much more rapidly than the rings, adding no less than 13.6 million (14.0 per cent) to their aggregate population, while the rings grew by a mere 7.1 million (5.2 per cent) and the non-metropolitan areas made slight gains; but during 1960–70 the positions were

Table 4.1a   Europe: metropolitan and non-metropolitan region population 1950–75

Population data for 1950, 1960, 1970 and 1975

Areal unit	1950[a] Total (thousands)	% of total	1960[a] Total (thousands)	% of total	1970[a] Total (thousands)	% of total	1950[b] Total (thousands)	% of total	1960[b] Total (thousands)	% of total	1970[b] Total (thousands)	% of total	1975[b] Total (thousands)	% of total
Core	97 082	35.89	110 652	38.00	120 805	38.21	75 314	38.20	85 261	40.17	94 479	40.86	95 190	40.18
Ring	135 510	50.11	142 612	48.97	158 219	50.04	88 441	44.85	93 351	43.98	103 368	44.71	109 093	46.06
Non-metropolitan	37 854	13.99	37 939	13.03	37 167	11.75	33 426	16.95	33 635	15.85	33 345	14.42	32 582	13.76
Total	270 446	100.00	291 203	100.00	316 191	100.00	197 181	100.00	212 248	100.00	231 192	100.00	236 865	100.00

Population change 1950–60, 1960–70 and 1970–5

Areal unit	1950–60[a] Absolute change (thousands)	% change	% of total	1960–70[a] Absolute change (thousands)	% change	% of total	1950–60[b] Absolute change (thousands)	% change	% of total	1960–70[b] Absolute change (thousands)	% change	% of total	1970–5[b,c] Absolute change (thousands)	% change	% of total
Core	13 570	13.98	65.38	10 153	9.18	40.63	9947	13.21	66.02	9218	10.81	48.66	711	0.75	12.53
Ring	7102	5.24	34.21	15 607	10.94	62.46	4910	5.55	32.59	10 017	10.73	52.88	5725	5.54	100.92
Non-metropolitan	85	0.22	0.41	-772	-2.04	-3.09	209	0.63	1.39	-290	-0.87	-1.53	-763	-2.28	-13.44
Total	20 757	7.68	100.00	24 988	8.58	100.00	15 067	7.64	100.00	18 944	8.93	100.00	5673	2.45	100.00

Notes: [a] Fifteen country comparison: all countries.
[b] Nine country comparison: Great Britain, Sweden, Norway, Denmark, France, Belgium, The Netherlands, Spain, Italy.
(separate core and ring figures not available for German Federal Republic)
[c] Quinquennial rate of change.

reversed, with the cores gaining 10.2 million (9.2 per cent) against 15.6 million (10.9 per cent) for the rings and against a small loss in the non-metropolitan areas. For 1970–5 the nine-country analysis shows a dramatic change: the cores gained a negligible 0.8 per cent, the rings grew at about the same rate as before (5.5 per cent over the five-year period), while the non-metropolitan loss actually accelerated.

The conclusion is inescapable and clear. In the 1950s, European population was concentrating remarkably into the metropolitan cores: a process of centralisation was taking place – above all by movements from the non-metropolitan rural peripheries. But by the 1960s, a reversal had taken place: though metropolitan areas were still growing, they were decentralising people from cores to rings. After 1970, this process accelerated, so that the cores virtually ceased to grow and – with continuing losses from the non-metropolitan areas – the rings actually accounted for more than the entire net gain of the population. This process corresponds closely to the sequence observed by Glickman for Japan (Glickman 1978) while it seems to have occurred rather earlier in the history of the United States, which was already recording mass decentralisation of people by the 1950s.

We can safely conclude, therefore, that something like a 'clean break' did occur in population trends during the 1960s and early 1970s. The urban cores, which had as much as two-thirds of net population growth in the 1950s, had less than one-half in the 1960s – and a negligible share in the early 1970s. The rings, conversely, took only one-third of the growth in the 1950s, over one-half in the 1960s – and the whole of the net share in the early 1970s. But in one important respect, the American hypotheses are not justified: on balance, population was still leaving non-metropolitan areas for metropolitan ones. It needs stressing here that the metropolitan areas used for this study are more generously bounded than the SMSAs used in most American work: they include what American researchers would call contiguous non-metropolitan counties. But they do exclude the non-contiguous areas, which have been shown to be taking such a substantial share of American population growth in the early 1970s. The drift back to remote rural areas, so strong in the America of the 1970s, is not yet evident in Europe.

Unfortunately, trends in employment change cannot be analysed so rigorously because of the scarcity of relevant data. Only a few European countries in the decade 1950–60 published employment at the workplace, although by 1970 the situation was substantially better. No figures exist for the period 1970–5 except for Sweden. In addition, where employment figures do exist for the first three dates there are sometimes difficulties of comparability because not all the data could be derived from the same sources. As an alternative we considered using employment by place of residence statistics as these were more universally available. The argument proposed was that, at a regional level, total employment by place of work and by place of residence ought to be reasonably similar, assuming regions were accurately defined, because the fundamental concept of the functional region is that in theory it should be a relatively closed system (though in intensely-urbanised areas this can never be entirely true). However, regardless of how precisely this situation is represented by the regions already defined, the application of employment by residence data would not provide any clear indication of trends in decentralisation or centralisation of employment at an intra-regional level; employment by place of residence conforms generally to basic population distributions. Therefore we are limited to the original workplace information; although we are fortunate enough to have at least one country with time-series data in each of the five conventional groupings

As far as we are able to judge, given the above-mentioned limitations, concentration of employment in metropolitan areas has been predictably greater than that of population (Table 4.1b). In those countries where data are available for all three dates – admittedly some of the more urbanised nations of Europe – employment concentration levels were static over the three dates at around 98.6 per cent. By 1960 four more countries are added to the list: Austria, Sweden, Belgium and Italy, resulting in lower levels of metropolitan area employment, but now indicating a slightly growing trend towards concentration over time (1960 – 93.1 per cent; 1970 – 93.8 per cent). For 1970 all but two countries (France and Ireland) have employment data, although the concentration level of 92.2 per cent is not comparable with other dates.

The employment level in the urban cores shows an increase in the period 1950–60 from 45.8 to 50.7 per cent for those countries for which 1950 data are available. In the same countries there is a fall-back to 49.5 per cent in 1970 indicating that the movement off the land and into the bigger cities had ceased by the early 1960s and employment had again become more dispersed into the rings. It is, however, unfortunate that the same data are not available for the less urbanised European countries as, perhaps, different trends might have been revealed.

Europe Region by Region: Atlantic Europe
Almost certainly, though, such an overview conceals very different – even contradictory – trends. The processes cannot have been identical as between an old industrial nation such as Britain, at one extreme, and a peasant country barely at the stage of take-off, such as Portugal, at the other. Therefore, it is critical to disaggregate by broad region of Europe – and if necessary by individual country.

Tables 4.2a and b present overall data for Atlantic Europe: Great Britain and Ireland. As with Europe as a whole, the metropolitan areas were dominant and were increasing their dominance over the period. Indeed, an exceptionally high proportion of the total population lived in them: 93.6 per cent in 1950, 94.3 per cent in 1970. Thence, a comparison from Great Britain only shows a further marginal increase, from 96.6 to 96.7 per cent between 1970 and 1975. But the distribution between metropolitan cores and rings was very different. As few as 51.3 per cent of the total population lived in core areas in 1950, and this share fell steadily to 46.3 per cent in 1970 – and, for Britain, from 48.0 to 46.6 per cent from 1970 to 1975. Thus the share of the rings increased markedly: from 42.3 per

Table 4.1b Europe: metropolitan and non-metropolitan region employment 1950–70

Employment data for 1950, 1960 and 1970

Areal unit	1950[a]		1960[a]		1970[a]		1960[b]		1970[b]		1970[c]	
	Total	% of total	Total	% of total	Total	% of total	Total	% of total	Total	% of total	Total	% of total
Core	23 786	45.78	27 124	50.68	27 195	49.53	37 827	46.68	38 617	46.66	44 772	45.90
Ring	27 419	52.77	25 649	47.94	26 908	49.00	37 639	46.45	39 001	47.13	45 212	46.35
Non-metropolitan	750	1.44	746	1.39	806	1.47	5562	6.87	5140	6.21	7564	7.75
Total	51 955	100.00	53 519	100.00	54 909	100.00	81 028	100.00	82 758	100.00	97 548	100.00

Employment change 1950–60 and 1960–70

Areal unit	1950–60[a]			1960–70[a]			1960–70[b]		
	Absolute change	% change	% of total	Absolute change	% change	% of total	Absolute change	% change	% of total
Core	3338	14.03	213.43	71	0.26	5.11	790	2.09	45.66
Ring	-1770	-6.46	-113.17	1259	4.91	90.58	1362	3.62	78.73
Non-metropolitan	-4	-0.53	-0.26	60	8.04	4.32	-422	-7.59	-24.39
Total	1564	3.01	100.00	1390	2.60	100.00	1730	2.14	100.00

Notes: [a] Britain, The Netherlands, Germany, Switzerland only.
[b] Britain, Sweden, Belgium, The Netherlands, Italy, Germany, Austria, Switzerland.
[c] All countries except Ireland and France.

Table 4.2a Atlantic Europe (Great Britain, Ireland): metropolitan and non-metropolitan region population 1950–75

Population data for 1950, 1960, 1970 and 1975

Areal unit	1950^a Total (thousands)	% of total	1960^a Total (thousands)	% of total	1970^a Total (thousands)	% of total	1950^b Total (thousands)	% of total	1960^b Total (thousands)	% of total	1970^b Total (thousands)	% of total	1975^b Total (thousands)	% of total
Core	27 322	51.25	27 833	50.01	27 160	46.29	26 155	53.39	26 665	51.87	25 992	47.99	25 364	46.58
Ring	22 575	42.34	24 550	44.12	28 178	48.02	21 078	43.03	23 012	44.77	26 354	48.65	27 305	50.15
Non-metropolitan	3419	6.41	3267	5.87	3340	5.69	1756	3.58	1728	3.36	1822	3.36	1781	3.27
Total	53 316	100.00	55 560	100.00	58 678	100.00	48 989	100.00	51 405	100.00	54 168	100.00	54 450	100.00

Population change 1950–60, 1960–70 and 1970–75

Areal unit	1950–60^a Absolute change (thousands)	% change	% of total	1960–70^a Absolute change (thousands)	% change	% of total	1950–60^b Absolute change (thousands)	% change	% of total	1960–70^b Absolute change (thousands)	% change	% of total	1970–5^b Absolute change (thousands)	% change	% of total
Core	511	1.87	21.92	-673	-2.42	-22.23	509	1.95	21.10	-673	-2.52	-24.36	-628	-2.42	-222.74
Ring	1975	8.75	84.63	3628	14.78	119.82	1934	9.18	80.04	3342	14.52	120.96	951	3.61	337.20
Non-metropolitan	-153	-4.47	-6.54	73	2.25	2.41	-28	-1.57	-1.14	94	5.44	3.40	-41	2.24	-14.46
Total	2334	4.38	100.00	3028	5.44	100.00	2416	4.93	100.00	2763	5.37	100.00	282	0.52	100.00

Notes: ^{a} Great Britain only.
^{b} Great Britain plus Ireland

**Table 4.2b   Atlantic Europe (Great Britain): metropolitan and
non-metropolitan region employment 1950–70**

Employment data for 1950, 1960 and 1970

| | 1950[a] | | 1960[a] | | 1970[a] | |
| | Total | % of | Total | % of | Total | % of |
Areal unit	(thousands)	total	(thousands)	total	(thousands)	total
Core	13 511	60.95	14 384	61.86	13 981	58.93
Ring	8011	36.14	8242	35.45	9098	38.35
Non-metropolitan	645	2.91	626	2.69	646	2.72
Total	22 167	100.00	23 251	100.00	23 726	100.00

Employment change 1950–60 and 1960–70

| | 1950–60[a] | | | 1960–70[a] | | |
| | Absolute change | % | % of | Absolute change | % | % of |
Areal unit	(thousands)	change	total	(thousands)	change	total
Core	873	6.46	80.52	−403	−2.80	−85.14
Ring	230	2.88	21.25	856	10.38	180.90
Non-metropolitan	−19	−2.97	−1.77	20	3.21	4.25
Total	1084	4.89	100.00	473	2.03	100.00

Notes: [a] Great Britain only.

cent to 48.0 per cent over the twenty-year period – and thence, for Britain, from
48.7 to 50.2 per cent from 1970 to 1975. The rings accounted for nearly 85 per
cent of total growth in the 1950s and for more than the total growth in the 1960s
– a product of the fact that by this time, the cores were suffering absolute losses of
people. By this time, also, even the non-metropolitan areas were gaining, albeit
modestly. Looking just at Great Britain, this trend accelerated in the 1970s, with
massive losses from the cores and gains in the rings; the non-metropolitan areas
showed a marginal decline.

Atlantic Europe is therefore a region exhibiting a remarkable degree of population decentralisation: relatively in the 1950s, in the sense that rings were gaining on cores; absolutely in the 1960s and 1970s, in the sense that core populations
were actually falling, and falling at a rapidly increasing rate. This is a picture
similar to the United States, and rather different from many other areas of
Europe. The position with employment is more complex.* Here the concentration into metropolitan areas was even more remarkable: 97.1 per cent of all jobs
in 1950, 97.3 per cent in 1970, were found here. Within them, the concentration
in the cores was greater than for population – as would be expected; and it
increased during the 1950s, from 61.0 to 61.9 per cent. But then it slipped back,

* Employment comparisons exclude Ireland.

to 58.9 per cent by 1970. During the 1960s, indeed, the cores suffered an absolute loss of jobs, while the rings made an 856 000 (10.4 per cent) gain. Thus, while the trend in population was from relative decentralisation to absolute decentralisation, in employment it was from relative centralisation to absolute decentralisation.

Atlantic Europe is of course dominated by Great Britain, and the trends described above reflect the position there – as Appendix Tables A.1 and A.2 show. However, the figures for Ireland (Appendix Tables A.3 and A.4) show an exceptionally high – albeit declining – proportion of the population living in non-metropolitan areas, and a suburbanisation of the population that interestingly parallels the trend in Britain. Because Ireland has only a few metropolitan areas, this suggests that the tendency to suburbanisation is equally strong in British and in Irish urban areas – a result perhaps of Anglo–Irish space and life-style preferences.

Figs. 4.1a, 4.1b and 4.1c show the patterns of population growth (or, less often, decline) for the 143 metroplitan areas of Atlantic Europe for the periods 1950–60, 1960–70 and 1970–5 respectively. (The patterns of employment growth are not mapped, because they tend to follow closely the patterns of population.) The cartographic convention, that is identical for all similar maps in this chapter, is based on an analysis for all Europe which subdivides the 539 metropolitan areas into five equal groups according to their growth performance over the two decades. The pattern in the 1950s was dominated by heavy growth in the ring around London, a product of decentralisation – partly planned, partly spontaneous – from the capital. Already, some of the greatest percentage increases were recorded by metropolitan areas containing the new towns. Slightly weaker, but still notable growth extended widely through the West and East Midlands, where it was shared fairly evenly by larger metropolitan areas based on major cities such as Birmingham, Nottingham and Leicester, and by smaller areas. Hardly any significant growth appeared in the northern half of England or in Scotland, Wales or Ireland.

The picture for the 1960s is rather different. By this time the ring of growth around London was more widely diffused, extending as much as 100 miles from the capital to envelop much of eastern England, the Midlands, and parts of the South-west; in fact, it had become a regional (southern) effect rather than a London-related effect, though the heaviest growth of all was still within the ring up to fifty miles from London. Birmingham, Manchester and Liverpool now also showed signs of local decentralisation to discontinuous rings of small metropolitan areas around them. Growth extended more widely in the north of England than before, especially in areas containing new towns or university towns; it was still however largely missing from Scotland and Ireland. Some of the Irish urban centres were, however, by now showing rapid increases. By this decade the largest English centres, with the exception of the Birmingham metropolitan system, were tending to show very low growth; in fact, though the map does not distinguish it, the London, Manchester and Newcastle systems were already in decline. Thus the process of stagnation and even decline of larger, older metropo-

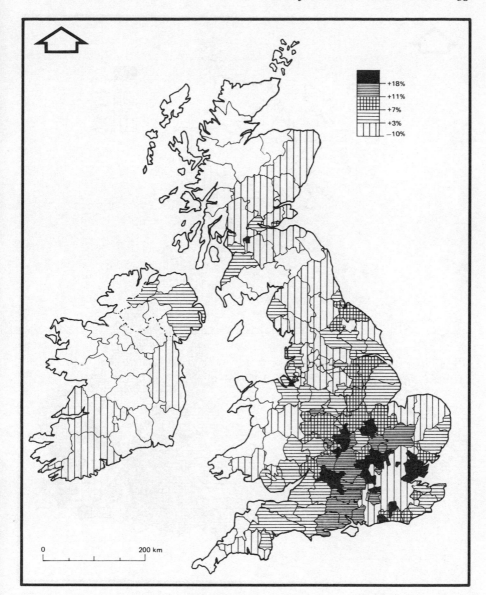

Fig. 4.1a   Atlantic Europe: population change 1950–60

lises was evident at least as early in Atlantic Europe as it was in the United States.

The pattern for the 1970s shows even more widely diffused growth around London, extending far into East Anglia and the South-west region as far as south Devon and south Cornwall. In contrast the northern half of the country, from Birmingham northwards, was almost universally showing stagnation or de-

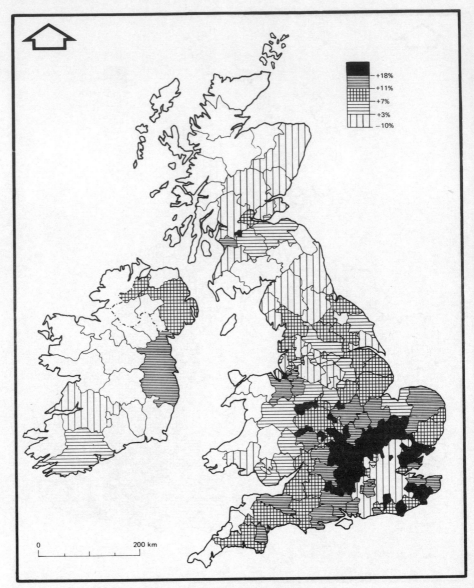

Fig. 4.1b   Atlantic Europe: population change 1960–70

cline. Particularly notable, again, was the loss from the big conurbation cities including London, Birmingham, Manchester, Liverpool and Glasgow.

With the metropolitan areas, as Figs. 4.2a and 4.2b show,* there was a rather pronounced reversal of population movement between the 1950s and the 1960s.

* For an explanation of the calculations for type of shift, see the Appendix at the end of this chapter.

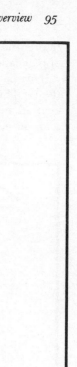

Fig. 4.1c   Atlantic Europe: population change 1970–75

In the 1950s a majority of areas were still centralising population in a relative sense; that is, the cores were growing faster than the rings. The exceptions were fairly well-distributed; they include most of the larger cities and also a number of smaller towns, including seaside resorts, in southern England. By the 1960s decentralisation was almost universal and the larger cities – together with some seaside resorts and a few other medium-sized towns – were demonstrating absolute loss of population from the cores.

This pattern continued and even accentuated into the 1970s, as Fig. 4.2c shows. The great majority of metropolitan areas were by then exhibiting decentralisation, and a significant number were showing absolute decentralisation with an actual loss of population from the core. Significantly also the biggest

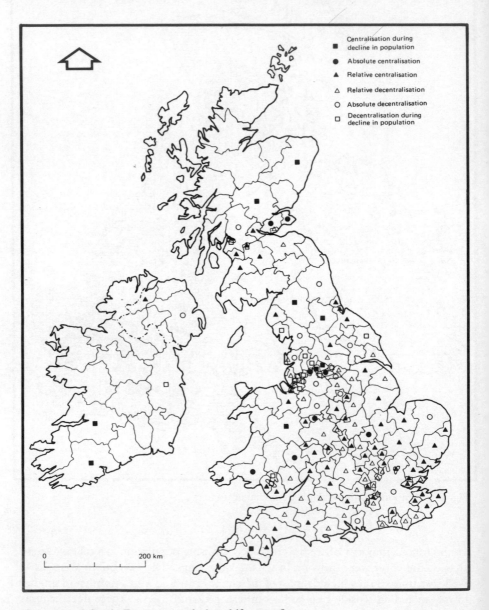

Fig. 4.2a   Atlantic Europe: population shift 1950–60

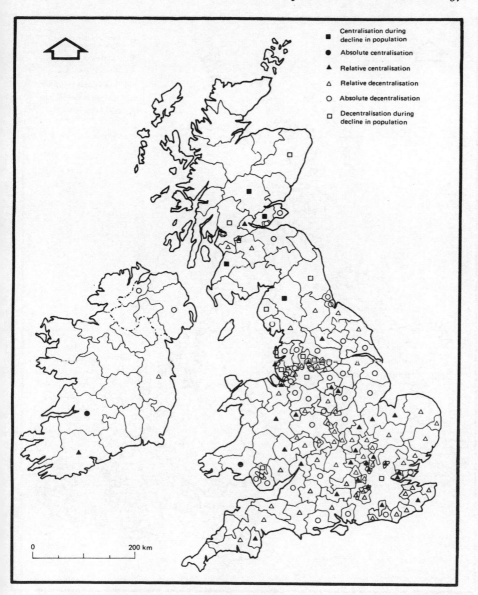

Fig. 4.2b   Atlantic Europe: population shift 1960–70

metropolitan areas – London, Birmingham, Manchester, Liverpool, Leeds, New-castle, Glasgow – were exhibiting decentralisation during loss; and this pattern had extended to many smaller areas in the industrial districts of northern England.

Comparison with Figs. 4.3a and 4.3b show that a similar reversal occurred for employment, but it was not nearly so pronounced. In the decade 1950–60 cen-

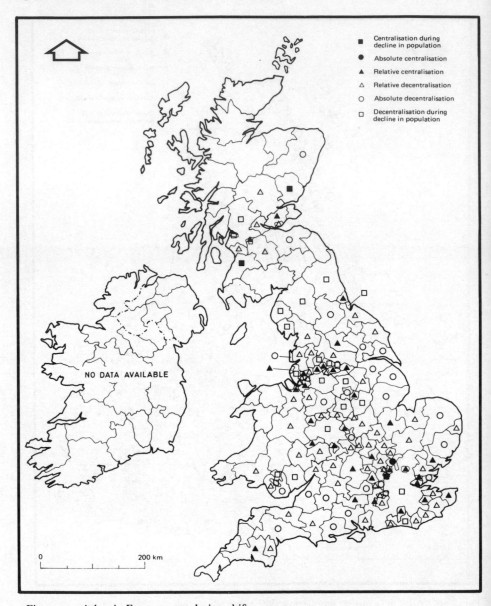

Fig. 4.2c   Atlantic Europe: population shift 1970–75

tralisation was the norm, with many examples of absolute losses from the rings; the exceptions to the general rule were widely distributed in areas such as the South Coast, the South Midlands, and Humberside. By the 1960s, in contrast, about half the total metropolitan areas were decentralising employment; again the bigger cities were prominent here, and in the case of some of the biggest of all – London, Liverpool, Manchester, Glasgow – there was a relative decentralisa-

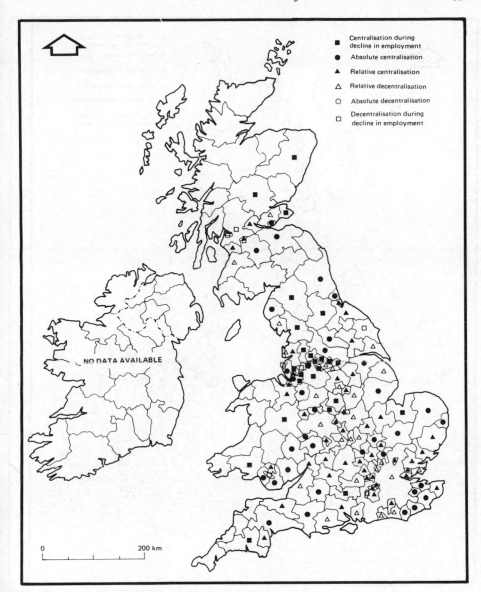

Fig. 4.3a   Atlantic Europe: employment shift 1950–60

tion associated with a decline in employment throughout the metropolitan system. In this regard, again, Atlantic Europe seems to have kept parallel with trends on the other side of the ocean.

Northern Europe
The three northern European countries are much less strongly urbanised – or

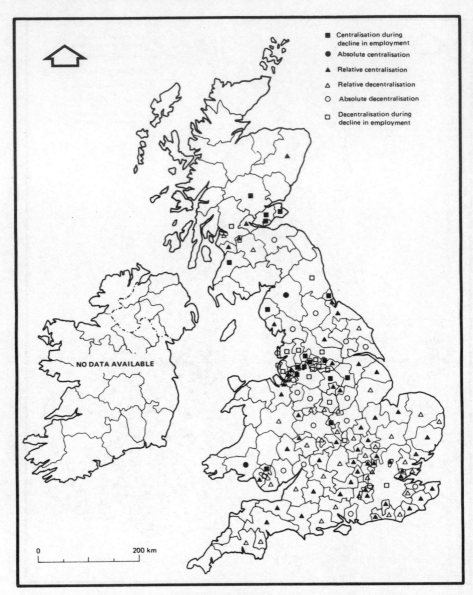

Fig. 4.3b   Atlantic Europe: employment shift 1960–70

'metropolitanised' than Atlantic Europe, or as Europe as a whole, as Tables 4.3a and 4.3b show. In 1950, only 76.9 per cent of the population lived in metropolitan areas as we have defined them in this study, and that proportion has risen only slowly to 79.2 per cent by 1975. Nor are the urban cores particularly prominent: they contained just under 34 per cent of the total population in 1950, climbed to 35.5 per cent in 1960 and then fell back, to 35.2 per cent in 1970 and

Table 4.3a   Northern Europe (Denmark, Sweden, Norway): metropolitan and non-metropolitan region population 1950–75

Population data for 1950, 1960, 1970 and 1975

Areal unit	1950 Total (thousands)	1950 % of total	1960 Total (thousands)	1960 % of total	1970 Total (thousands)	1970 % of total	1975 Total (thousands)	1975 % of total
Core	4959	33.94	5554	35.54	5950	35.23	5683	32.90
Ring	6274	42.94	6589	42.16	7403	43.83	8007	46.35
Non-metropolitan	3378	23.12	3485	22.30	3536	20.93	3585	20.75
Total	14 612	100.00	15 628	100.00	16 889	100.00	17 275	100.00

Population change 1950–60, 1960–70 and 1970–75

Areal unit	1950–60 Absolute change (thousands)	1950–60 % change	1950–60 % of total	1960–70 Absolute change (thousands)	1960–70 % change	1960–70 % of total	1970–75 Absolute change (thousands)	1970–75 % change	1970–75 % of total
Core	594	11.99	58.49	395	7.14	31.45	−267	−4.49	−69.17
Ring	315	5.02	30.98	814	12.35	64.54	604	8.16	156.48
Non-metropolitan	107	3.17	10.53	51	1.45	4.01	49	1.39	12.69
Total	1016	6.95	100.00	1261	8.07	100.00	386	2.29	100.00

Table 4.3b   Northern Europe (Denmark, Sweden, Norway): metropolitan and non-metropolitan region employment 1950–70

	Employment data for 1950, 1960 and 1970							
	1950		*1960ᵃ*		*1970ᵃ*		*1970ᵇ*	
	Total	*% of*	*Total*	*% of*	*Total*	*% of*	*Total*	*% of*
Areal unit	*(thousands)*	*total*	*(thousands)*	*total*	*(thousands)*	*total*	*(thousands)*	*total*
Core	na	na	1359	41.01	1520	44.76	2996	43.31
Ring	na	na	1245	37.57	1148	37.42	2582	37.33
Non-metropolitan	na	na	710	21.42	680	17.82	1339	19.35
Total	na	na	3314	100.00	3347	100.00	6917	100.00

	Employment change 1950–60 and 1960–70					
	1950–60			*1960–70ᵃ*		
	Absolute	*%*	*% of*	*Absolute*	*%*	*% of*
	change	*change*	*total*	*change*	*change*	*total*
Areal unit	*(thousands)*			*(thousands)*		
Core	na	na	na	161	11.85	480.40
Ring	na	na	na	−97	7.82	−290.45
Non-metropolitan	na	na	na	−30	4.25	−89.95
Total	na	na	na	33	1.01	100.00

Notes: ᵃ Sweden.
   ᵇ Denmark, Sweden and Norway.
   na – data not available.

32.9 per cent in 1975. Conversely a high proportion – 42.9 per cent in 1950, falling to 42.1 per cent in 1960, then rising to 43.8 per cent in 1970 and 46.4 per cent in 1975 – lived in the rings of the metropolitan areas, indicating a rather dispersed population within the spheres of influence of the major cities. In this sense Scandinavia is quite suburbanised, and the suburban trend has grown markedly stronger with metropolitan rings accounting for 31 per cent of total population growth in the 1950s, for less than 64.5 per cent in the following decade, and then for well over the net growth (156.5%) in the 1970s as core populations fell. Employment trends are harder to analyse due to the non-existence of workplace data for Norway and Denmark in 1950 and 1960 and for Sweden in 1950. However, the 1970 figures indicate a relatively low concentration of employment in metropolitan regions (80.6 per cent) compared with the other European national groupings; in fact, only 1.5 per cent more employment than population is located in the Scandinavian metropolitan regions. The cores themselves have a sizeable share of the national employment totals in 1970 (43.3 per cent) although, again this is a lower figure than equivalent proportions in other groupings.

We can therefore sum up the Scandinavian experience as far as we are able: a substantial, but falling, proportion of the total population lives and works outside metropolitan areas. Within the metropolitan areas, population was concentrating in the cores in the 1950s; but later began to decentralise at an accelerated rate into the metropolitan rings. This parallels European experience as a whole and may indicate that Scandinavia is fairly typical of general trends, being in this regard at a slightly earlier stage of evolution than Atlantic Europe.

Appendix Tables A.5 to A.10 show that the individual northern European countries did not diverge very markedly from this general pattern. The degree of metropolitan concentration of population was a little below the general level in Sweden, more noticeably below it in Norway and above it in Denmark; but in all three countries it rose over the twenty-year period.

Even national totals tend to mask spatial variations, however. Figs. 4.4a, 4.4b and 4.4c show the pattern of population change for the two decades. In the 1950s growth in Sweden in Sweden peaked in the region around Stockholm, with the Göteborg region in second place. In Norway the heaviest growth tended to be along the south coast; the Oslo complex of metropolitan areas was showing considerably less dynamism than the Stockholm complex. In both countries, the metropolitan areas of the extreme north did not display conspicuous growth. In Denmark the main development was again around Copenhagen, but the metropolitan area of the capital city was growing less rapidly than two smaller areas in the thirty-mile range, Helsingør and Roskilde. Already, here, there is evidence of local decentralisation from the biggest metropolitan area to adjacent ones. Fig. 4.4b shows that in the 1960s this process accentuated; otherwise a notable feature was the development of a belt of strong growth in central Jutland, along the Århus–Herning axis, in stark contrast to the stagnation and decline further north. In Sweden the heaviest growth had polarised in the Stockholm, Göteborg and Malmö–Lund regions; there was no evidence here of a slowing-down in the growth of the biggest regions, but Stockholm was showing a tendency to decentralise towards Södertälje in rather the same way as Copenhagen towards Roskilde. Norway had an even pattern of growth, with the highest levels recorded in the south-west coastal areas.

In the 1970s population growth was rather weak everywhere, a result of falling birth-rates. Much of the interior area of Sweden had static declining population by this time. The larger urban areas on the whole continued to attract modest rates of growth with the exception of Copenhagen, where local decentralisation to Helsingør and Roskilde persisted. Within Denmark eastern Jutland again continued to be an area of rather stronger growth. In Norway the heaviest growth was on the south coast and in the Trondheim area. The growth of Luleå in northern Sweden marks the impact of a vigorous regional policy to develop the northern region of that country.

These patterns need to be seen in relation to the internal shifts recorded in Figs. 4.5a 4.5b and 4.5c. Very evident here is the dominant pattern of centralisation shown for both decades in Sweden and Denmark, contrasted with the tendency towards decentralisation in much of Norway. In the 1950s the two capital regions were the only ones recording decentralisation in the first two countries (Copenhagen absolutely, Stockholm relatively); in Norway decentralisation was

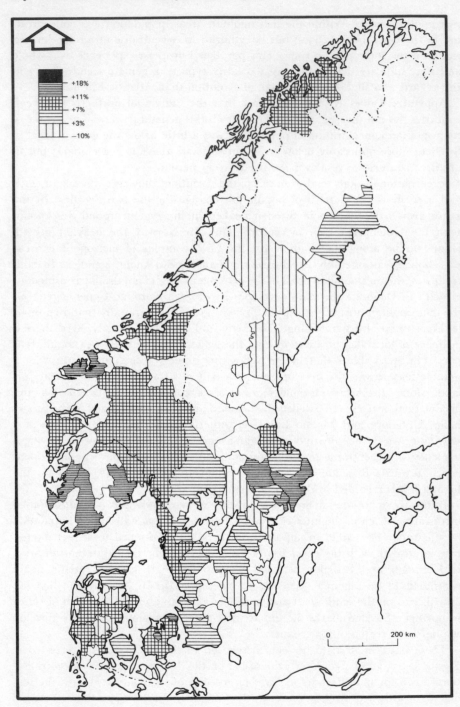

Fig. 4.4a   Northern Europe: population change 1950–60

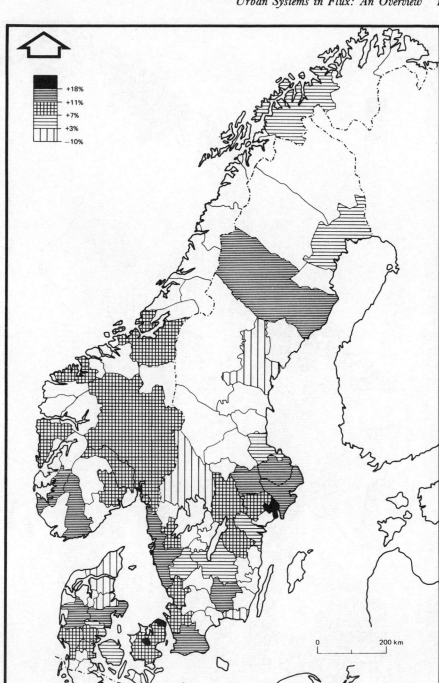

+18%
+11%
+7%
+3%
−10%

0   200 km

Fig. 4.4b   Northern Europe: population change 1960–70

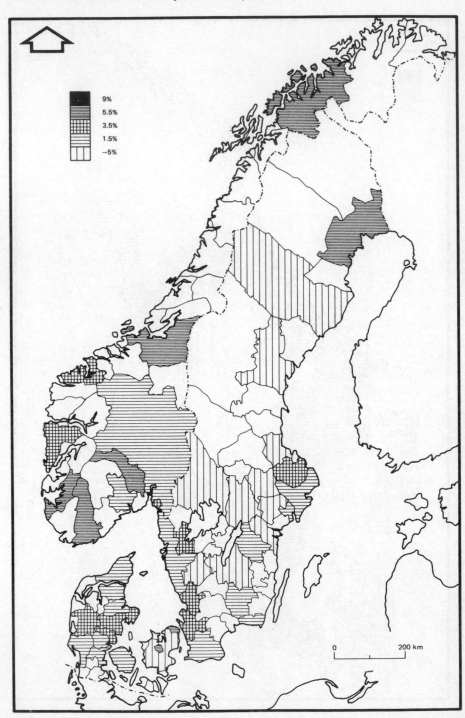

Fig. 4.4c   Northern Europe: population change 1970–75

general in the Oslo complex and in other major urban centres. Nor had this picture changed strikingly by the 1960s. In Sweden, Göteborg and Helsingborg joined Stockholm in the process of decentralisation; in Norway, the major centres continued to deconcentrate; but in Denmark, only Copenhagen's near neighbour Helsingør joined it in this process. Particularly significant is that the aggregate pattern of decentralisation in Denmark, earlier noted, was almost wholly due to the anomalous behaviour of its biggest urban system. But by the 1970s the picture was very different: decentralisation was the rule everywhere, with a considerable amount of absolute decentralisation as core cities began to lose to their hinterlands. The exceptions appear to be special cases of towns growing strongly in near proximity to capital cities, such as Västerås and Gävle near Stockholm or Porsgrunn–Skien near Oslo. Clearly, the 1970s marked a 'clean break' in Scandinavian population trends.

Only for Sweden – and only for the decade 1960–70 – can any comment be made on employment change and shift in northern Europe; although it would be dangerous to infer that this sample was totally representative of northern European employment trends over this period (Fig. 4.6). Strong centralisation of employment, exceeded only by Switzerland, was the basic pattern in Sweden (Appendix Table A.6) during this decade; the overall increase of 11.8 per cent in the cores suggesting that the trend towards employment deconcentration, experienced by several other European nations, is a feature of the most densely populated zones. Indeed, only Stockholm, with a relative loss of jobs between 1960 and 1970, contradicted the general pattern. But with this one exception, the picture of population and, as far as we are able to judge, employment trends only confirms the conclusion earlier reached: that in important respects, the evolution of urban systems in northern Europe is at a slightly earlier stage than in atlantic Europe. We shall return to this important conclusion later in the chapter.

Western Europe
It might at first be thought that western Europe – embracing as it does some of the urban heartland of mainland Europe such as the Dutch Randstad, Flanders and the Paris Basin – would be one of the most heavily urbanised regions of Europe. But it embraces also the great rural expanses of southern and western France, and so the proportion of its population that lives in metropolitan areas is actually lower than the European aggregate: 83.9 per cent in 1950, rising to 86.0 per cent by 1970 and very marginally from then to 1975 (see Table 4.4a). Within this total, the proportion living in the cores was close to the European average: 37.8 per cent in 1950, rising steadily to 41.6 per cent in 1970; thence, excluding Luxembourg, the proportion fell from 41.7 per cent in 1970 to 40.9 per cent in 1975. In other words, until 1970 the tendency here was strongly towards centralisation; the rings' share of total population actually fell in both decades, and in both a majority of the total population growth – nearly 64 per cent in the 1950s, over 53 per cent in the 1960s – occurred in the metropolitan core areas. But then came a 'clean break': excluding Luxembourg, the com-

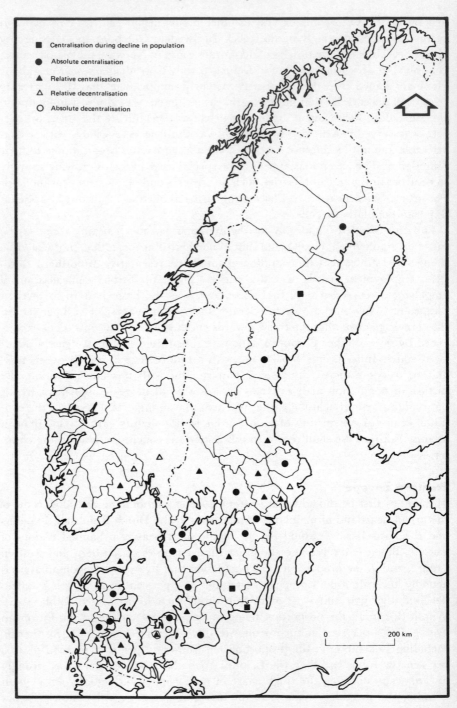

Fig. 4.5a Northern Europe: population shift 1950–60

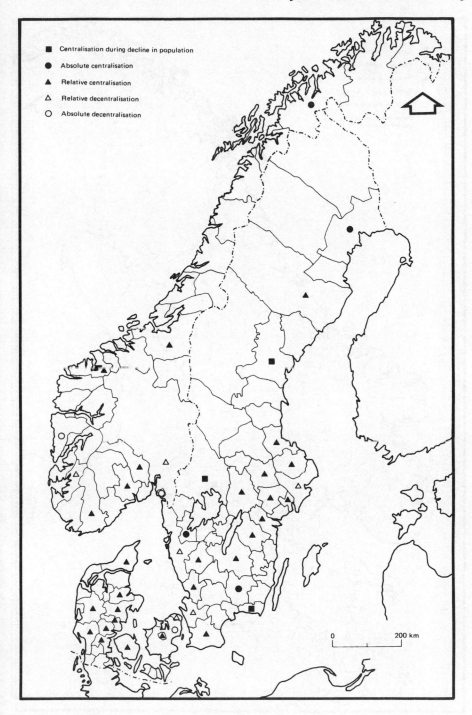

Fig. 4.5b   Northern Europe: population shift 1960–70

Fig. 4.5c   Northern Europe: population shift 1970–75

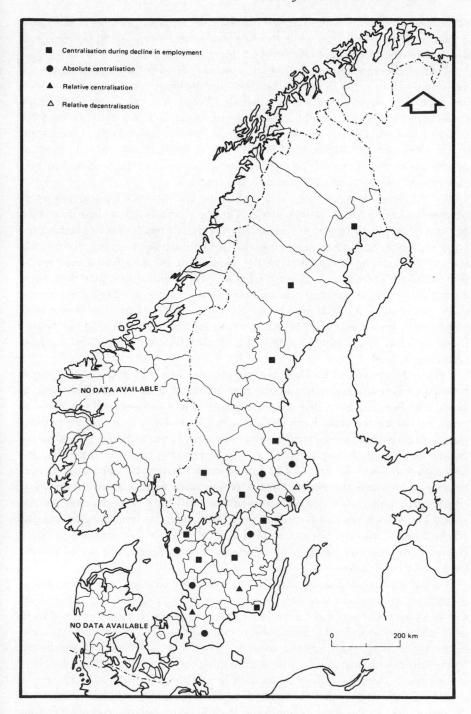

■ Centralisation during decline in employment

● Absolute centralisation

▲ Relative centralisation

△ Relative decentralisation

NO DATA AVAILABLE

NO DATA AVAILABLE

0   200 km

Fig. 4.6   Northern Europe: employment shift 1960–70

parison shows that the core share fell dramatically from 53 per cent in the 1960s to 20 per cent in the 1970s, while the ring share rose from 40 to 69 per cent and the non-metropolitan share rose from 6.2 to 11.5 per cent.

Much of the 1950–70 centralisation, however, disguises the performances of individual countries. Both the Netherlands and Belgium experienced much earlier population decentralisation as Appendix Tables A.11 and A.13 show, with consistent ring growth, mainly at the expense of cores, throughout the twenty-five-year period. France, on the other hand, moved towards decentralisation much more slowly (Appendix Table A.15); indeed, strong centralisation of population occurred even up to 1970 whereas much of Europe by this time had experienced the beginnings of outward movement.

The employment figures for western Europe are more difficult to interpret, because we have a full set only for 1960. Table 4.4b shows that at that date, 86.1 per cent of employment was in metropolitan regions. French data are lacking for 1950 and 1970, making time comparisons impossible; Belgian data are missing for 1950, restricting comparison to the 1960s. But the Dutch statistics reveal that, although cores were receiving a higher proportion of new jobs than rings during the 1950s, the process was reversed in the 1960s with high gains in the rings contrasted with zero growth in the cores. In Belgium, also, hinterland employment grew faster than in the cores during the 1960s marking the beginnings, as far as we are able to judge, of a greater dispersal of jobs – in the Low Countries at least.

Despite deficiencies in the data, we can say that western Europe has exhibited internally contradictory trends in the post-World War II period. The Netherlands and Belgium have decentralised population from metropolitan cores to rings. France on the other hand showed a strong tendency to centralise population, but even here, a contrary trend set in after 1970, with the core share of population growth falling from 73.0 to 43.1 per cent and the rings showing faster growth than the cores. The employment change is regrettably harder to review, although the results for the Netherlands and Belgium suggest that employment patterns in total are coincident with those of population by the 1960s. The French position is unclear, but, intuitively, the continuing movement off the land, at least up to 1970, implies a decline of jobs in metropolitan rings. However, the buoyant nature of the French economy during this period cannot lend itself to such inferences.

It is particularly interesting therefore to look more closely at the geographical patterns of growth and internal change. Figs. 4.7a, 4.7b and 4.7c show that within western Europe, there have been great variations in growth rates during the period 1950–75. Partly, these reflect national demographic experience: thus in the 1950s there was a striking contrast between the dynamism of the urban Netherlands (with particularly strong growth in the Catholic, south-eastern part of the country) and the relative stagnation in neighbouring Belgium. France was somewhat intermediate between the two, with strong growth in Lorraine, in Provence, and in the Paris region as well as in some isolated coastal locations such as Nantes–St Nazaire and Boulogne–Dunkerque. In the 1960s the same

Table 4.4a Western Europe (France, Belgium, Netherlands): metropolitan and non-metropolitan region population 1950-75

Population data for 1950, 1960, 1970 and 1975

Areal unit	1950^a Total (thousands)	% of total	1960^a Total (thousands)	% of total	1970^a Total (thousands)	% of total	1950^b Total (thousands)	% of total	1960^b Total (thousands)	% of total	1970^b Total (thousands)	% of total	1975^b Total (thousands)	% of total
Core	22 744	37.84	26 725	40.29	30 717	41.60	22 682	37.92	26 653	40.37	30 641	41.69	31 169	40.93
Ring	27 674	46.05	29 711	44.79	32 760	44.36	27 445	45.89	29 468	44.63	32 496	44.21	34 308	45.05
Non-metropolitan	9683	16.11	9900	14.92	10 368	14.04	9683	16.19	9900	15.00	10 368	14.10	10 673	14.02
Total	60 101	100.00	66 336	100.00	73 845	100.00	59 810	100.00	66 021	100.00	73 505	100.00	76 150	100.00

Population change 1950-60, 1960-70 and 1970-75

Areal unit	1950-60^a Absolute change (thousands)	% change	% of total	1960-70^a Absolute change (thousands)	% change	% of total	1950-60^b Absolute change (thousands)	% change	% of total	1960-70^b Absolute change (thousands)	% change	% of total	1970-75^b Absolute change (thousands)	% change	% of total
Core	3981	17.50	63.85	3992	14.94	53.16	3971	17.51	63.93	3988	14.96	53.29	528	1.72	19.96
Ring	2037	7.36	32.67	3049	10.26	40.60	2023	7.73	32.57	3028	10.28	40.46	1812	5.58	68.51
Non-metropolitan	217	2.24	3.48	468	4.73	6.23	217	2.24	3.49	468	4.73	6.25	305	2.94	11.53
Total	6235	10.38	100.00	7509	11.32	100.00	6211	10.38	100.00	7484	11.34	100.00	2645	3.60	100.00

Notes: *a* Including Luxembourg.
b Excluding Luxembourg.

Table 4.4b Western Europe (France, Belgium, Netherlands): metropolitan and non-metropolitan region employment 1950–70

| | Employment data for 1950, 1960 and 1970 | | | | | | | | | |
| | 1950[a] | | 1960[a] | | 1970[a] | | 1970[b] | | 1960[c] | |
Areal unit	*Total (thousands)*	*% of total*	*Total (thousands)*	*% of total*	*Total (thousands)*	*% of total*	*Total (thousands)*	*% of total*	*Total (thousands)*	*% of total*
Core	1647	44.89	1893	46.74	1894	45.90	3295	41.98	11 682	44.48
Ring	1779	48.48	1913	47.22	1994	48.33	4273	54.43	10 922	41.59
Non-metropolitan	243	6.63	244	6.04	238	5.78	282	3.59	3657	13.92
Total	3669	100.00	4050	100.00	4126	100.00	7850	100.00	26 260	100.00

| | Employment 1950–60 and 1960–70 | | | | | |
| | 1950–60[a] | | | 1960–70[a] | | |
Areal unit	*Absolute change (thousands)*	*% change*	*% of total*	*Absolute change (thousands)*	*% change*	*% of total*
Core	246	14.94	64.61	1	0.03	0.68
Ring	134	7.52	35.11	81	4.26	107.45
Non-metropolitan	1	0.44	0.28	−6	−2.52	−8.12
Total	381	10.38	100.00	76	1.87	100.00

Notes: [a] Netherlands only.
      [b] Netherlands and Belgium only.
      [c] Netherlands, Belgium and France.

contrasts are evident: the belt of very rapid growth in the Netherlands now runs north–south from the area bordering the IJsselmeer, down to Eindhoven, while parts of the western Randstad are growing much more slowly. In Belgium growth is generally modest but fairly even except for the stagnating southern coalfield; in France, the particularly striking feature is the development of the zone of most rapid growth in the whole south-eastern part of the country, embracing most of the southern coastal area from the Spanish to the Italian border, but extended inland, particularly up the Rhône corridor. Only slightly less notable is the continued dynamism of the Paris region, now extending from the capital itself to a ring of subordinate metropolitan areas up to 200 kilometres distant such as Tours, Chartres, Orléans, Rennes, Rouen–Le Havre, Evreux and Amiens. Strong growth also continues in Alsace–Lorraine. But outside these favoured zones, relative stagnation continued to characterise 'le désert français' of southern and western France.

The 1970s saw some modification of these trends. By then, rapid growth was generally characteristic of the whole of the eastern Netherlands, including the extreme north-east (the province of Groningen) that had previously been lagging. The southern half of the country was also growing strongly, and contrasted with more modest growth in Randstad Holland. In Belgium, on the other hand, growth was everywhere weaker except for the Hasselt area next to the Dutch growth zone. To the south, on the coalfield across the Belgian–French frontier, there was clear evidence of the recession in coal and associated heavy industries. The Paris region was decentralising strongly to centres up to 150 or 200 kilo-

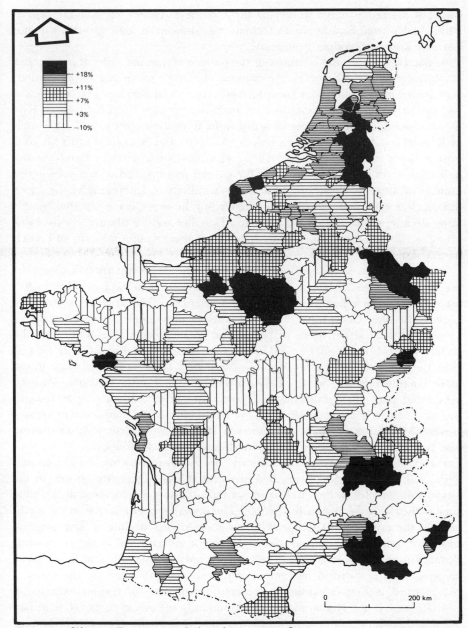

Fig. 4.7a   Western Europe: population change 1950–60

metres distant, such as Evreux, Chartres, Orléans, Rennes and Amiens. Resort
areas such as Brest and Quimper in far western Brittany, as well as the Nantes–
St Nazaire *métropôle d'equilibre*, were also demonstrating extremely strong growth.
In the south, Toulouse and Montpellier were islands of growth; the Rhône
corridor appeared to be growing less strongly than in the 1960s, and the main

emphasis seemed to have shifted to the Grenoble–Annecy region. The upper Rhine valley from Strasbourg to Colmar was showing modest growth, but the Lorraine area was tending to stagnate.

As notable also are the contrasts in the pattern of internal shifts of people and employment. Figs. 4.8a–c show the patterns of relative movement of population, and confirm that in the 1950s both the Netherlands and Belgium were characterised by fairly strong tendencies to decentralisation from metropolitan cores. Particularly notable here were the outward shifts from the bigger urban areas such as Rotterdam, The Hague, Amsterdam, Antwerp and Brussels. France in contrast shows a strong centralising trend, with only a few areas – mainly in the industrial north and east – breaking the overall pattern, and with a substantial number of areas demonstrating absolute centralisation. Interestingly, the 1960s show a clear continuation in France. Significant, however, is the fact that by this latter decade, three major cities – Paris, Marseilles and Strasbourg – were exhibiting relative decentralisation, thus appearing among a select minority of French metropolitan areas.

The 1970s show some continuity but also some important modifications. In the Netherlands and Belgium, decentralisation was by then the general rule, and many areas – including the big cities (Amsterdam, The Hague, Rotterdam, Utrecht; Brussels, Gent, Liège) but also many smaller ones – were decentralising absolutely, with actual losses of population in the core cities. In France the picture is much more mixed, and seems to represent a transition. The biggest cities were decentralising relatively, but there are a large number of areas in the more dynamic regions – west of Paris, in the south, and in the Grenoble–Annecy area – that were still centralising as the core cities attracted new people. And, in the rural centre of the country, there are still some smaller metropolitan areas – Nevers, Montluçon, Vichy – that showed the pattern of centralisation during loss, typical of an early stage of industrialisation and urbanisation.

For employment, the analysis has to be restricted to Benelux. Figs. 4.9a and 4.9b confirm the conclusion reached in the analysis of aggregate figures: in the 1950s, a majority of Netherlands cities were centralising employment at the same time as they were decentralising people. The probable reason is that in the Netherlands, the rapid population growth was coupled with decline of farm employment due to mechanisation, so that employment concentrated in the cities while people found new homes outside them, with only Amsterdam and The Hague showing signs of outward movement of jobs to the rings. But, by the 1960s, a more mixed picture is evident: an increasing number of regions exhibit decentralisation in the Netherlands – predominantly the major cities; while in Belgium, although overall deconcentration is indicated by the aggregate data, centralisation of jobs occurred in no fewer than ten metropolitan regions, including Brussels, no doubt partly as a result of the country's strong leanings towards the encouragement of foreign investment.

In summary, therefore, a confused situation is evident. The Low Countries seem to be at a slightly later phase of metropolitan evolution than is France. During the 1950s and 1960s they were still centralising jobs (with the exception of a few

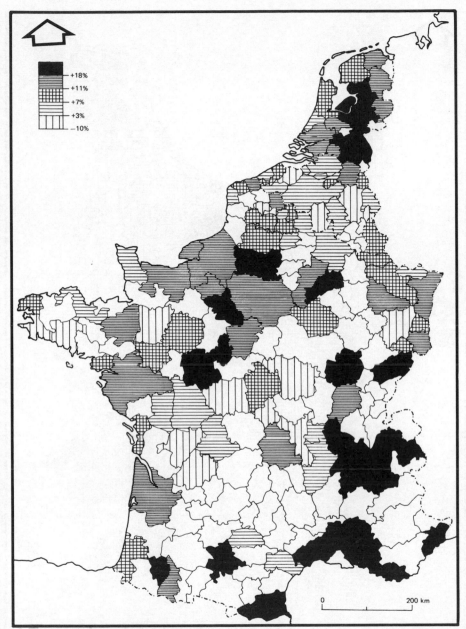

Fig. 4.7b   Western Europe: population change 1960–70

large cities) but decentralising people; this, as already seen, was fairly characteristic also for Atlantic Europe in this period. France, on the other hand, tended to
centralise population as well – except for a very few large cities in the 1960s.
This is consistent with an economy where very large numbers were still leaving
the land, often from remote non-metropolitan areas, and were migrating to cen-

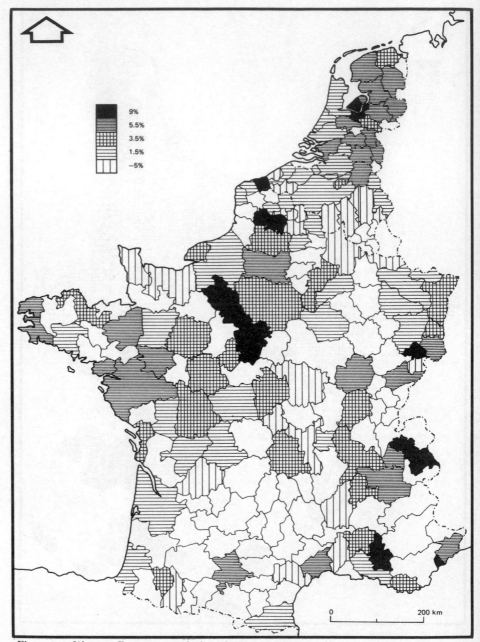

Fig. 4.7c   Western Europe: population change 1970–75

tral cities in search of expanding job opportunities in the manufacturing and service sectors. This pattern, we earlier saw, was also characteristic of much of northern Europe. By the 1970s, population decentralisation was at full flood in the Benelux countries; but France seemed to be in a stage of transition, with de-

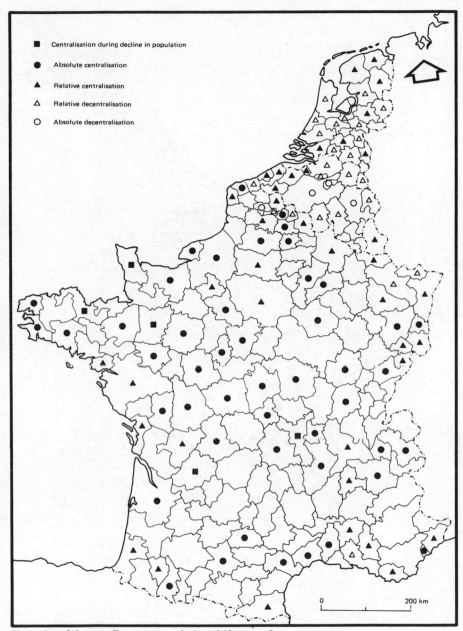

Fig. 4.8a   Western Europe: population shift 1950–60

centralisation from the larger cities but a form of local centralisation into some core cities of dynamic regions, into which migration currents were strongly flowing.

Southern Europe
At first sight, the summary figures for the countries of Europe's southern peri-

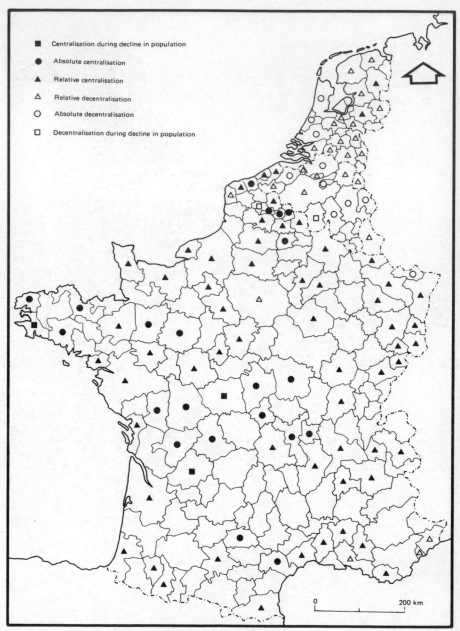

Fig. 4.8b   Western Europe: population shift 1960–70

phery recall those for the northern periphery. Table 4.5a shows that like northern Europe, southern Europe has a rather low proportion of its population
living in metropolitan areas and also a low proportion living in their urban core
areas. But in southern Europe, unlike Scandinavia, there has been a strong tendency towards concentration. In 1950, only 74.2 per cent of the population lived

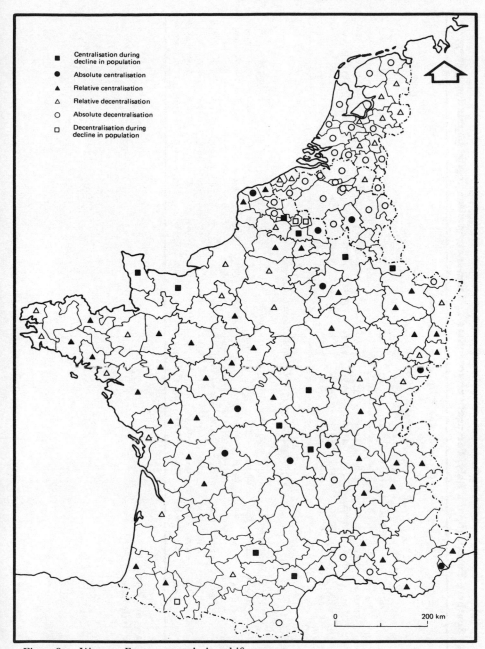

Centralisation during
decline in population

Absolute centralisation

Relative centralisation

Relative decentralisation

Absolute decentralisation

Decentralisation during
decline in population

0   200 km

Fig. 4.8c   Western Europe: population shift 1970–75

in metropolitan areas; by 1970, that proportion had risen to 79.3 per cent.
Again, in 1950 only 27.9 per cent lived in metropolitan cores; but by 1970 that
figure had jumped to 35.4 per cent. The cores took over 85 per cent of growth in
the 1950s, over 80 per cent in the 1960s – though by this latter decade, the rings

Table 4.5a   Southern Europe (Spain, Italy, Portugal): metropolitan and non-metropolitan region population 1950–75

Population data for 1950, 1960, 1970 and 1975

Areal unit	1950[a]		1960[a]		1970[a]		1950[b]		1960[b]		1970[b]		1975[b]	
	Total	% of total	Total	% of total	Total	% of total	Total	% of total	Total	% of total	Total	% of total	Total	% of total
Core	22 801	27.94	27 821	31.82	33 346	35.37	21 518	29.17	26 389	33.32	31 896	36.81	32 974	37.05
Ring	37 747	46.26	38 696	44.25	41 425	43.93	33 644	45.61	34 282	43.29	37 115	42.84	39 473	44.36
Non-metropolitan	21 045	25.79	20 927	23.93	19 515	20.69	18 609	25.22	18 522	23.39	17 619	20.33	16 543	18.59
Total	81 593	100.00	87 444	100.00	94 286	100.00	73 771	100.00	79 193	100.00	86 630	100.00	88 990	100.00

Population change 1950–60, 1960–70 and 1970–5

Areal unit	1950–60[a]			1960–70[a]			1950–60[b]			1960–70[b]			1970–5[b]		
	Absolute change	% change	% of total	Absolute change	% change	% of total	Absolute change	% change	% of total	Absolute change	% change	% of total	Absolute change	% change	% of total
Core	5020	22.02	85.80	5525	19.86	80.75	4871	22.64	89.84	5507	20.87	74.05	1078	3.38	45.68
Ring	949	2.51	16.22	2729	7.05	39.89	638	1.90	11.76	2833	8.26	38.09	2358	6.35	99.92
Non-metropolitan	−118	−0.56	−2.02	−1413	−6.75	−20.65	−87	−0.47	−1.60	−993	−4.88	−12.16	−1076	−6.10	−45.56
Total	5851	7.17	100.00	6842	7.82	100.00	5422	7.35	100.00	7437	9.39	100.00	2360	2.72	100.00

Notes: [a] Spain, Italy and Portugal.
[b] Spain and Italy only.

were taking over one-third of total growth. In both decades, the non-metropolitan areas lost people absolutely, the loss increasing from 118 000 in the 1950s to over 1.0 million in the 1960s.

Here, as elsewhere, the 1970s saw a break – though not of quite the same character as already observed for other parts of Europe. The figures for Spain and Italy (no Portuguese figures are available for this period) show that the cores continued to grow and to increase their total share of population, from 36.8 per cent in 1970 to 37.1 per cent in 1975. But the rate of core growth dramatically slowed, and the rings were growing twice as fast. Indeed they accounted for virtually the whole of the total net growth, with the more modest gains of the cores being offset by continuing decline in the non-metropolitan areas. So here, too, there were beginnings of the sign of the 'clean break' – though certainly, it was not transferring population back to the rural areas.

There are no time-comparable employment figures for all three countries in the southern group. Table 4.5b shows that in 1970, over 40 per cent of their total employment was in the cores and altogether more than 81 per cent was in metropolitan areas; however, this is an exaggerated total since the Spanish figures omit farm workers. Italy, the only country for which employment data are available for an earlier year, had seen the share of the metropolitan areas climb from 77.3 per cent in 1960 to 79.6 per cent in 1970 – and the share of the cores rise in parallel, from 36.1 to 39.4 per cent. But, this was in the context of a very puzzl-

Table 4.5b Southern Europe (Spain, Italy, Portugal): metropolitan and non-metropolitan region employment 1950–70

Areal unit	Employment data for 1950, 1960 and 1970							
	1950[a]		1960[a]		1970[a]		1970[b]	
	Total (thousands)	% of total	Total (thousands)	% of total	Total (thousands)	% of total	Total (thousands)	% of total
Core	na	na	6452	36.06	6981	39.36	10 888	40.33
Ring	na	na	7381	41.25	7146	40.29	11 115	41.17
Non-metropolitan	na	na	4061	22.70	3610	20.36	4995	18.50
Total	na	na	17 894	100.00	17 737	100.00	26 999	100.00

Areal unit	Employment change 1950–60 and 1960–70					
	1950–60[a]			1960–70[a]		
	Absolute change (thousands)	% change	% of total	Absolute change (thousands)	% change	% of total
Core	na	na	na	529	8.19	−337.26
Ring	na	na	na	−235	−3.18	149.69
Non-metropolitan	na	na	na	−451	−11.10	287.57
Total	na	na	na	−157	−0.88	100.00

Notes: [a] Italy only.
          [b] Italy, Spain and Portugal.
          na – Data not available.

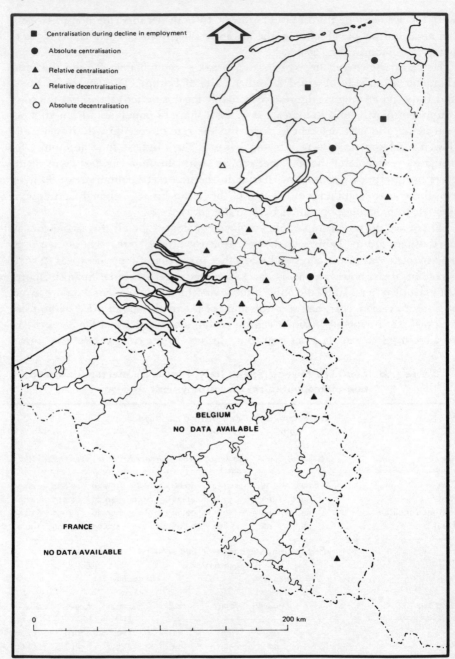

Fig. 4.9a   Western Europe: employment shift 1950–60

ing marginal fall in total employment, which possibly reflects deficiencies in the employment data.

Appendix Tables A.17 to A.22 present population and, where possible, em-

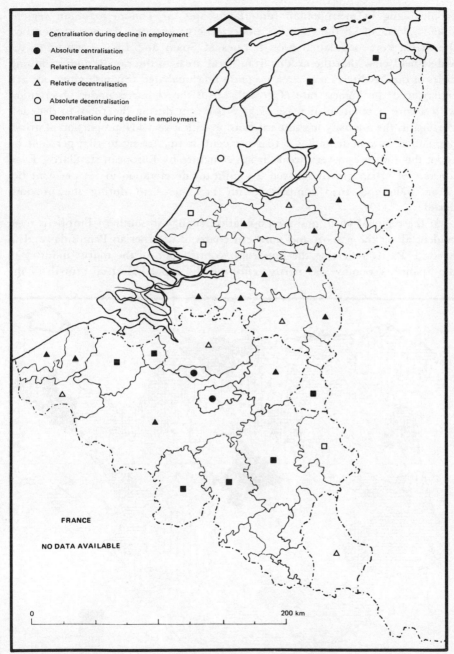

Fig. 4.9b Western Europe: employment shift 1960–70

ployment change in the individual countries of southern Europe over the 1950–75 period. Both Spain and Italy, as would be expected, experienced rapid core population growth throughout with corresponding declines in the percentages of people living in metropolitan hinterlands and the non-metropolitan regions alike. Indeed, of all the countries under observation, only France approached the urban core population growth rates of Spain and Italy, confirming the widely-held view that the exodus from rural areas to the rapidly industrialising cities of the Mediterranean area is continuing unabated (Spanish cities, in fact, experienced the highest rate of growth of all the countries under observation with a core population increase of 31.2 per cent during the 1960–70 decade). Portugal is the anomaly in southern Europe with a very low proportion of urban population by our definition – 16.4 per cent in 1950 rising to 18.3 per cent by 1970; this indicates a very weak urban structure by European standards. Even the rate of urban growth showed a significant deceleration to 1.3 per cent between 1960 and 1970 compared with 11.5 per cent during the previous decade.

At the regional level, positive population change in southern Europe is most evident along the eastern and northern coasts of the Iberian Peninsula, and in Madrid. Partly reflecting the important contribution of the tourist industry to the Spanish economy and partly reflecting the rapid industrial growth of the

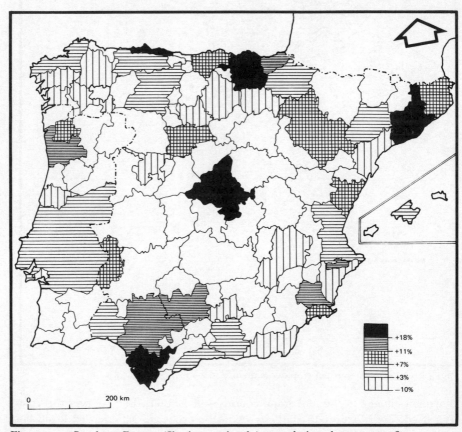

+18%
+11%
+7%
+3%
–10%

0   200 km

Fig. 4.10a   Southern Europe (Iberian peninsula): population change 1950–60

Basque and Catalan regions, the population increases are most dramatic in the 1960–70 time period with no fewer than eleven metropolitan regions in these two coastal areas exhibiting growth rates in excess of 18 per cent (Figs. 4.10a and 4.10c). In Italy the fastest growing regions are predictably in the North-west and the Rome area, although consistent population growth over both decades is apparent around Florence and Bologna in north-central Italy (Figs. 4.10b and 4.10d). Predictable, also, is the accelerating population decline of the Mezzogiorno with six metropolitan regions out of sixteen actually experiencing negative growth in the 1950s; this increased to nine in the 1960s.

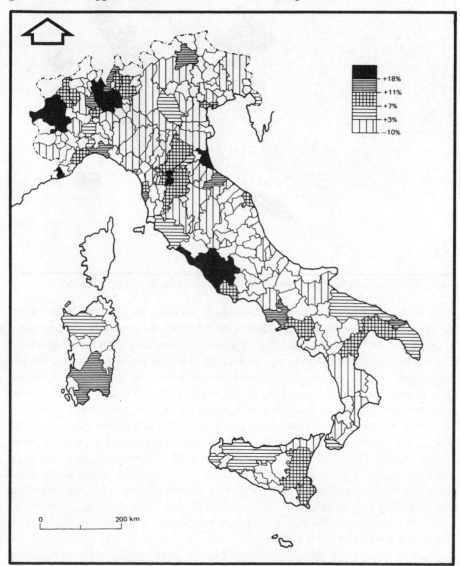

Fig. 4.10b   Southern Europe (Italy): population change 1950–60

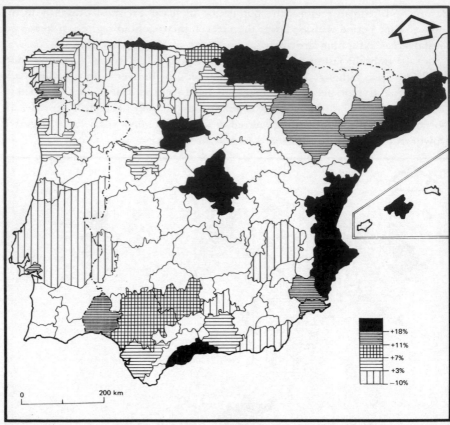

Fig. 4.10c   Southern Europe (Iberian peninsula): population change 1960–70

In the 1970s there was again exceptionally rapid growth all along the Mediterranean coasts of Spain, together with Madrid and the Basque provinces. Here, as in the previous decade, the biggest metropolitan areas were still showing extremely large increases; but once again the interior of the country showed stagnation or decline, save for isolated islands (generally representing planned growth poles) at Huelva and Jaén in the South and in the Zaragoza–Pamplona corridor (Fig. 4.10e). In Italy, however, there was a decided reversal. The large metropolitan areas of the centre and north showed much slower rates of growth and in one case (Milan) stagnation, while metropolitan areas in the Mezzogiorno recorded quite strong gains (Fig 4.10f). The explanation, presumably, is the mass return of guest workers from the northern cities and from other parts of urban Europe, impelled by the recession of the mid-1970s. This may represent some parallel to the de-metropolitan trend in the United States – though, as already noted, and as Table A.21 emphasises, there is no suggestion that it is yet aiding the really remote rural areas.

Type of population shift in southern Europe, however, is surprisingly by no means dominated by the trend towards centralisation (Figs. 4.11a to 4.11f). The

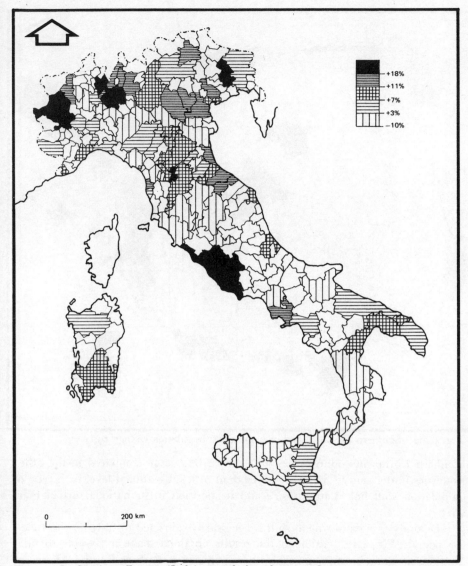

Fig. 4.10d   Southern Europe (Italy): population change 1960–70

1950s saw relative decentralisation in the Lisbon, Valencia, Cádiz and Granada metropolitan areas in Iberia as well as in some parts of the Italian Riviera. By 1960–70 the pattern becomes clearer: Lisbon is still decentralising people, but is now joined by Porto, Madrid, Barcelona, Bilbao, San Sebastián and by several more cities in northern Italy, including Milan, Turin and Genoa. The smaller and medium-sized urban cores, however, were still generally attracting people up to 1970 throughout southern Europe. This suggests, perhaps, that stages of urban development are not only discernable at the national grouping level – the

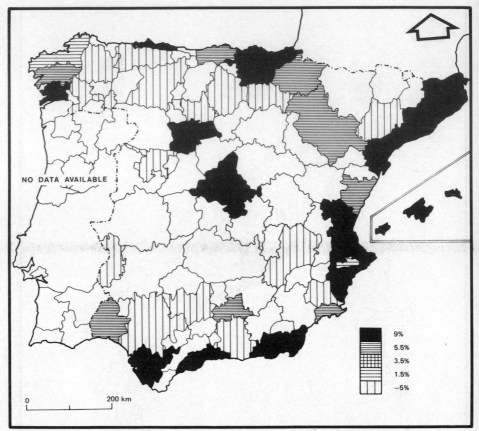

Fig. 4.10e   Southern Europe (Iberian peninsula): population change 1970–75

southern European countries being at the earliest stage compared to the other countries under study – but also are evident at a sub-national level with type of population shift linked to city-size and its position in its national urban hierarchy.

The analysis of employment shift is necessarily restricted to Italy for the 1960–70 period (Fig. 4.12), although the results obtained make it possible to infer that this situation is common to the other countries in southern Europe. There are many more regions exhibiting employment decentralisation in northern Italy than were expected, especially when viewed in relation to population shifts over the same period. Those regions indicating decentralisation during decline in employment appear to reflect the possible deficiencies in the data mentioned earlier. But the very striking losses in hinterland and non-metropolitan area employment shown in Appendix Table A.22 – confirming the rapid movement out of agricultural employment – may, indeed, be partly the cause of the unexpected results, with the remaining balance of the labour-force perhaps being attracted to more lucrative employment opportunities within the EEC. After 1970, however, the evidence of population trends suggest that this migration

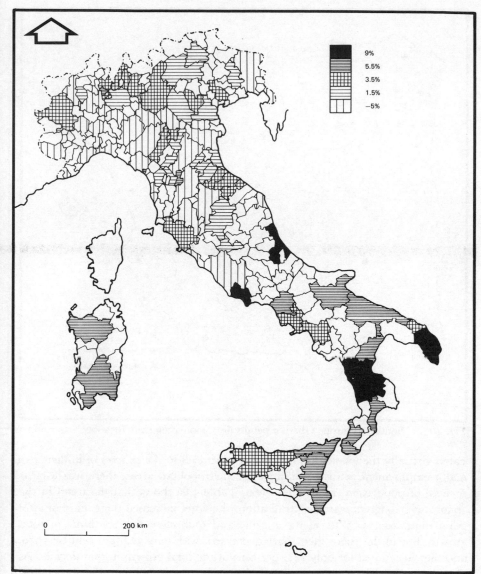

Fig. 4.10f   Southern Europe (Italy): population change 1970–75

pattern was reversed; and, with employment opportunities still limited in the Mezzogiorno, despite considerable government subsidies to industry, the implications of this return to an already depressed area are obvious.

Central Europe

Central Europe is slightly special in that only a negligible proportion of its administrative areas have been allocated to non-metropolitan areas; the central place regions, largely used by the IIASA team to produce the regionalisations, allo-

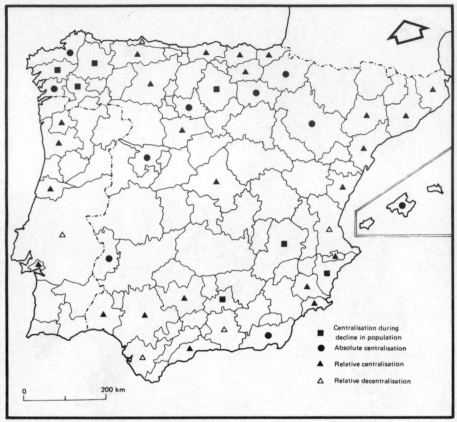

Fig. 4.11a   Southern Europe (Iberian peninsula): population shift 1950–60

cated virtually the whole of the national territories to the spheres of influence of major employment centres. Within these metropolitan areas, there was a clear reversal of population trends after 1960. Table 4.6a shows that the trend in the 1950s was strongly towards centralisation: the cores increased their share of total population from 31.7 to 34.4 per cent, and took close on two-thirds of total growth. But in the 1960s their share decreased, with only 32.6 per cent by 1970, and they accounted for only 14.4 per cent of the total growth in that decade. As already explained, core-ring analysis beyond 1970 is not possible for central Europe.

For employment, in contrast, centralisation was typical of both decades. Table 4.6b shows that in the 1950s (for which no Austrian data are available) the cores increased their share sharply, from 34.0 per cent in 1950 to 41.2 per cent in 1960; thence, in the 1960s (for all three countries) the core share increased marginally, from 42.3 to 42.6 per cent. The cores, which dominated the pattern of growth in the 1950s, took just over half in the 1960s. Thus central Europe was typical of Europe as a whole: its population began to disperse after 1960 but its employment continued to concentrate – albeit with diminishing force.

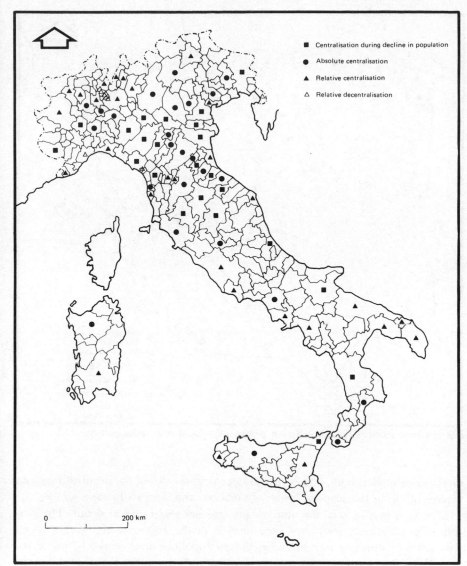

Fig. 4.11b   Southern Europe (Italy): population shift 1950–60

The Appendix Tables A.23 to A.28 show that for population, all three countries replicated the general trend. For employment, however, the continuing
tendency towards centralisation after 1960 is a result of the dominance of the
aggregate figures by Germany – which continued to increase its core share of
employment, though with sharply reduced speed. In the other two countries, the
core share of jobs actually fell in the 1960s, and the rings accounted for a major
share of the increase: nearly two-thirds of it in Switzerland, the whole of it in
Austria. Thus by the 1960s, two of the three countries of central Europe were
decentralising both resident population and jobs – a pattern characteristic also of

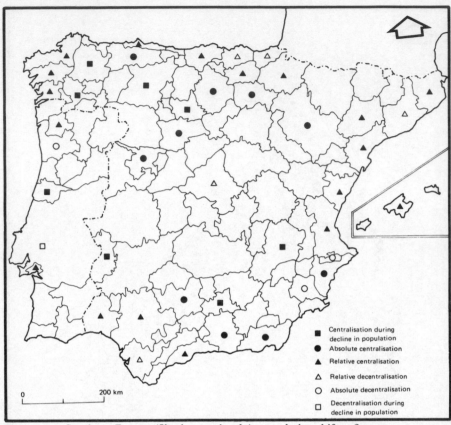

Fig. 4.11c   Southern Europe (Iberian peninsula): population shift 1960–70

Great Britain. Germany, however, was decentralising homes but centralising jobs
– resembling, in this respect, much of northern and western Europe.

Figs. 4.13 to 4.15 take the analysis into greater geographical detail. The pattern of population growth was very uneven in the 1950s, as Fig. 4.13a shows.
The zones of strongest increase were the metropolitan areas of the Rhine–Ruhr
and Rhine–Main zones of Germany, together with the upper Rhine and Neckar
valleys from Basle to Stuttgart. This zone of growth extended into northern
Switzerland in the Basle and Zürich metropolitan areas. Zones of slightly less
dynamic growth were the Rheinland–Pfalz and Saarland areas of Germany and
most of the Swiss Mittelland from Geneva east to Lucerne. Austria, in general,
showed extremely weak growth in comparison, except in the Villach area adjacent to the Italian border. In both Germany and Austria there was a distinct Iron
Curtain effect, with stagnation or decline close to the borders with Russian-
occupied territory; and in the Austrian case, it should be remembered, the Rus-
sians were actually in occupation in the eastern part until 1955.

In the 1960s the patterns were rather different, as Fig. 4.13b shows. Within

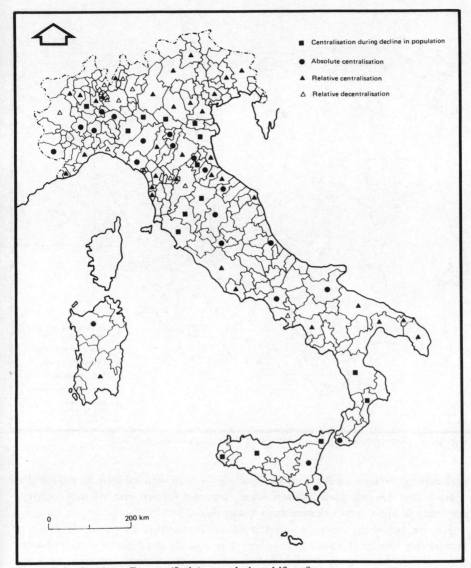

Fig. 4.11d   Southern Europe (Italy): population shift 1960–70

Germany, while the Iron Curtain effect was still evident, the new trend was for a north–south division to appear, with stagnation or decline in the Ruhr area and the strongest growth concentrated in the Stuttgart and Munich areas. In general, however, there was still reasonably vigorous growth up the western side of the country from Basle almost to the North Sea coast (with the sole exception of the Ruhr area) in comparison with weak growth or decline farther east. The prevailing high rates of growth in south Germany again extended across the Swiss frontier into the Fribourg, Lucerne and Zürich areas. By this time growth

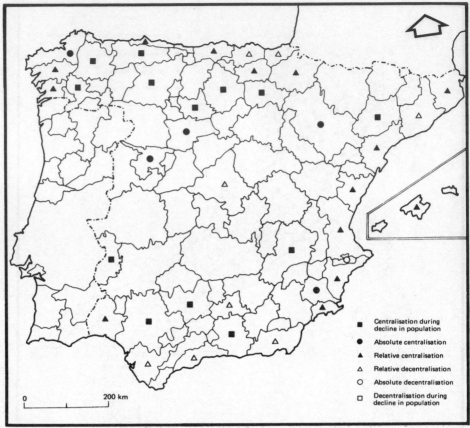

Fig. 4.11e   Southern Europe (Iberian peninsula): population shift 1970–75

was slightly stronger in Austria, especially in a south-central belt including the Villach and Leoben metropolitan areas; but the eastern end of the country, including Vienna, again demonstrated stagnation.

For the 1970s, the analysis is restricted to Germany (Fig. 4.13c). It shows a remarkable change. Growth everywhere has slowed, and high rates are observable only in three zones: in the far North-west, where development may have resulted from regional development policies; around the Bonn–Koblenz area; and discontinuously in the South, where Freiburg, Tübingen, Heidenheim, Munich and Regensburg are the fastest growing areas. Particularly notable is the slow growth or stagnation of some formerly fast-growing centres such as Stuttgart, Nürnberg, Karlsruhe and Mannheim–Ludwigshafen. Almost certainly, this change results from a combination of very low birth-rates and the return migration of the guest worker.

There is an interesting relationship between these patterns and those of internal population shift, as Figs. 4.14a and 4.14b demonstrate. Thus in the 1950s with the centralisation trend dominant, the exceptions tended to occur in those

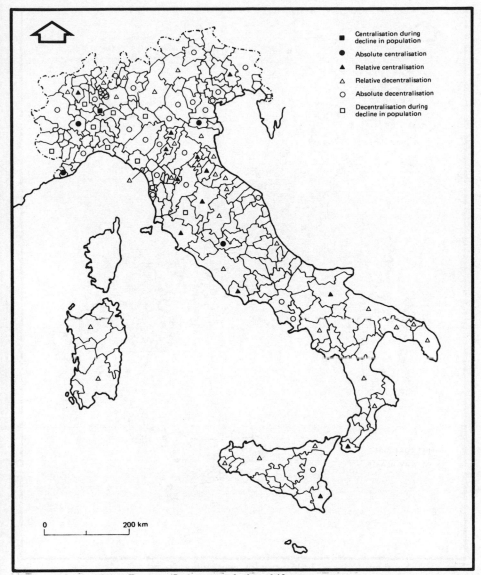

Fig. 4.11f Southern Europe (Italy): population shift 1970–75

metropolitan areas with the strongest growth. Conversely, the areas of weak
population growth – such as the eastern borders of the Federal Republic and
eastern Austria – tended to show absolute centralisation, or even centralisation
during loss, indicating a rapid loss of people from the hinterland zones. By the
1960s the opposite decentralisation trend was in evidence, right across the region;
no ready distinction can be drawn in this regard between growth and non-growth
areas, except that some of the latter were exhibiting the phenomenon of absolute

Fig. 4.12   Southern Europe (Italy): employment shift 1960–70

decentralisation – often associated with quite small core towns which were suffer-ing from the competition of neighbouring centres (as Amberg, Bamberg and Coburg *vis-à-vis* Bayreuth, Nürnberg and Würzburg). Some larger cities, too, were affected by the same phenomenon – notably Hamburg, Braunschweig, Düs-seldorf, Duisburg, Dortmund and Frankfurt-am-Main. In Switzerland the three major cities of Geneva, Bern and Zürich all demonstrated it, as did Vienna. Elsewhere, among some other large cities and many medium-sized ones, relative decentralisation had become the general rule. But there were still numerous cases

Table 4.6a   Central Europe (Austria, Switzerland, West Germany): metropolitan and non-metropolitan region population 1950–75

Population data for 1950, 1960, 1970 and 1975

Areal unit	1950[a] Total (thousands)	1950[a] % of total	1960[a] Total (thousands)	1960[a] % of total	1970[a] Total (thousands)	1970[a] % of total	1950[b] Total (thousands)	1950[b] % of total	1960[b] Total (thousands)	1960[b] % of total	1970[b] Total (thousands)	1970[b] % of total	1975[b] Total (thousands)	1975[b] % of total
Core	19 256	31.66	22 719	34.35	23 632	32.60	15 221	31.12	18 404	34.51	19 186	32.86	na	na
Ring	41 240	67.80	43 066	65.11	48 453	66.84	33 683	68.88	34 919	65.49	39 194	67.14	na	na
Non-metropolitan	329	0.54	360	0.54	408	0.56	0	0.00	0	0.00	0	0.00	0	0.00
Total	60 825	100.00	66 144	100.00	72 493	100.00	48 904	100.00	53 322	100.00	58 380	100.00	59 802	100.00

Population change 1950–60, 1960–70 and 1970–5

Areal unit	1950–60[a] Absolute change (thousands)	1950–60[a] % change	1950–60[a] % of total	1960–70[a] Absolute change (thousands)	1960–70[a] % change	1960–70[a] % of total	1950–60[b] Absolute change (thousands)	1950–60[b] % change	1950–60[b] % of total	1960–70[b] Absolute change (thousands)	1960–70[b] % change	1960–70[b] % of total	1970–75[b] Absolute change (thousands)	1970–75[b] % change	1970–75[b] % of total
Core	3463	17.98	65.11	914	4.02	14.39	3182	20.91	72.04	782	4.25	15.46	na	na	na
Ring	1825	4.43	34.32	5387	12.51	84.85	1235	3.67	27.96	4276	12.25	84.54	na	na	na
Non-metropolitan	31	9.28	0.57	48	13.38	0.76	0	0.00	0.00	0	0.00	0.00	0	0.00	0.00
Total	5319	8.74	100.00	6349	9.60	100.00	4418	9.03	100.00	5058	9.49	100.00	1422	2.44	100.00

Notes: [a] Austria, Switzerland and West Germany.

[b] Germany only.

na – separate core and region figures not available.

Table 4.6b Central Europe (Austria, Switzerland and West Germany): metropolitan and non-metropolitan region employment 1950–70

Employment data for 1950, 1960 and 1970

Areal unit	1950[a] Total (thousands)	% of total	1960[a] Total (thousands)	% of total	1970[a] Total (thousands)	% of total	1960[b] Total (thousands)	% of total	1970[b] Total (thousands)	% of total
Core	9066	33.99	11 383	41.23	11 889	41.80	12 916	42.33	13 499	42.59
Ring	17 474	65.52	16 076	58.22	16 369	57.55	17 444	57.17	17 889	56.82
Non-metropolitan	129	0.48	153	0.55	183	0.65	153	0.50	183	0.58
Total	26 669	100.00	27 611	100.00	28 441	100.00	30 513	100.00	31 481	100.00

Employment change 1950–60 and 1960–70

Areal unit	1950–60[a] Absolute change (thousands)	% change	% of total	1960–70[a] Absolute change (thousands)	% change	% of total	1960–70[b] Absolute change (thousands)	% change	% of total
Core	2317	25.56	245.91	506	4.44	60.94	492	3.81	50.87
Ring	−1398	−8.00	−148.41	293	1.83	35.35	445	2.55	45.94
Non-metropolitan	23	18.17	2.49	31	20.21	3.72	31	20.21	3.19
Total	942	3.53	100.00	830	3.01	100.00	968	3.17	100.00

Notes: [a] Germany and Switzerland only.

[b] Germany, Switzerland and Austria.

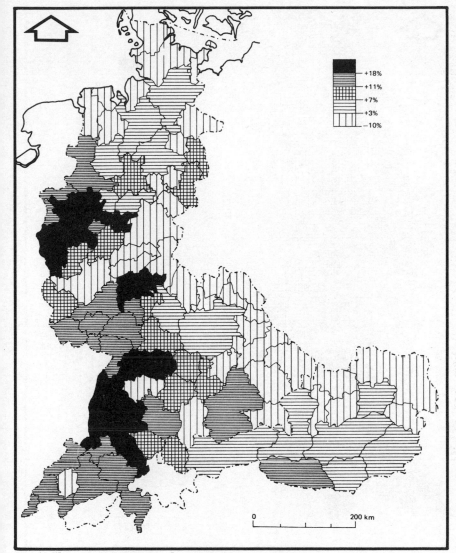

Fig. 4.13a   Central Europe: population change 1950–60

of centralising areas, generally affecting middle-sized cities but in one case (Munich) a very large one.

The picture for the 1970s (Fig. 4.14c) is very sketchy because it is limited to a relatively small number of metropolitan areas where boundary changes were nil or slight. It is also a very mixed picture. Most areas are now showing decentralisation; some indeed are showing absolute decentralisation, and a very few in the Ruhr area (Dortmund, Essen, Wuppertal) are showing the pattern of decentralisation during loss, characteristic of older industrial regions. But some other

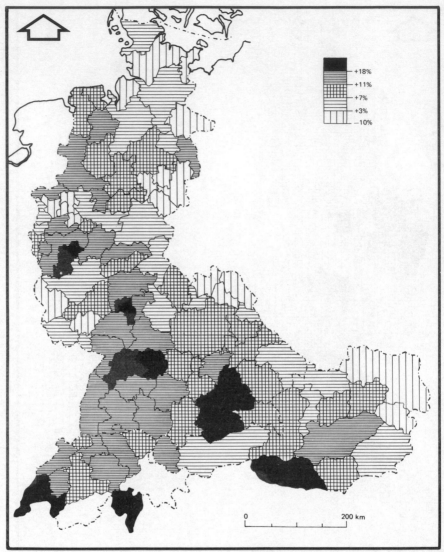

Fig. 4.13b   Central Europe: population change 1960–70

areas in the less thickly populated parts of the country – Oldenburg, Paderborn, Siegen, Kaiserslautern – are actually demonstrating centralisation, and surprisingly this also extends to Mainz–Wiesbaden.

Employment shift for the 1950s is mapped in Fig. 4.15a in respect of Germany and Switzerland only. Centralisation was everywhere dominant, with some notable exceptions in the cases of Düsseldorf, Basle and Zürich where industrial growth occurred in adjacent towns. The picture for the 1960s is more mixed, with a much greater number of decentralising cities in all three countries, as Fig.

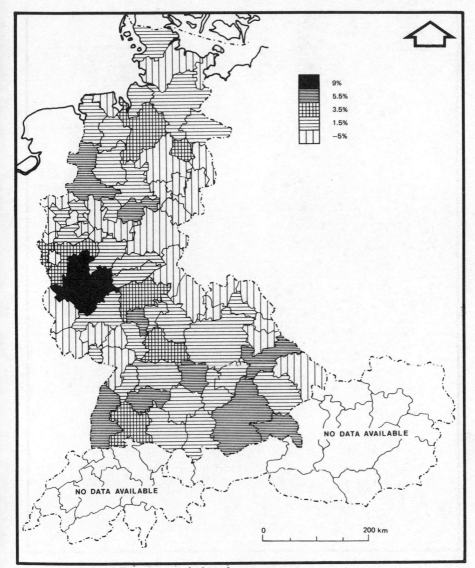

Fig. 4.13c   Central Europe: population change 1970–75

4.15b shows. There is no particular pattern to this decentralisation but it does seem to affect many of the biggest cities in all three countries. This is important because it suggests that here as elsewhere, these big cities may have been begin-ning to lead the process of outward movement of jobs.

The conclusion is that during the 1950s and 1960s – as the patterns of popula-tion growth switched and finally settled in western and southern Germany, middle Switzerland and southern Austria – a general process of decentralisation

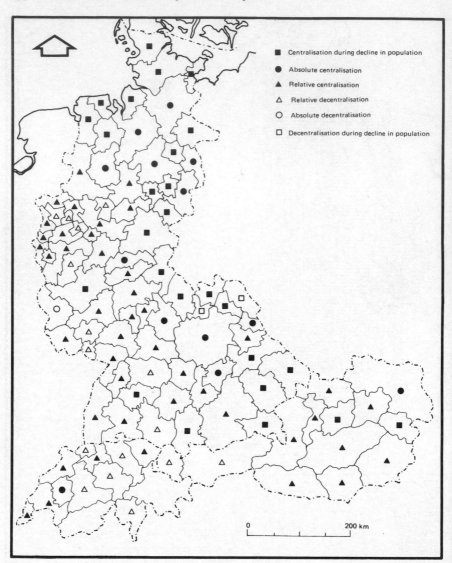

Fig. 4.14a   Central Europe: population shift 1950–60

began to set in. By the 1960s it was very usual for population, rather less so for employment. But generally, the bigger cities were leading the process. There are odd exceptions to this rule – notably the pattern of population concentration (but not employment concentration) in Munich – but overall it is a striking trend.

Some conclusions: European Urban Dynamics
In conclusion, it is useful to return to the European scale and to ask: what were

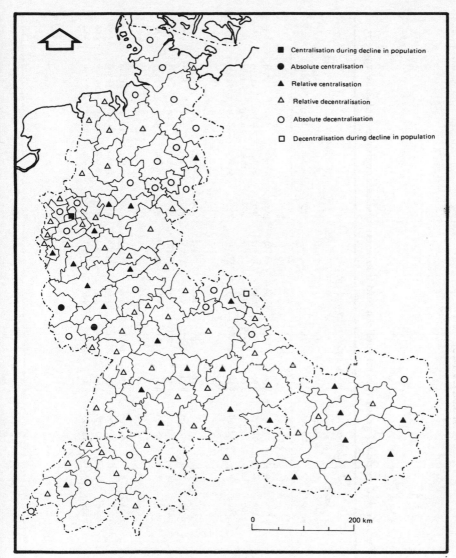

Fig. 4.14b   Central Europe: population shift 1960–70

the most striking features of urban evolution, across the continent, in the quarter-century from 1950 to 1975?

Table 4.7a is a starting-point. It simply re-groups the regional data from Tables 4.3–4.6, and sets them in relation to the aggregate European data of Tables 4.1–4.2. Thus it allows us to look at the broad regional shifts in urban development patterns, as a preliminary to a more fine-focused view. The first point to emerge from it is that only a very small part of Europe's urban population lives in northern Europe, but among the other four divisions there is a re-

Table 4.7a   Summary table. Europe and regional groups: metropolitan and non-metropolitan region population 1950–75

| | Population data for 1950, 1960, 1970 and 1975 | | | | | | | | | | | | | |
| | 1950a | | 1960a | | 1970a | | 1950b | | 1960b | | 1970b | | 1975b | |
	Total (thousands)	%	Total (thousands)	%	Total (thousands)	%	Total (thousands)	%	Total (thousands)	%	Total (thousands)	%	Total (thousands)	%
Atlantic Europe														
Core	27 322	10.10	27 833	9.56	27 160	8.58	26 155	10.63	26 665	10.04	25 992	8.98	25 364	8.55
Ring	22 575	8.35	24 550	8.43	28 178	8.91	21 078	8.57	23 012	8.67	26 354	9.10	27 305	9.20
Non-metropolitan	3419	1.26	3267	1.12	3340	1.06	1756	0.71	1728	0.65	1822	0.63	1781	0.60
Total	53 316	19.71	55 650	19.11	58 678	18.56	48 989	19.91	51 405	19.36	54 168	18.71	54 450	18.35
Northern Europe														
Core	4959	1.83	5554	1.91	5960	1.88	4959	2.02	5554	2.09	5950	2.06	5683	1.92
Ring	6274	2.32	6589	2.26	7403	2.34	6274	2.55	6589	2.48	7403	2.56	8007	2.70
Non-metropolitan	3378	1.25	3485	1.20	3536	1.12	3378	1.37	3485	1.31	3536	1.22	3585	1.21
Total	14 612	5.40	15 628	5.37	16 889	5.34	14 612	5.94	15 628	5.88	16 889	5.83	17 275	5.82
Western Europe														
Core	22 744	8.41	26 725	9.18	30 717	9.71	22 682	9.22	26 653	10.04	30 641	10.59	31 169	10.51
Ring	27 674	10.23	29 711	10.20	32 760	10.36	27 445	11.15	29 468	11.10	32 496	11.22	34 308	11.56
Non-metropolitan	9683	3.58	9900	3.40	10 368	3.28	9683	3.93	9900	3.73	10 368	3.58	10 673	3.60
Total	60 101	22.22	66 336	22.78	73 845	23.35	58 910	24.30	66 021	24.86	73 595	25.38	76 150	25.67

Southern Europe														
Core	22 801	8.43	27 821	9.55	33 346	10.55	21 518	8.74	26 389	9.94	31 896	11.02	32 974	11.11
Ring	37 747	13.95	38 696	13.29	41 425	13.10	33 644	13.67	34 282	12.91	37 115	12.82	39 473	13.31
Non-metropolitan	21 045	7.78	20 927	7.19	19 515	6.17	18 609	7.56	18 522	6.97	17 619	6.08	16 543	5.58
Total	81 593	30.17	87 444	30.03	94 286	29.82	73 771	29.98	79 193	29.82	86 630	29.92	88 990	30.00
Central Europe														
Core	19 256	7.12	22 719	7.80	23 632	7.47	15 221	6.19	18 404	6.93	19 186	6.63	na	na
Ring	41 240	15.29	43 066	14.79	48 453	15.32	33 683	13.69	34 919	13.15	39 194	13.54	na	na
Non-metropolitan	329	0.12	360	0.12	408	0.13	0	0.00	0	0.00	0	0.00	0	0.00
Total	60 825	22.49	66 144	22.71	72 493	22.93	48 904	19.87	53 322	20.08	58 380	20.16	59 802	20.16
Europe														
Core	97 082	35.89	110 652	38.00	120 805	38.20	90 535	36.79	103 665	39.03	113 665	39.25	na	na
Ring	135 510	50.11	142 612	48.97	158 219	50.04	122 124	49.63	128 270	48.30	142 562	49.23	na	na
Non-metropolitan	37 854	13.99	37 939	13.03	37 167	11.75	33 426	13.58	33 635	12.67	33 345	11.52	32 582	10.98
Total	270 446	100.00	291 203	100.00	316 191	100.00	246 085	100.00	265 570	100.00	289 572	100.00	296 667	100.00

Notes: [a] All countries.
[b] Great Britain, Sweden, Norway, Denmark, France, Belgium, (excluding Luxembourg), The Netherlands, Spain, Italy and Germany only.

na – separate core and region figures not available for Germany.

Table 4.7b Summary table. Europe and regional groups: metropolitan and non-metropolitan region population 1950–75

Population change 1950–60, 1960–70 and 1970–5

	1950–60a			1960–70a			1950–60b			1960–70b			1970–75b		
	Absolute change (thousands)	% change	% of total	Absolute change (thousands)	% change	% of total	Absolute change (thousands)	% change	% of total	Absolute change (thousands)	% change	% of total	Absolute change (thousands)	% change	% of total
Atlantic Europe															
Core	511	1.87	2.46	−673	−2.42	−2.69	509	1.95	2.61	−673	−2.52	−2.80	−628	−2.42	−8.85
Ring	1975	8.75	9.52	3628	14.78	14.52	1934	9.18	9.93	3342	14.52	13.92	951	3.61	13.40
Non-metropolitan	−153	−4.47	−0.74	73	2.25	0.29	−28	−1.57	−0.14	94	5.44	0.39	−41	2.24	−0.58
Total	2334	4.38	11.24	3028	5.44	12.11	2416	4.93	12.40	2763	5.37	11.51	282	0.52	3.97
Northern Europe															
Core	594	11.99	2.86	396	7.14	1.58	594	11.99	3.05	396	7.14	1.65	−267	−4.49	−3.76
Ring	315	5.02	1.52	814	12.35	3.26	315	5.02	1.62	814	12.35	3.39	604	8.16	8.51
Non-metropolitan	107	3.17	0.52	51	1.45	0.20	107	3.17	0.55	51	1.45	0.21	49	1.39	0.69
Total	1016	6.95	4.89	1261	8.07	5.05	1016	6.95	5.21	1261	8.07	5.25	386	2.29	5.44
Western Europe															
Core	3981	17.50	19.18	3992	14.94	15.98	3971	17.51	20.38	3988	14.96	16.61	528	1.72	7.44
Ring	2037	7.36	9.81	3049	10.26	12.20	2023	7.73	10.38	3028	10.28	12.62	1812	5.58	25.54
Non-metropolitan	217	2.24	1.05	468	4.73	1.87	217	2.24	1.11	468	4.73	1.95	305	2.94	4.30
Total	6235	10.38	30.04	7509	11.32	30.05	6211	10.38	31.88	7484	11.34	31.18	2645	3.60	37.28

Southern Europe															
Core	5020	22.02	24.19	5555	19.86	22.11	4371	22.64	25.00	5507	20.57	22.94	1078	3.38	15.19
Ring	949	2.51	4.57	2729	7.05	10.92	538	1.90	3.27	2833	6.58	11.80	358	6.35	33.23
Non-metropolitan	−118	−0.56	−0.57	−1413	−7.25	−5.65	−87	−0.47	−0.45	−903	−4.88	−3.75	−1076	−6.11	−15.17
Total	5851	7.17	28.19	6341	7.82	27.38	5422	7.35	27.83	7437	9.39	30.98	2360	2.72	33.26
Central Europe															
Core	3463	17.98	16.68	914	4.02	3.66	3182	20.91	16.33	782	4.25	3.26	na	na	na
Ring	1825	4.43	8.79	5387	12.51	21.56	1235	3.67	6.34	4276	12.25	17.82	na	na	na
Non-metropolitan	31	9.28	0.15	48	13.38	0.19	0	0.00	0.00	0	0.00	0.00	0	0.00	0.00
Total	5319	8.74	25.63	6349	9.60	25.41	4418	9.03	22.67	5058	9.49	21.07	1422	2.44	20.04
Europe															
Core	13 570	13.98	65.38	10 153	9.18	40.63	13 130	14.50	67.39	10 000	9.65	41.67	na	na	na
Ring	7102	5.24	34.21	15 607	10.94	62.46	6146	5.03	31.54	14 292	11.14	59.55	na	na	na
Non-metropolitan	85	0.22	0.41	−772	−2.32	−3.09	209	0.63	1.07	−290	−0.87	−1.21	−763	−2.29	−10.75
Total	20 757	7.68	100.00	24 988	8.58	100.00	19 485	7.92	100.00	24 002	9.03	100.00	7095	2.45	100.00

Notes: [a] All countries.
[b] Great Britain, Sweden, Norway, Denmark, France, Belgium (excluding Luxembourg), The Netherlands, Spain, Italy and Germany only.

na – separate core and region figures not available for Germany.

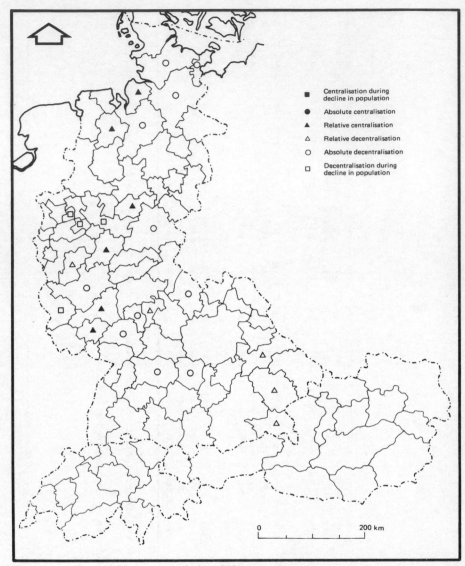

Fig. 4.14c   Central Europe: population shift 1970–75

markably even balance. In 1950, 86.0 per cent of Europe's total population lived in metropolitan areas, divided as follows: Atlantic 18.4; Northern 4.2; Western 18.6; Southern 22.4; Central 22.4 per cent. By 1970, 88.2 per cent lived in metropolitan areas; divided as follows: Atlantic 17.5; Northern 4.2; Western 20.1; Southern 23.7; Central 22.8 per cent. Thus western, southern and central Europe had gained, relatively, at the expense of atlantic and northern Europe – though in all regions, the metropolitan areas had of course made absolute gains.

This appears even more clearly from Table 4.7b, which looks at changes over

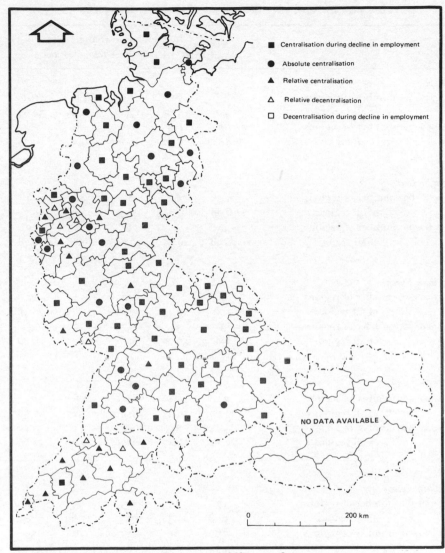

Centralisation during decline in employment

Absolute centralisation

Relative centralisation

Relative decentralisation

Decentralisation during decline in employment

NO DATA AVAILABLE

0   200 km

Fig. 4.15a   Central Europe: employment shift 1950–60

the quarter-century. In the 1950s, of the population growth of the fifteen
countries, nearly 100 per cent occurred in the metropolitan areas – to be exact,
99.6 per cent. No less than 29.0 per cent of net overall growth occurred in the
metropolitan areas of Western Europe, another 28.8 per cent in those of Southern
Europe, and 25.5 per cent in those of central Europe. In comparison the metropolitan growth in Atlantic and Northern Europe was modest: 12.0 and 4.4 per
cent of the total respectively. And this pattern was maintained in the 1960s. In
that decade, 103.1 per cent of total growth occurred in the metropolitan areas,

Table 4.8   Europe: rate of metropolitan growth 1950–60–70

	% Population change				
	+18.00	*+11.00*	*+7.00*	*+3.00*	
Europe					
1950–60: number of regions	81	81	94	121	161
% of all regions	15.03	15.03	17.44	22.45	30.05
1960–70: number of regions	102	113	116	104	104
% of all regions	18.92	20.96	21.52	19.30	19.30
Atlantic Europe					
1950–60: number of regions	23	14	20	42	44
% of all regions	16.08	9.79	13.99	29.37	30.77
1960–70: number of regions	30	30	30	24	29
% of all regions	20.98	20.98	20.98	16.78	20.28
Northern Europe					
1950–60: number of regions	0	9	12	14	9
% of all regions	0.00	20.45	27.27	31.82	20.45
1960–70: number of regions	3	11	27	10	3
% of all regions	6.82	25.00	38.64	22.73	6.82
Western Europe					
1950–60: number of regions	24	22	24	29	21
% of all regions	20.00	18.33	20.00	24.17	17.50
1960–70: number of regions	35	23	24	24	14
% of all regions	29.17	19.17	20.00	20.00	11.66
Southern Europe					
1950–60: number of regions	17	15	25	23	50
% of all regions	13.08	11.54	19.23	17.69	38.46
1960–70: number of regions	25	21	19	26	39
% of all regions	19.23	16.15	14.62	20.00	30.00
Central Europe					
1950–60: number or regions	17	21	13	13	38
% of all regions	16.67	20.59	12.75	12.75	37.25
1960–70: number of regions	9	28	26	20	19
% of all regions	8.82	27.45	25.49	19.61	18.63

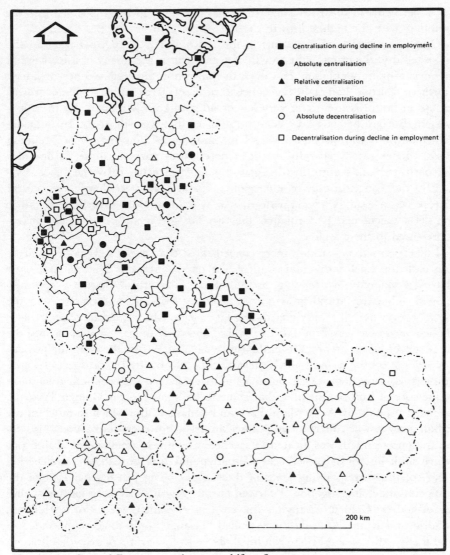

Fig. 4.15b   Central Europe: employment shift 1960–70

and of this 28.2 per cent was in Northern Europe, 32.2 per cent in southern Europe and 25.2 per cent in Central Europe; Atlantic Europe again had only 11.8 per cent and Northern Europe 4.8 per cent. Thus 83 per cent of total population growth in the 1950s, and 87 per cent in the 1960s, was concentrated in the metropolitan areas of three European regional divisions: Western, Southern and Central.

However, both within and outside these regions the growth was quite un-evenly distributed. Table 4.8 shows that a mere eighty-one of the 539 regions

(15.0 per cent) in the 1950s, and 102 (18.9 per cent) in the 1960s, fell into the quintile* with the highest growth rates of 18 per cent or over per decade.

Conversely, 162 (30.0 per cent) in the 1950s and 104 (19.3 per cent) in the 1960s fell into the group with growth of 3 per cent or less; many of these were in fact declining in population. However, the pattern in the regions differed widely. Northern Europe had a heavy concentration of areas in the middle growth groups in both decades, with very few or no strong growth areas. By the 1960s western Europe had a heavy concentration of high-growth areas. In both decades southern Europe had a very large number of slow-growth or declining areas, concentrated generally in the remoter rural parts. Central Europe also demonstrated this feature in the 1950s but had corrected it by the 1960s. Evidently, the concentration of metropolitan growth into southern and central Europe was a result of a good performance by many middle-growth areas, rather than of a spectacular performance; the very fast growers were generally under-represented in these regions.

In fact, growth was rather more concentrated than a coarse regional analysis can indicate. Each individual country had parts that were dynamic and parts that were stagnant or declining, as the maps earlier in this chapter graphically showed. Though natural growth was generally high in some countries in the 1950s, everywhere it was falling by the late 1960s. More important, probably – though as yet we lack firm data – was the pattern of migration streams into the more successful urban areas from the rural backwaters and also from the peasant countries of southern and south-eastern Europe, drawn by the prospect of secure employment and high wages. But that in turn reflected the economic dynamism of the core of Europe: the area that came to be known as the Golden Triangle, bounded roughly by Amsterdam, Paris and Milan, within which so much of the urban growth was concentrated. Closer analysis, however, shows that this concentration of growth was located in seventeen relatively small zones (Table 4.9) which took just over 54 per cent of total population growth over the period 1950–70; the corresponding areas of these zones being just 8.5 per cent of the countries under investigation. Fourteen of the growth areas were located within an extended 'Golden Triangle', the corners of which were North Holland, Madrid and Rome. Outside the extended 'Triangle' only Stockholm, Valencia and the North London Fringe exhibited above average rates of growth, although the last two areas, can only be considered as marginally peripheral to the extended 'Triangle' (Fig. 4.16).

Two broad categories of growth can be identified. First, a pronounced axial development along the Rhine, with lesser concentrations along its tributaries, the Rhône–Saône valleys and the Côte d'Azur. Most of this growth was based on

---

* Evidently the 'quintiles', used in these and subsequent analyses, are not exactly so. They were chosen on the basis of a convenience – especially that the intervals should be expressed in round numbers. Additionally, as the fifth quintile classifies regions growing by less than 3 per cent, negative growth is not discernible. We refer the reader back to the maps and tables of population (or employment) shifts. Regions undergoing either centralisation or decentralisation during loss are by definition experiencing negative growth.

Table 4.9 European 'megalopolitan' growth zones 1950–70^a

	Population, 1950	Population, 1970	% change 1950–70	National rates of change 1950–70
1. Madrid	1 984 033	3 950 686	99.13	21.58
2. Basque Coast (Spain)	1 133 238	1 992 833	75.85	21.58
3. Turin^b	1 228 320	2 037 738	65.90	13.94
4. Lorraine	708 886	1 160 381	63.69	22.80
5. Milan^c	2 896 628	4 558 966	57.39	13.94
6. Rome	2 532 233	3 970 345	56.79	13.94
7. Barcelona	2 510 382	3 827 988	52.49	21.58
8. Provence–Côte d'Azur^d	2 788 690	4 242 828	52.14	22.80 (France) 13.94 (Italy)
9. North London Fringe	3 054 552	4 578 760	49.90	10.58
10. Lyon–Grenoble^e	1 767 740	2 548 729	44.18	22.80
11. East Randstad–North Rhine	8 690 394	12 312 128	41.66	
(German component)	3 792 987	5 383 917	41.94	19.38
(Dutch component)	4 532 534	6 383 590	40.84	30.60
(Belgian component)	364 873	544 621	49.26	14.26
12. Geneva–Lausanne–Annecy^{b, e, f}	1 031 072	1 499 659	40.59	32.35 (Switzerland) 22.80 (France)
13. Paris	7 230 690	10 068 911	39.25	22.80
14. Upper Rhine (East Bank)–Central Switzerland	9 975 364	13 855 652	38.90	
(German component)	7 684 137	10 729 651	39.63	19.38
(Swiss component)	2 291 227	3 126 001	36.43	32.35
15. Munich	1 814 585	2 508 972	38.27	19.38
16. Stockholm	1 354 434	1 828 893	35.03	14.58
17. Valencia	1 952 185	2 582 482	32.29	21.58
Total	52 653 426	77 475 951	47.14	16.82 (Europe)

Notes: ^a Defined as individual metropolitan regions of aggregates of contiguous metropolitan or non-metropolitan regions having growth rates of more than 30
per cent (1950–70) and which reached one million population by 1970.

^b Turin–Geneva–Lausanne–Annecy zones contiguous via Mont Blanc Tunnel.

^c Milan–Central Switzerland zones contiguous via San Gottardo.

^d Includes San Remo and Ventimiglia in Italy.

^e Lyon–Grenoble–Geneva–Lausanne–Annecy zones just contiguous.

^f Geneva–Lausanne–Annecy astride French–Swiss frontier.

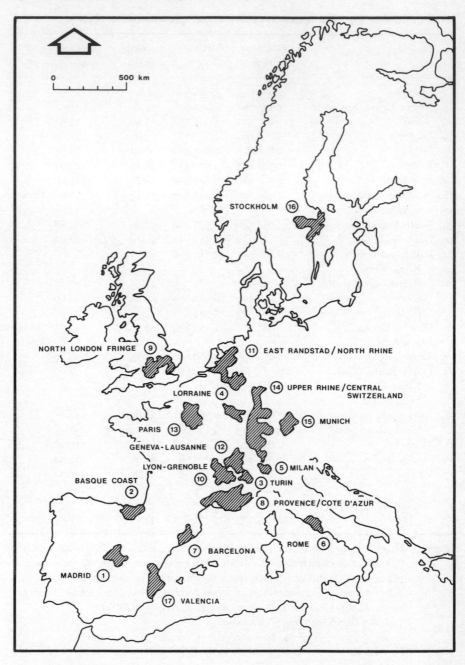

Fig. 4.16   Megalopolitan growth zones of Europe

medium-sized rather than very large cities; little of it took place in what could be categorised as the older industrial areas of Europe – although, unlike their American counterparts, these areas are not yet exhibiting absolute declines of population. Second, growth in southern Europe: this appears to be in stark contrast to the central European patterns, with dramatic increases in the biggest cities – Madrid, Barcelona, Bilbao, Valencia, Rome, Turin and Milan. What is certain is that much growth in these southern areas results from rapid migration from the land – so that it is an essentially different phenomenon from the American one, where rural migration occurred in the 1940s and early 1950s and resulted in the growth of the industrial heartland. Corresponding enormous declines of population in the rural areas of the Spanish Meseta and the Italian Mezzogiorno certainly do not suggest evidence for a 'drift to the sunbelt', on the basis of the model of American trends reported in Chapter 1; the growth in the largest metropolitan areas being more a response to attractive levels of employment and wages relative to the depressed areas within each country rather than relative to other parts of Europe. Indeed the labour migration patterns identified by Salt (Salt and Clout 1976) and others imply that, up to 1973, there was still a 'drift away from the sunbelt' with West Germany and France as massive importers of southern European labour; though, as already seen, this was rudely reversed in the early 1970s.

There are some other interesting points about these seventeen growth zones. First, none of them is in a truly peripheral part of Europe. Only one is in northern Europe, and the one in atlantic Europe is near its south-eastern extremity, closest to the rest of Europe. Second, only one is based on a giant metropolitan area (Paris, with 9.50 million in 1970). Several of the others contain a single metropolitan area in the 2 to 4 million range (Barcelona, 3.75 million; Madrid, 3.95 million; Milan, 3.74 million; Rome, 3.75 million; Frankfurt, 2.25 million; Stuttgart, 2.47 million), but others do not have a single area as big as 2 million. Two of them, London north-west fringe and eastern Randstad, indeed exclude large neighbouring metropolitan areas (London, The Hague, Amsterdam) on the grounds of a weak growth record; these can indeed be regarded as growth zones arising from the deconcentration of larger metropolitan areas to adjoining suburban ones. Significantly, both these are in regions of Europe where the decentralisation trend was strong.

Certainly, Europe lacks the homogeneity of language and culture that makes it possible for Americans to move readily for retirement to the climatically-favoured regions; while many locational decisions by European entrepreneurs are still similarly constrained by barriers that are not present in the United States. But there are two features that Europe does share with the United States, and increasingly so: the development of the tourist and ancillary industries in amenity-rich areas and the deliberate location by bigger companies – especially multinationals – in areas of more laggard economic development and consequently lower wages plus greater freedom from union pressures. How far these have contributed to the extraordinary development of the southern European growth must, however, remain a topic for further study.

In any event, a striking difference betweeen the European and American patterns is the continuing strength of Europe's industrial heartland. The relative decline of what Wilbur Thompson has called the American Ruhr – the whole belt stretching from New England and New York as far as Chicago and St Louis – has no real parallel, so far, in Europe. True, some industrial areas have shown serious structural weakness in the post-World War II period: notably northern England and central Scotland (both outside the extended 'Golden Triangle'), the southern Belgian–northern French coalfield and the Ruhr region after 1960. But counteracting that have been the conspicuous success stories such as the eastern Randstad, Cologne-Bonn and above all the upper Rhine region. Here, growth has been based on a solid foundation in dynamic manufacturing industries including electrical goods, cars, and a wide range of engineering and chemical industries, together with tertiary industry that serves a more-than-local function. These elements will be considered more closely in the follow-up study on industrial structure, introduced in Chapter 6 of the book.

If we seek to identify areas of low growth or decline in Europe, significantly, they are conspicuously peripheral to the industrial centre of gravity – again in contrast to the USA. They include areas such as much of Scotland, Wales and northern England; most of rural Ireland; (perhaps surprisingly) the London area; northern Jutland in Denmark; northern Sweden and Norway; western and central France; southern and eastern Belgium; central and north-western Spain; much of Portugal; and, as mentioned earlier, parts of northern and central Italy and (down to 1970) the Mezzogiorno; the upland periphery of Germany, especially that bordering the DDR and Czechoslovakia; and eastern Austria. Among these, only the London and Glasgow areas are regions, based on big cities, which have since 1950 undergone absolute decline. Elsewhere, Liverpool, Manchester, Duisburg, Essen, Bochum are areas of minimal growth or more recent decline; so too are smaller-centred regions in northern England and parts of Belgium.

But most of the declining metropolitan regions of Europe are in peripheral areas, somewhat distant from the main metropolitan areas of their respective countries, and often near the national frontier. Many also are in thinly-populated rural areas, and are based on quite small towns (that is, towns in the 50 000–100 000 range). We can conclude, then, that only in Great Britain – and to a limited extent in the Franco–Belgian coalfield and the German Ruhrgebiet – is there so far any inkling of the decline of older industrial-urban regions.

The Urban Hierarchy

There is quite a different, but equally useful way of looking at urban change: in terms of movements in the hierarchy of sizes. Geographers have devoted much study to the size-distribution of cities in different countries and at different times. They have concluded, for instance, that countries in an early stage of development are characterised by a *primate* distribution, in which one (or less often, two) major cities contrast sharply with a large number of small cities. But as economic and social development takes place, so the hierarchy evolves into a *rank-size distribution,* in which city sizes can be plotted (in log form) against their ranking in the hierarchy to give a straight line (log-normal) distribution. For such analysis to be meaningful, a prerequisite is to define urban areas in a rigorous, fully-comparable way – which is what the European Urban Systems study has aimed to do. The results should therefore be of some interest; they are plotted in Figs. 4.17a to 4.17e for each European group and then in Figs. 4.18a to 4.18n for each country, at the four dates 1950, 1960, 1970 and 1975 (where available). Addi-

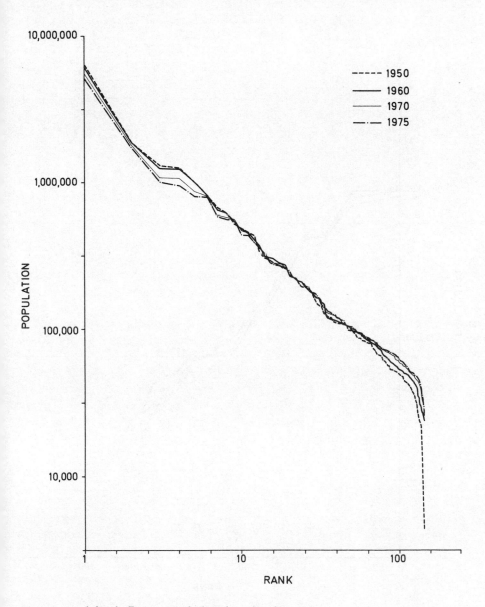

Fig. 4.17a   Atlantic Europe: rank-size plot 1950–60–70

tionally, Table 4.10 gives a summary quantification of the results, by dividing the 1960 European size distribution into approximate quintiles.

It is evident that the hierarchies in the regional divisions have been far from identical. Atlantic Europe is characterised by a large number of small regions, and corresponds closely to the rank-size rule. Northern Europe has a very similar distribution. But western Europe is dominated by medium-sized urban areas,

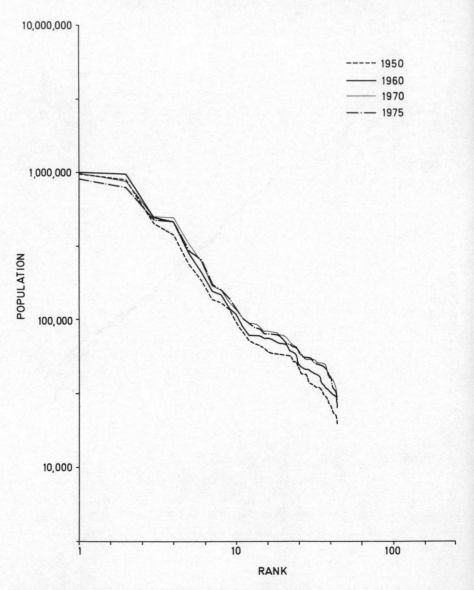

Fig. 4.17b   Northern Europe: rank-size plot 1950–60–70

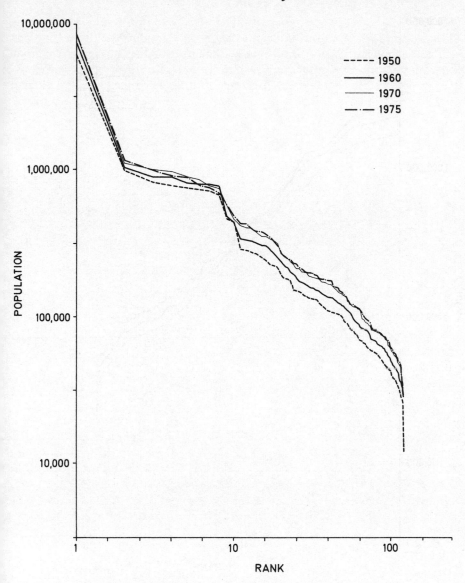

Fig. 4.17c   Western Europe: rank-size plot 1950–60–70

while Southern Europe has a rather large number of regions in the biggest size-class. The extreme case however is Central Europe, where the largest size class actually contains the biggest number of cases. These last areas, as the graphs show, differ considerably from the ideal rank-size distribution.

In general, of course, there was a progression up the hierarchy as urban growth took place; this was characteristic of all regional divisions, but it was

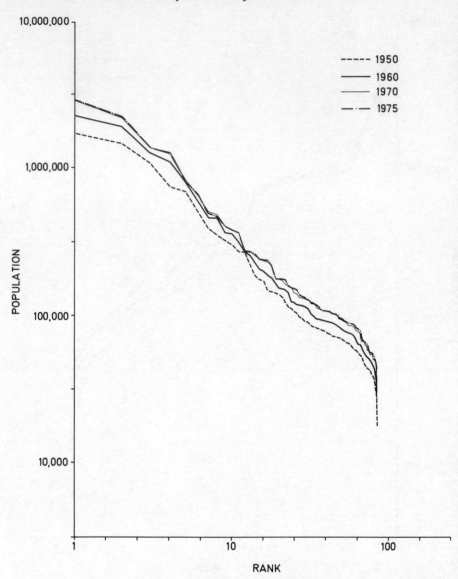

Fig. 4.17d   Southern Europe: rank-size plot 1950–60–70

most marked in those divisions where urban growth was most rapid. Thus in slower-growing Atlantic and Northern Europe it increased the numbers in the medium-sized categories (225 000–325 000 in Atlantic Europe; 150 000–325 000 in northern Europe); but in Western Europe it led to increases in the categories above 325 000, and in Southern and Central Europe to big jumps in the numbers

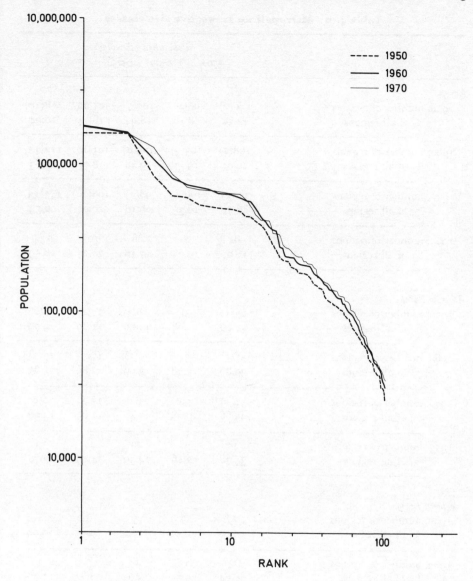

Fig. 4.17e Central Europe: rank-size plot 1950–60–70

in the half-million group. So not only were Southern and Central Europe dominated by the bigger urban areas; this dominance was growing over the period.

The rank-size plots for the individual countries, Figs. 4.18a to 4.18n, bring out
some even sharper contrasts. Great Britain, Norway, Belgium, Spain, Italy, Germany and Switzerland approach close to perfect rank-size relationships, though
with some minor distortions: Britain has a tail of very small areas in 1950, that

Table 4.10   Metropolitan areas: five size classes

| | *Population (thousands)* | | | |
	150.0	*225.0*	*325.0*	*500.0*
Europe				
1950, number of regions	130(2) 98(4)	102(7)	101(12)	108(10)
% of all regions	24.12 18.18	18.92	18.74	20.04
1960, number of regions	108(2) 103(3)	105(8)	101(10)	122(12)
% of all regions	20.04 19.11	19.48	18.74	22.63
1970, number of regions	90(2) 100(1)	98(2)	108(10)	143(13)
% of all regions	16.70 18.55	18.18	20.04	26.53
1975, number of regions	84 96	88	102	134
% of all regions	16.67 19.05	17.46	20.24	26.59
Atlantic Europe				
1950, number of regions	63(1) 31	18(1)	17(1)	14(2)
% of all regions	44.06 21.68	12.59	11.89	9.79
1960, number of regions	57(1) 32	20(1)	17(1)	17(2)
% of all regions	39.86 22.38	13.99	11.89	11.89
1970, number of regions	51(1) 30	25(1)	17(1)	20(2)
% of all regions	35.66 20.98	17.48	11.89	13.99
1975, number of regions	48 31	20	20	19
% of all regions	34.78 22.46	14.49	14.49	13.77
Northern Europe				
1950, number of regions	22 9	5	4	4
% of all regions	50.00 20.45	11.36	9.09	9.09
1960, number of regions	17 13	6	3	5
% of all regions	38.64 29.55	13.64	6.82	11.36
1970, number of regions	15 14	7	3	5
% of all regions	34.09 31.82	15.91	6.82	11.36
1975, number of regions	14 15	7	3	5
% of all regions	31.82 34.09	15.91	6.82	11.36

Table 4.10 – *continued*

	Population (thousands)			
	150.0	225.0	325.0	500.0
Western Europe				
1950, number of regions	19	24	37(1)	22	18
% of all regions	15.83	20.00	30.83	18.33	15.00
1960, number of regions	13	22	35(1)	29	21
% of all regions	10.83	18.33	29.16	24.17	17.50
1970, number of regions	9	22	26	31(1)	32
% of all regions	7.50	18.33	21.67	25.83	26.67
1975, number of regions	7	19	28	32	33
% of all regions	5.88	15.97	23.53	26.89	27.73
Southern Europe				
1950, number of regions	23(1)	24(0)	24(0)	26(2)	33(2)
% of all regions	17.69	18.46	18.46	20.00	25.38
1960, number of regions	18(1)	27(0)	28(0)	20(1)	37(3)
% of all regions	13.85	20.77	21.54	15.38	28.46
1970, number of regions	13(1)	28(0)	24(0)	26(1)	39(3)
% of all regions	10.00	21.54	18.46	20.00	30.00
1975[b], number of regions	13	26	23	25	38
% of all regions	10.40	20.80	18.40	20.00	30.40
Central Europe				
1950, number of regions	3(0)	10(4)	18(5)	32(9)	39(6)
% of all regions	2.94	9.80	17.65	31.37	38.24
1960, number of regions	3(0)	9(3)	16(6)	32(8)	42(7)
% of all regions	2.94	8.82	15.69	31.37	41.18
1970, number of regions	2(0)	6(1)	16(8)	31(7)	47(8)
% of all regions	1.96	5.88	15.69	30.39	46.08
1975[d], number of regions	2	5	10	22	39
% of all regions	2.56	6.41	12.82	28.21	50.00

Notes: [a] Excluding Ireland [b] Excluding Portugal.
[c] Excluding Luxembourg. [d] Excluding Switzerland, Austria.
Figures in brackets show regions excluded from the 1975 analysis but which are included in the other dates.

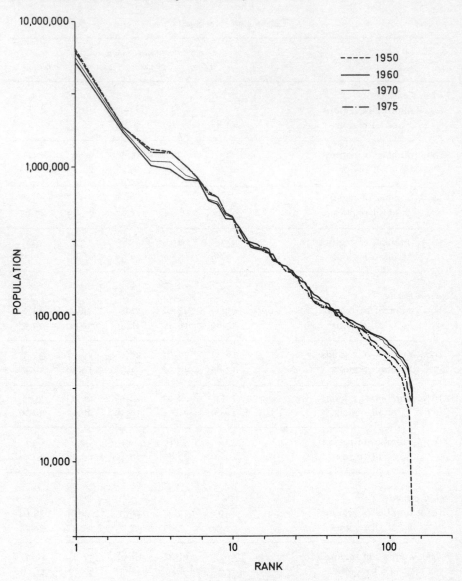

Fig. 4.18a   Great Britain: rank-size plot 1950–60–70–75

were to become the bases for new towns in the following two decades; in Norway, Oslo shows slight primacy; in Spain, Madrid and Barcelona similarly provide a slight distortion; Italy has a tail of small areas; and in Germany, the linear relationship shows an inflexion which reflects the rather large number of major provincial capitals towards the top end. In contrast, Ireland, Sweden, Denmark and the Netherlands, France and Austria tend towards primacy; and

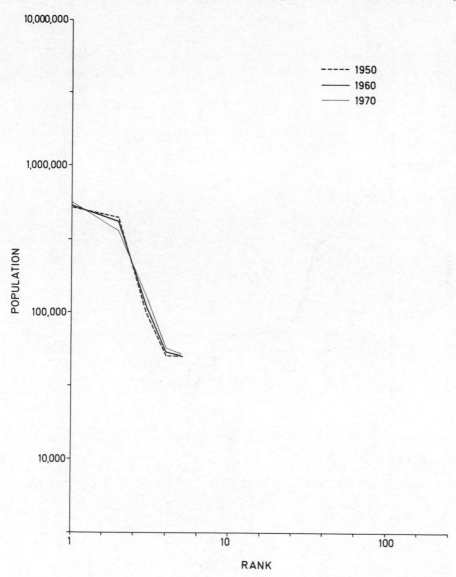

Fig. 4.18b   Ireland: rank-size plot 1950–60–70

interestingly, in a number of these there is more than one 'primate' city. Ireland clearly has two while the Netherlands have three – a reflection of the poly-nuclear structure of the Randstad. Clearly, it is not possible to relate these differences in any simple way to stages of economic development. The urban hierarchy in the countries of Europe reflects far more their individual historical paths of development and in particular the date by which each of them first achieved effective unification.

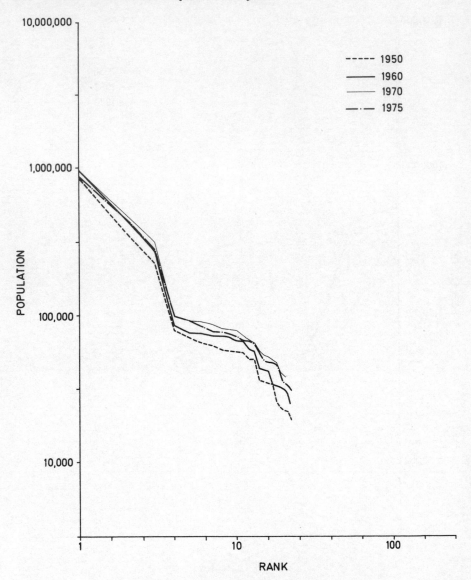

Fig. 4.18c   Sweden: rank-size plot 1950–60–70–75

The plots also show shifts in the patterns over the twenty-five-year period. Particularly significant here is the relative stability of the systems, though in virtually every case – as is only to be expected – there is a tendency for population sizes to grow at almost every level of the hierarchy. Notable however for many countries – Sweden, Norway, Denmark, the Netherlands, France, and to some degree, Austria – is the tendency for the curves to remain convergent at the top

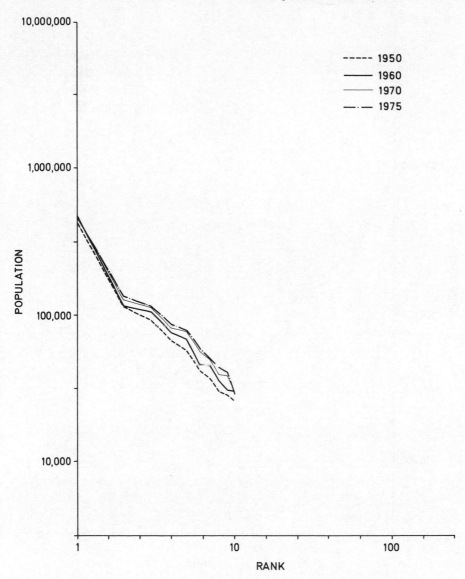

Fig. 4.18d   Norway: rank-size plot 1950–60–70–75

and to diverge towards the base, indicating faster growth for the smaller areas and relative stagnation for the largest ones. Spain, Italy and Germany are significant exceptions: in these countries, the largest urban systems achieved very vigorous growth. Switzerland, in contrast, exhibits remarkably even growth at every level of the urban hierarchy. During 1970–75, however, significant changes occur. Most countries demonstrate great stability in the system, a function of

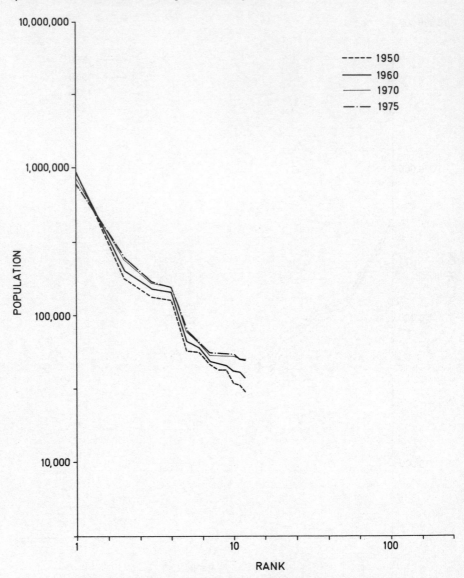

Fig. 4.18e   Denmark: rank-size plot 1950–60–70–75

drastic reductions in population growth. Britain shows a definite pivotal effect, with higher-ranking places in decline and lower-ranking places still in the ascendant. Almost everywhere in Europe, higher-ranking places are stagnating or marginally declining.

These measures treat each metropolitan area as an aggregate. But finally, it is useful to supplement them by looking at the pattern of internal shifts within

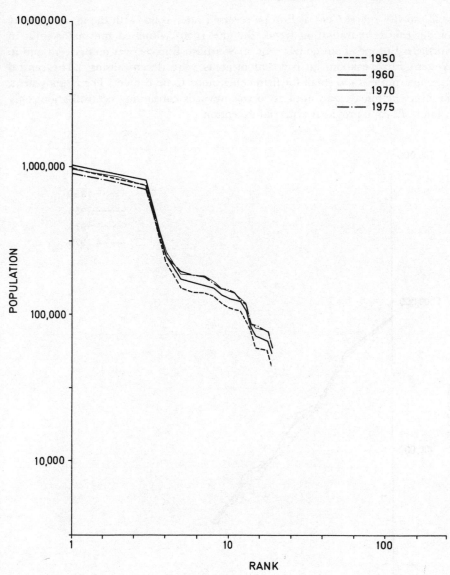

Fig. 4.18f The Netherlands: rank-size plot 1950–60–70–75

metropolitan areas. Tables 4.11 and 4.12 summarise the information about type of shift that we earlier saw mapped for each main region of Europe, and bring out the sharp contrast between these regions in this regard. While in Atlantic Europe nearly one half of the areas were already decentralising people in the 1950s and nearly three-quarters were doing so in the 1960s and 1970s, in Northern, Western and Southern Europe the majority of areas were still centralising well into the 1960s; Central Europe reversed after 1960, with the great majority joining the decentralisation trend. But the 1970s witnessed the major shift: in Northern Europe about 90 per cent, in Southern Europe over 60 per cent and in Western Europe about 50 per cent of areas were decentralising. (The central Europe sample is too small for firm conclusions to be drawn.) For employment, the overwhelming trend until 1970 was towards continuing centralisation; only Atlantic Europe provided a partial exception.

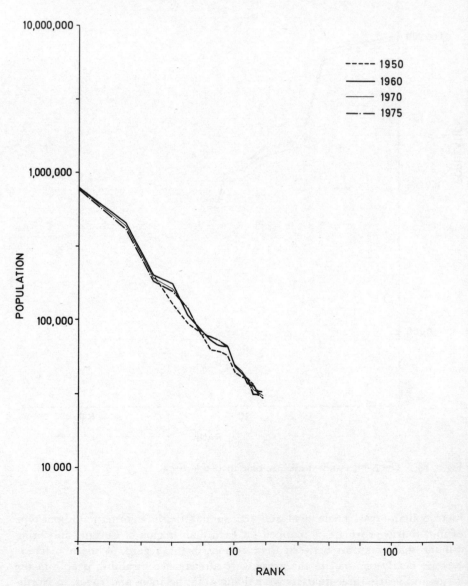

Fig. 4.18g   Belgium and Luxembourg: rank-size plot 1950–60–70–75

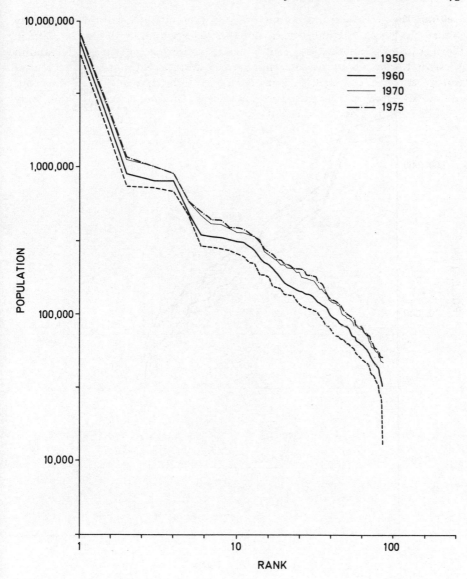

Fig. 4.18h   France: rank-size plot 1950–60–70–75

Forces behind Urban Growth

Thus, between 1950 and 1975, an already urban continent underwent further urbanisation: metropolitan areas, defined as those parts of Europe within the sphere of major urban concentrations of employment, gained over 39 million people while non-metropolitan areas stagnated. This process of urban growth was especially marked in Western, Southern, and Central Europe – though all

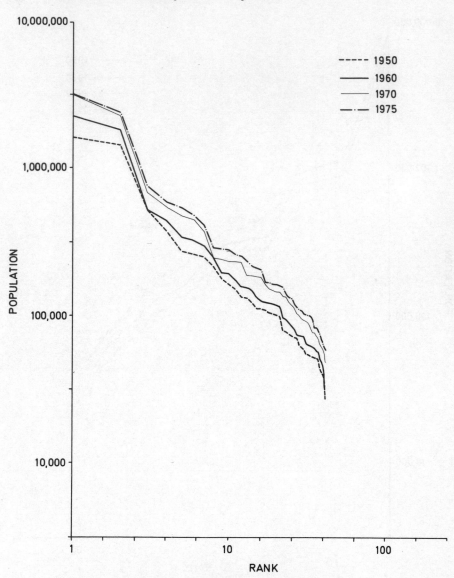

Fig. 4.18i   Spain: rank-size plot 1950–60–70–75

these regions included a large number of slow-growth areas affected by heavy population loss from their hinterlands, and sometimes even from their core cities.

The main explanation was of course migration in search of employment opportunities – a factor worthy of further detailed research. Throughout most of the post-World War II era, natural increase in European countries was on the

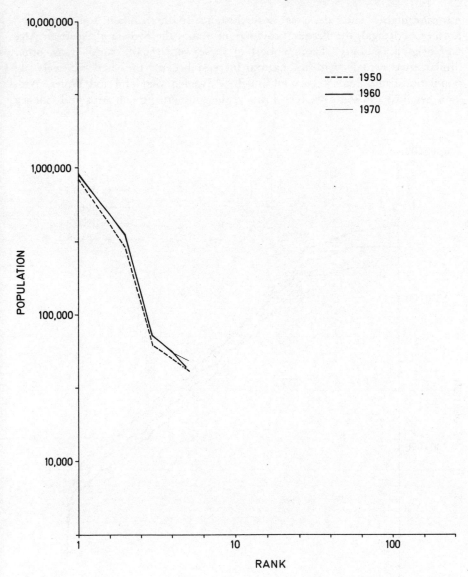

Fig. 4.18j   Portugal: rank-size plot 1950–60–70

decline – and though there were still strong differences between one country and another, with higher-than-average rates persisting in countries like the Netherlands, Portugal, Spain and Switzerland, it was also notable that these differences were diminishing over time (Salt and Clout 1976, pp. 8–14; Benjamin 1976, pp. 502–3). There were even regional differences within countries in their rates of natural growth: areas with high concentrations of young people tended to have the highest natural excess, as for instance southern Spain, southern Italy, northern Portugal, the Basque provinces of Spain, the Swiss and Austrian Alps and Belgian Limburg. Though most of these were remote rural areas, other similar areas actually had low natural increase because they had relatively old populations: into this category fell much of Sweden, Scotland and Wales, Walloon Belgium and south-western France, the southern French Alps and Corsica

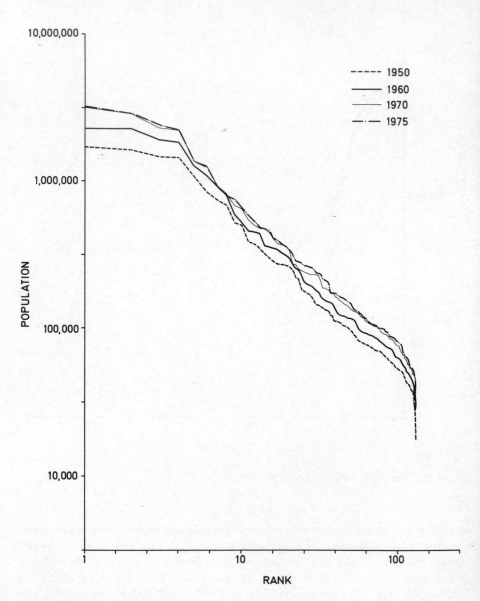

Fig. 4.18k   Italy: rank-size plot 1950–60–70–75

(Biraben and Duhourcau 1973, 1166). No simple explanation of these differences is possible: while many of the rural high growth areas were Catholic, so were some of the low growth ones.

More important was the indirect impact of natural increase on migration flows. Occasionally, areas of strong natural increase could absorb it locally. But more usually, the regional economy of these remoter agrarian parts of Europe

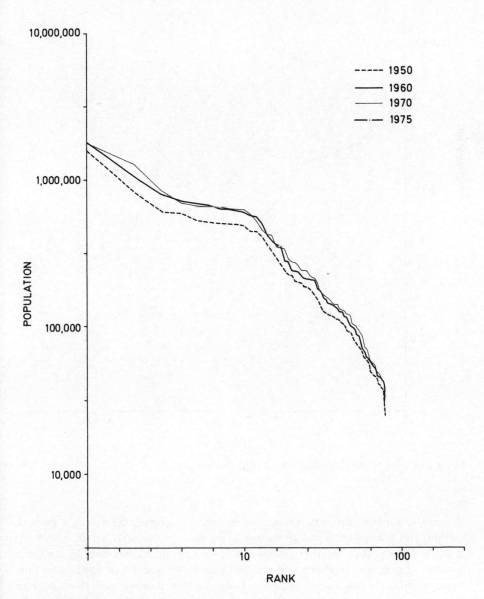

Fig. 4.181   Federal Republic of Germany: rank-size plot 1950–60–70

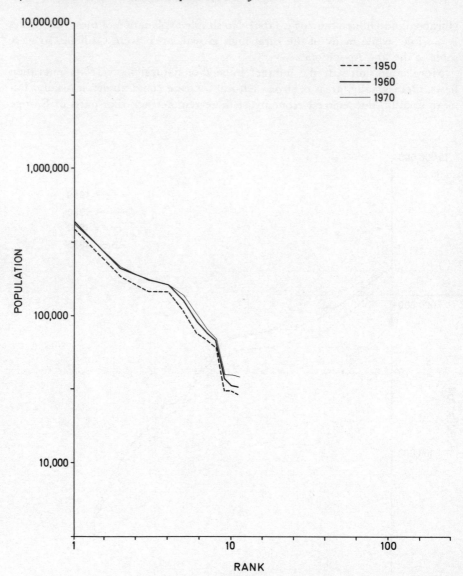

Fig. 4.18m   Switzerland: rank-size plot 1950–60–70

was not capable of the feat. During these years, therefore, there was a massive out-migration from the rural periphery of Europe and into its urban–industrial heartland: away from northern Norway, western Denmark, western Ireland, the Scottish Highlands, southern and western France, almost all of Spain and Portugal outside the big cities, southern Italy, eastern Austria and Bavaria; into southern Norway and Sweden and eastern Denmark, south-east England, the

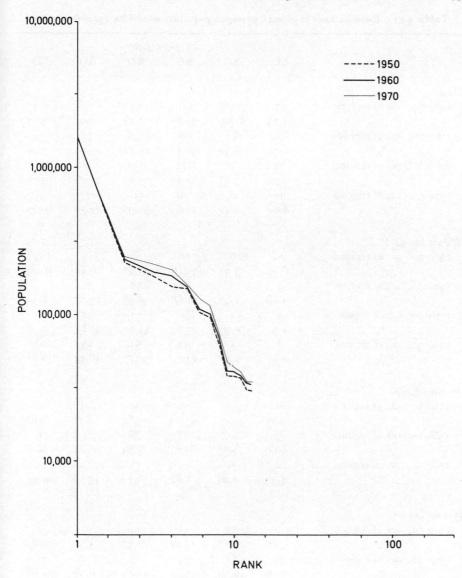

Fig. 4.18n   Austria: rank-size plot 1950–60–70

Rhine Valley and south-west Germany, western Austria, almost all of Switzerland, northern Italy, the axial belt of France from Normandy to Provence, and north-eastern Spain (Biraben and Duhourcau 1973, p. 1167; Salt and Clout 1976, pp. 27, 36). The areas of out-migration had very diverse economic systems, demographic patterns and physical environments; what tended to unite them all – apart from a few with declining older industries – was a dependence on agri-

Table 4.11   Europe and regional groups: population shifts 1950–60–70–75

	LC	AC	RC	RD	AD	LD
			Type of shift*			
Europe						
1950–60, no. of regions	74	118	215	93	21	18
%	13.73	21.89	39.89	17.25	3.90	3.34
1960–70, no. of regions	35	61	196	158	74	15
%	6.49	11.32	36.36	29.31	13.73	2.78
1960–70[a], no. of regions	33	60	174	120	51	14
%	7.30	13.27	38.49	26.55	11.28	3.10
1970–5[a], no. of regions	30	20	107	140	111	44
%	6.64	4.42	23.67	30.97	24.56	9.73
Atlantic Europe						
1950–60, no. of regions	10	8	56	39	15	15
%	6.99	5.59	39.16	27.27	10.49	10.49
1960–70, no. of regions	4	2	31	58	36	12
%	2.80	1.40	21.68	40.56	25.17	8.39
1960–70[b], no. of regions	4	1	30	57	34	12
%	2.90	0.72	21.74	41.30	24.64	8.70
1970–5[b], no. of regions	3	1	32	54	25	23
%	2.17	0.72	23.19	39.13	18.12	16.67
Northern Europe						
1950–60, no. of regions	3	15	19	6	1	0
%	6.82	34.09	43.18	13.64	2.27	0.00
1960–70, no. of regions	3	4	28	6	3	0
%	6.82	9.09	63.64	13.64	6.82	0.00
1970–5, no. of regions	2	0	3	16	19	4
%	4.55	0.00	6.82	36.36	43.18	9.09
Western Europe						
1950–60, no. of regions	5	47	41	22	4	1
%	4.17	39.17	34.17	18.33	3.33	0.83
1960–70, no. of regions	3	21	59	25	10	2
%	2.50	17.50	49.17	20.83	8.33	1.67
1960–70[c], no. of regions	3	21	59	24	10	2
%	2.52	17.65	49.58	20.17	8.40	1.68
1970–5[c], no. of regions	11	9	40	26	30	3
%	9.24	7.56	33.61	21.85	25.21	2.52
Southern Europe						
1950–60, no. of regions	30	35	55	10	0	0
%	23.08	26.92	42.31	7.69	0.00	0.00
1960–70, no. of regions	24	32	53	19	2	0
%	18.46	24.62	40.77	14.62	1.54	0.00

Table 4.11 – *continued*

	LC	AC	Type of shift* RC	RD	AD	LD
1960–70^d, no. of regions	22	32	51	19	1	0
%	17.60	25.60	40.80	15.20	0.80	0.00
1970–5^d, no. of regions	14	9	26	40	26	10
%	11.20	7.20	20.80	32.00	20.80	8.00

Central Europe

	LC	AC	RC	RD	AD	LD
1950–60, no. of regions	26	13	44	16	1	2
%	25.49	12.75	43.14	15.67	0.98	1.96
1960–70, no. of regions	1	2	25	50	23	1
%	0.98	1.96	24.51	49.02	22.55	0.98
1960–70^e, no. of regions	1	2	6	14	3	0
%	3.85	7.69	23.08	53.85	11.54	0.00
1970–5^e, no. of regions	0	1	6	4	11	4
%	0.00	3.85	23.08	15.38	42.31	15.38

Notes: ^{a} Excluding Ireland, Luxembourg, Portugal, Germany (most areas), Switzerland
and Austria.
  ^{b} Excluding Ireland.
  ^{c} Excluding Luxembourg.
  ^{d} Excluding Portugal.
  ^{e} Excluding Germany (most areas), Switzerland and Austria.

*Key: LC–Centralisation during region decline in population.
    AC–Absolute centralisation.
    RC–Relative centralisation.
    RD–Relative decentralisation.
    AD–Absolute decentralisation.
    LD–Decentralisation during region decline in population.

culture, a lack of alternative employment and mean incomes below their respective national averages (Salt and Clout 1976, pp. 38–9).

For France, Merlin has made a useful distinction between those areas of out-migration where the local urban centres can absorb the flows (the Paris Basin, the northern industrial region, Lorraine, Rhône–Alpes, Provence–Côte d'Azur) and those that could not (Centre, Bourgogne, Normandie, Picardie, Champagne–Ardennes, Franche–Comté, Languedoc–Roussillon). A third type has less intense out-migration, but the local economy had even less capacity to absorb it (Merlin 1971). Where the local economy lacks the absorptive capacity, long-distance migration is the result. Applying Merlin's analysis to the EEC, Clout identifies the following regions that have been unable to absorb their own rural out-migration: Corsica, Sardinia, parts of southern Italy, Scotland and Ireland, the Massif Central of France and the so called *Zonenrandgebiet* (border area) on the Federal Republic's eastern frontier (Clout 1976, p. 5). While many

Table 4.12   Europe and regional groups: employment shifts 1950–60–70

	LC	AC	RC	RD	AD	LD
			*Type of shift**			
Europe						
1950–60[a], no. of regions	74	57	72	34	1	8
%	30.08	23.17	29.27	13.82	0.41	3.25
1960–70[b], no. of regions	103	33	92	68	32	35
%	28.37	9.09	25.34	18.73	8.82	9.64
Atlantic Europe						
1950–60, no. of regions	25	34	45	26	1	7
%	18.12	24.64	32.61	18.84	0.72	5.07
1960–70, no. of regions	17	2	52	34	17	16
%	12.32	1.45	37.68	24.64	12.32	11.59
Northern Europe						
1950–60, no. of regions	na	na	na	na	na	na
1960–70[a], no. of regions	11	8	2	1	0	0
%	50.00	36.36	9.09	4.55	0.00	0.00
Western Europe[e]						
1950–60, no. of regions	2	4	11	2	0	0
%	10.53	21.05	57.89	10.53	0.00	0.00
1960–70, no. of regions	3	3	8	2	1	4
%	15.79	5.26	42.11	10.53	5.26	21.05
Southern Europe						
1950–60, no. of regions	na	na	na	na	na	na
1960–70[f], no. of regions	38	12	7	12	7	8
%	45.24	14.29	8.33	14.29	8.33	9.52
Central Europe						
1950–60[g], no. of regions	47	19	16	6	0	1
%	52.81	21.35	17.98	6.74	0.00	1.12
1960–70, no. of regions	34	10	23	19	7	7
%	34.00	10.00	23.00	19.00	7.00	7.00

Notes: [a] Excluding Ireland, Norway, Denmark, Sweden, France, Spain, Portugal, Italy, Austria.

      [b] Excluding Ireland, Norway, Denmark, France, Spain, Portugal.

      [c] Excluding Ireland.   [d] Sweden only.

      [e] Netherlands only.   [f] Italy only.

      [g] Excluding Austria.   na – not available.

*Key: LC–Centralisation during region decline in population.

      AC–Absolute centralisation.

      RC–Relative centralisation.

      RD–Relative decentralisation.

      AD–Absolute decentralisation.

      LD–Decentralisation during region decline in population.

of the migrants from these areas move to more heavily urbanised regions within the same country, others cross international frontiers: the enlarged EEC in 1972 had more than 6 million international migrant workers (Böhning 1974, p. 7).

Behind this great migration lies not merely the fact of varying rates of natural increase in the rural areas of out-migration, but far more potently the changes in their mode of economic support. Agricultural regions contained 54 per cent of the area of the original EEC and a little under 30 per cent of their population – though this figure was more than 50 per cent in Italy and nearly 70 per cent in France (Clout 1976). But between 1950 and 1972, employment in primary industry (agriculture, forestry and fishing) in these six countries fell from 30 million to 8.4 million – by nearly 70 per cent; these industries employed about 29 per cent of the total workforce in 1950, but only just over 11 per cent by 1972 (Salt and Clout 1976, pp. 34–5).

The industrial cities that attracted these migrants were very variously located. While some kinds of capital-intensive heavy industry (oil refining, petrochem-icals, iron and steel) were attracted to tidewater locations on estuaries (Wickham 1969, pp. 172–5), and though the presence of a major port drew other industry, many of the faster-growing industrial cities were in fact inland: London, Paris, the upper Rhine, Madrid. All, however, tended to be on strong natural corri-dors of transportation and trade that had persisted over centuries, or that had been created by centralised political power. This is the message of the zones of fastest growth in Fig. 4.16. The growing industrial cities were well connected to their sources of raw materials and markets. Analysis of 'contact potentials' within Europe, by the Swedish geographer Gunnar Törnqvist, brings this out (Törnqvist in Kawashima 1980).

Beyond that, the precise reasons for the location of Europe's network of cities defy any simple explanation. A multitude of historical factors, generally peculiar to the nation and even to the province in which the city is located, must be invoked. What recent European urban history does demonstrate, if anything, is the agglomerative power which cities – even bigger ones – can exert in periods of rapid rural–urban migration. This provides the only possible explanation of the anomaly that in some parts of Europe – especially Southern Europe – the largest urban systems were actually among the fastest growing. These countries appear to be in some respects transitional between fully-industrialised nations and de-veloping countries. Whatever the diseconomies of continued agglomeration, they have not yet been perceived either by ordinary migrants or by urban policy makers.

The so-called problem regions of Europe are for the most part those where still a much higher than average proportion work on the land, where low incomes persist, and where new alternative employment is not developing sufficiently fast to counterbalance the decline of farming opportunities. Thus in Italy's Mez-zogiorno, certainly the largest and almost certainly the most problematic of all such problem regions, 1.5 million farmworkers left the land between 1951 and 1968 but only 1.1 million new jobs (0.6 million in manufacturing, 0.5 million in the services) were created; the total out-migration of people over the entire period 1951-71 reached a staggering 4 million, yet unemployment in the early 1970s was still double the national average (Clout 1976, pp. 15–16, 21–2).

This evidence helps to explain not merely the relative rates of growth of metropolitan and non-metropolitan areas of Europe, and some of the differences in growth between one metropolitan area and another; it also helps powerfully to explain patterns of internal shift. Typically, a sequence of internal shifts can be distinguished, each corresponding roughly to a stage of economic development. In the earlier stage, people begin to leave the land but find that the local urban employment centre will not absorb them: in such urban systems, modest continuing growth in the urban core is offset by massive migration losses from the rural hinterland, leading to the phenomenon of *centralisation during loss*. A little later, regional policies may succeed in creating a growth centre in the core town; this helps turn the loss into a slight growth, leading to the stage of *absolute centralisation* (loss in the rural hinterland, gain in the core). As the city grows, it may overspill its boundaries; even the hinterland now begins to grow overall, giving the stage of *relative centralisation*.

Then comes the critical 'pivotal point', characteristic of the mature industrial-urban society: continued growth and deconcentration finally lead to the phenonomen of *relative decentralisation,* whereby growth in the suburban-exurban rings exceeds that of the central city. In the later stage of the same process, population (or employment) in the central city may actually start to decline: this is the stage of *absolute decentralisation*. Lastly – a stage reached only in some special cases, particularly in some very large agglomerations and in older industrial areas – the entire metropolitan area begins to decline, but with the contraction more marked in the core than in the ring: this stage of *decentralisation during loss* is exactly the reverse of the first stage of the process.

To try to trace this pattern of evolution more precisely, a set of matrices was compiled which permitted identification not only of the metropolitan regions that were passing through the sequence, but of the approximate time lapse involved. Tables 4.13a and 4.13b show that the overall European picture of these 1950–75 *population sequential shift* trends. The vertical axes give the shift type over the first decade, while the horizontal axes give the shift type over the second decade. Thus, in Table 4.13a (1950–60 compared with 1960–70) ninety (76.3 per cent) of the regions which had undergone absolute centralisation in the 1950–60 decade either revealed the same trend in the following decade or underwent relative centralisation. Of the 215 regions in the relative centralisation category during 1950–60, no fewer than 184 (85.5 per cent) remained stable or crossed the 'pivotal point' to relative decentralisation. Relative decentralisation followed by relative decentralisation or absolute decentralisation accounted for seventy-four out of ninety-three regions (79.6 per cent); while thirteen out of twenty-one regions (61.9 per cent) in the 1960–70 decade revealed patterns of absolute decentralisation followed by absolute decentralisation or decentralisation during loss.

Much the same pattern of sequential shifts occurred during the 1960–70 period (Table 4.13b) with a higher total proportion of metropolitan regions being situ-

Table 4.13a   Europe: population sequential shifts 1950–70

		LC	AC	RC	RD	AD	LD
Type of shift 1950–60	LC	18	15	17	14	8	2
	AC	10	33	57	13	5	0
	RC	6	8	108	76	16	1
	RD	1	4	12	45	29	2
	AD	0	1	1	6	8	5
	LD	0	0	1	4	8	5

Type of shift 1960–70

Key: LC–Centralisation during region decline in population.
AC–Absolute centralisation.
RC–Relative centralisation.
RD–Relative decentralisation.
AD–Absolute decentralisation.
LD–Decentralisation during region decline in population.

Table 4.13b   Europe: population sequential shifts 1960–75

		LC	AC	RC	RD	AD	LD
Type of shift 1960–70	LC	7	2	4	10	4	6
	AC	13	7	19	8	6	7
	RC	9	8	62	59	29	7
	RD	0	2	18	50	42	8
	AD	1	1	4	13	27	5
	LD	0	0	0	0	3	11

Type of shift 1970–5

Notes: Excludes Ireland, Portugal, Austria, Switzerland and some of Germany.

ated lower down and further to the right of the matrix indicating a stage-by-stage progression. (It should be remembered that the total number of observations for Europe is less during this period due to the absence of 1975 population data from Ireland, Luxembourg, Portugal, Austria, Switzerland and part of the Federal Republic of Germany.) Of course, some regions may pass through the sequence faster than the ten-year or five-year intervals can reveal; and others, which are in the minority (as the bottom left corners of the European matrices show), do not conform at all. Additionally, the overall European picture does not clearly establish that absolute centralisation predominantly follows centralisation during loss. This is a phenomenon through which most regions in Europe have probably already passed, although the Southern Europe matrix (Table 4.14a) of 1950–70 trends suggests that there is still some validity to the argument.

Accordingly, it is possible to disaggregate the European matrices into our conventional country groupings and even into the single countries themselves so that a clearer picture is gained. In addition, individual regions which conform to the expected sequences are listed underneath the matrices; although this list only includes regions which have passed through a maximum of two stages of the sequences during each of the two periods (1950–70, 1960–75) under observation – the maximum considered likely within ten years (Appendix Tables A.29–A.50).

The southern European matrix for 1950–70 clearly indicates a preponderance of centralising regions at the beginning of the sequence (Table 4.14a), although the 1960–75 matrix (Table 4.14b) gives a more confused picture with some decentralisation already following the earliest centralisation stages.

However, nearly all of this discrepancy arises from the reversal of flows back to the Italian Mezzogiorno in the 1970–5 period – i.e. a return migration to the regional hinterlands rather than a sudden movement out of the cities (Appendix

Table 4.14a   Southern Europe: population sequential shifts 1950–70

		LC	AC	RC	RD	AD	LD
	LC	14	10	6	0	0	0
Type of shift 1950–60	AC	6	15	13	1	0	0
	RC	4	6	29	14	2	0
	RD	0	1	5	4	0	0
	AD	0	0	0	0	0	0
	LD	0	0	0	0	0	0

Type of shift 1960–70

Table 4.14b Southern Europe: population sequential shifts 1960–75

		LC	AC	RC	RD	AD	LD
	LC	6	1	2	8	2	3
Type	AC	6	5	8	6	3	4
of							
shift	RC	2	2	16	16	14	1
1960–							
70	RD	0	0	0	10	7	2
	AD	0	1	0	0	0	0
	LD	0	0	0	0	0	0

Type of shift 1970–5
Note: Spain and Italy only.

Tables A.29 and A.30). The position in Spain is much clearer; Appendix Tables A.31 and A.32 reveal a definite sequence in most regions from centralisation during loss through to the beginnings of relative decentralisation which by 1970 affected five cities: Madrid, Barcelona, Bilbao, San Sebastián and the industrial centre of Alcoy. By 1975 four more regions had arrived at the 'pivotal point' of relative decentralisation, all of them notably located in southern Spain.

France could also be included at a similar stage of urban and regional change, with very clear sequential shifts between 1950 and 1975 (Tables A.33 and A.34). Indeed, after inspection of the Belgian and Dutch shifts, the inclusion of France in a western Europe grouping (Tables 4.15a and 4.15b) seems highly questionable; the other countries are both at a later stage of development. The sequential shifts of these two smaller nations, however, provide an almost perfect confirmation of the phases of metropolitan region population dynamics. Not only do the general sequences correspond to the model, but also the individual regions themselves pass progressively, with varying time lapses, through relative centralisation, relative decentralisation and absolute decentralisation in virtually every case (Tables A.35 and A.36, A.37 and A.38). Especially notable are the performances of the three largest regions: Amsterdam, Rotterdam and The Hague.

Again, in Northern Europe, the sequential shifts are clearly identifiable, with the 'pivotal point' having been passed in most regions during 1970–5 (Tables 4.16a and 4.16b). Sweden appears to have the most rapidly-evolving urban system (Tables A.39 and A.40), with many regions moving from a stage of *absolute centralisation* in 1950 to *absolute decentralisation* by 1975. Denmark's and Norway's systems evolved more slowly, but the general trends are still readily discernible (Tables A.41 to A.44); here the latest developmental stages are reserved for the bigger regions.

Table 4.15a   Western Europe: population sequential shifts 1950–70

		LC	AC	RC	RD	AD	LD
	LC	1	3	1	0	0	0
Type	AC	2	15	29	1	0	0
of shift	RC	0	1	28	11	1	0
1950– 60	RD	0	2	1	12	6	1
	AD	0	0	0	1	2	1
	LD	0	0	0	0	1	0

Type of shift 1960–70

Table 4.15b   Western Europe: population sequential shifts 1960–75

		LC	AC	RC	RD	AD	LD
	LC	0	1	1	1	0	0
Type	AC	7	2	9	1	0	2
of shift	RC	4	5	28	17	4	1
1960– 70	RD	0	1	2	7	14	0
	AD	0	0	0	0	10	0
	LD	0	0	0	0	2	0

Type of shift 1970–5

Lack of 1975 data precludes a comprehensive view of Central Europe, although it is evident that between 1950 and 1970 many regions moved rapidly into the decentralisation phases (Table 4.17). Without comparable 1960–75 data it is more difficult, however, to ascertain whether or not individual central European countries or regions can be allocated to precise stages in the sequence. Only partial 1970–5 results for Germany were available for analysis (Tables A.45 and A.46), but these do not reveal any predominant sequential shifts. Individually, Austria and Switzerland conformed to the model for the 1950–70 period, but again no conclusions are possible without further data (Tables A.47 and A.48).

We leave Atlantic Europe until last both because of its more complex results and also because, although at first sight the patterns appear similar to some other

Table 4.16a   Northern Europe: population sequential shifts 1950–70

		LC	AC	RC	RD	AD	LD
	LC	1	1	1	0	0	0
Type	AC	1	2	10	2	0	0
of							
shift	RC	1	1	16	1	0	0
1950–							
60	RD	0	0	1	3	2	0
	AD	0	0	0	0	1	0
	LD	0	0	0	0	0	0

Type of shift 1960–70

Table 4.16b   Northern Europe: population sequential shifts 1960–75

		LC	AC	RC	RD	AD	LD
	LC	0	0	0	0	2	1
Type	AC	0	0	1	0	3	0
of							
shift	RC	2	0	2	13	8	3
1960–							
70	RD	0	0	0	2	4	0
	AD	0	0	0	1	2	0
	LD	0	0	0	0	0	0

Type of shift 1970–5

older industrialised European nations, there is evidence to suggest that Great Britain is the only European country exhibiting trends which conform to the American model. The key can be found by comparing the matrices of Atlantic Europe and Great Britain (Tables 4.18 and A.49 and A.50) with the matrices for Europe combined (Tables 4.13a and 4.13b), with particular reference to the bottom three squares of the extreme right-hand column: decentralisation during region population decline following relative decentralisation, absolute decentralisation or decentralisation during loss itself. Of the twelve regions in these categories in the 1950–70 period, nine are in Great Britain and they are either regions with a decaying economic base (Whitehaven, Burnley, Greenock, Merthyr

Table 4.17   Central Europe: population sequential shifts 1950–70

		LC	AC	RC	RD	AD	LD
	LC	0	0	6	12	8	0
Type	AC	0	0	3	6	4	0
of shift	RC	0	0	13	24	7	0
1950–60	RD	1	1	3	8	3	0
	AD	0	1	0	0	0	0
	LD	0	0	0	0	1	1

Type of shift 1960–70

Tydfil, Rhondda) or they are centred on large, old, industrial cities (London, Manchester, Newcastle, Glasgow).

By the second period, a further eleven regions exhibit decentralisation during loss following other decentralisation categories. Again, all but one (Brighton) can be classed as regions where industrial decline is rife. Only seven other European regions progress to the same point over the quarter-century period (Charleroi, Bruay-en-Artois, Geneva, Trieste, Dortmund, Wuppertal, Hof). A number of these, significantly, are also older industrial regions.

The model could certainly benefit from further development and refinement, particularly through the addition of data on employment trends – though lack of information would probably prove an insuperable problem here. Nevertheless, it does potentially provide a way of predicting future regional performance. Faced

Table 4.18   Atlantic Europe: population sequential shifts 1950–70

		LC	AC	RC	RD	AD	LD
	LC	2	1	3	2	0	2
Type	AC	1	1	2	3	1	0
of shift	RC	1	0	22	26	6	1
1950–60	RD	0	0	2	18	18	1
	AD	0	0	1	5	5	4
	LD	0	0	1	4	6	4

Type of shift 1960–70

Table 4.19 Rate of shift and type of shift: three theoretical examples

	Total			*Core*			*Hinterland*		
	1950	*1960*	*1950–60*	*1950*	*1960*	*1950–60*	*1950*	*1960*	*1950–60*
Area A									
Population (thousands)	100	120	+20	70	85	+15	30	35	+5
Change, %			+20			+21[a]			+17[a]
Share of total, %				70	71[a]	+1[a]	30	29[a]	−1[a]
Type of shift	Relative centralisation (core and hinterland increasing, core relatively faster than hinterland)								
Area B									
Population (thousands)	100	100	—	50	49	−1	50	51	+1
Change, %			—			−2			+2
Share of total, %				50	49	−1	50	51	+1
Type of shift:	Absolute decentralisation (core decreasing, hinterland increasing)								
Area C									
Population (thousands)	100	150	+50	50	60	+10	50	90	+40
Change, %			+50			+20			+80
Share of total, %				50	40	−10	50	60	+10
Type of shift:	Relative decentralisation (core and hinterland increasing, hinterland relatively faster than core)								

Note: [a] To nearest 1%.

with it, the urban or regional policy-maker may want to try to manipulate the process. And this may be possible – within limits. During the 1950s and 1960s most European nations were officially using a variety of regional policies to try to steer growth into their lagging regions, with varying degrees of success. By the mid-1970s, national–regional policies of various kinds covered no less than half the area and one-third of the population of the enlarged Community – or, taking also into account the areas of restriction around London, Paris and Amsterdam, no less than three-fifths of the area and more than two-fifths of the population (Romus in Vaizey 1975, pp. 125–6). These national efforts are now supplemented by the European Regional Fund, created in 1973 to try to standardise policies and so ease the path to Economic and Monetary Union (Romus in Vaizey 1975, pp. 129–31; Clout 1976, pp. 54–5). Yet even at that point, the expectation was that further large reductions in agricultural workers would still occur, especially in France and Italy. All this raised challenges for European

regional policies, but perhaps weakened their chances of success; we try to analyse their impact in the chapter that follows.

All these pieces of evidence suggest powerfully that Europe in the quarter
century after 1950 was still a continent in course of rapid industrialisation and
urbanisation. People were pouring off the land and into the cities. They were
strongly concentrating into a relatively few highly urbanised areas. This process
was especially marked in western, southern, and central Europe. The industrial
heartland of Europe showed little tendency to slow growth or decline. Indeed, in
many countries there was actually a movement up the urban hierarchy, with
even bigger metropolitan areas showing marked growth. Though a substantial
proportion of the fastest-growing areas were in Europe's 'Sunbelt', the reasons
were very different from those generating growth in the American South and
West: in Europe they were concerned with movement out of adjacent rural
areas. These rural or non-metropolitan areas – especially the more remote and
thinly populated ones – were still tending to lose people. And, though Great
Britain was decentralising both people and jobs out of its central cores by the
1960s, elsewhere there was at most a limited amount of decentralisation of residential populations; generally, jobs were still centralising, while in France and
southern Europe people were continuing to flood into central cities.

Thus, the observed trends were quite contrary to those observed for the
United States – and they persisted into the early 1970s. The obvious explanation
is that Europe was in an earlier stage of industrial-urban evolution. People were
still leaving the land and flooding into the cities. The suburbanisation process
had not yet, or only just, set in. To these generalisations, Great Britain provides
the conspicuous exception. But, as the oldest industrial and urban nation, it
could be expected to behave differently.

Appendix to Chapter 4:
Type of Shift: Explanation and Calculation

Two main groups of shift are identified: centralisation and decentralisation. Differentiation within each group is made according to whether a region is gaining or losing population (or employment) and according to the performance of the two components within the region (core and hinterland). The typology is as follows:

1. Centralisation during decline in population (or employment): positive shift.
2. Absolute centralisation: positive shift (core increasing, hinterland decreasing).
3. Relative centralisation: positive shift (core and hinterland increasing, core relatively faster than hinterland).
4. Relative decentralisation: negative shift (core and hinterland increasing, hinterland relatively faster than core).
5. Absolute decentralisation: negative shift (core decreasing, hinterland increasing).
6. Decentralisation during decline in population (or employment): negative shift.

As Table 4.19 illustrates by theoretical examples, it is possible to have a *high* percentage shift figure associated with *relative* centralisation (or decentralisation) while a much *lower* figure is associated with *absolute* centralisation (or decentralisation). This is because the type of shift depends principally on the absolute change in the population of the central core.

Chapter 5
Explaining the Patterns:
A Statistical Experiment

In the previous chapter, we already began to develop some tentative hypotheses about the behaviour of Europe's urban systems. American geographers, working with the uniformly defined metropolitan areas and their rich data base, have developed and tested such hypotheses in great detail and with considerable success. In this chapter, we try to go on to do the same for Europe, using fairly familiar statistical techniques.

The Variables and Their Expression
What we shall do is to take four *dependent variables* – percentage population change, percentage population shift, percentage employment change and percentage employment shift – and seek to 'explain' them in terms of a series of *independent variables*. The hypothesis in each case is that changes in the dependent variable are systematically associated with variations in the independent variable and that this association may be interpreted as causal. Below we separately consider both the dependent variables and the independent variables. We outline the hypothesis we are trying to test for each, and we explain how the variables are expressed.

Dependent Variable 1: Population Change
This is the inter-censal population change for each metropolitan area, considered as an aggregate. (The non-metropolitan areas are excluded from this, and from all other analyses considered in this chapter.) The change is considered as a percentage which is standardised for a decade (that is, if the original figures referred to a period more or less than ten years, they are deflated or inflated). These figures are available for each of the 539 metropolitan areas.

Dependent Variable 2: Employment Change
This is a standardised decennial percentage change, as already explained for population. It is however available for only some of the 539 metropolitan areas:

for 254 in 1950–60 and for 451 in 1960–70. For some countries it is available for neither of these decades, and for some only for the 1960–70 decade.

Dependent Variable 3: Population Shift
It was deemed unsuitable to use the 'type of shift' analysis used in Chapter 4 in the regressions. Instead, the dependent variable is the percentage gain or loss in the core share of the total metropolitan area population, again expressed as a standard decennial rate. These figures are available for each of the 539 metropolitan areas and for two intercensal periods.

Dependent Variable 4: Employment Shift
This is a standardised percentage rate of shift, as already explained for population. Its availability is the same as for dependent variable 2.

Independent Variable 1: Population
This is total population size of the metropolitan area at the start of the period. The hypothesis for population change and for employment change is that the bigger the population at the start of the period, the lower the subsequent rate of growth. This is a general rule found to apply to American metropolitan areas. The hypothesis for population shift and for employment shift is that the bigger the population at the start of a period, the higher the subsequent tendency towards decentralisation (negative shift). This again has been found to apply to American metropolitan areas; it is related to other factors such as the age of the city, the physical condition of the housing stock in the central core, the racial composition of the core city and the presence of unfavourable social indicators there.

Independent Variable 2: Employment
This is used (and measured) in the same way as population, to provide a further measure for testing against employment change and shift only. The hypothesis is the same as for population size. Its availability is the same as for dependent variable 2.

Independent Variable 3: Population Density
This is the population per hectare over the whole metropolitan area at the start of the period. The hypothesis for population change is that the higher the density, the lower the rate of subsequent growth. This is related to simple lack of available space as well as to associated variables such as the age of the central city (on the assumption that older cities are denser). The hypothesis for population shift is that the higher the density, the greater the tendency to subsequent outward movement. This can be regarded as a simple physical response to population pressure and also as a reaction against associated housing conditions and/or negative social indicators.

Independent Variable 4: Employment Density
This is measured and used in association with employment change and shift, in the same way as population density is used in association with population change and shift. Its availability again is the same as for dependent variable 2.

Independent Variable 5: Population Concentration
This is the percentage of total metropolitan population living in the core at the start of the period. The hypothesis for change is that the higher the concentration, the lower the rate of subsequent growth in the urban region as a whole. The hypothesis for shift is that the greater the concentration, the greater the subsequent tendency to outward shift. The reasoning is similar to that for independent variable 3.

Independent Variable 6: Employment Concentration
This is measured and used in association with employment change and shift, in the same way as population concentration is used in association with population change and shift. Its availability is the same as for dependent variable 2.

Independent Variable 7: Latitude
This is the latitude of the core city of each metropolitan area, as shown in the index to *The Times Atlas*: it is 'metricised' for ease of computation. The hypothesis for population and employment change is that the lower the latitude, the greater the subsequent growth; this, it is suggested, will be associated with the 'drift to the sun' and with the later date of industrialisation and urbanisation in southern Europe. The hypothesis for population and employment shift is that the lower the latitude, the less the subsequent tendency to outward movement; it is hypothesised that southern Europeans retain a greater preference for central city location than northern Europeans, associated in part with later economic development and lower ownership of consumer durables, especially cars.

Independent Variable 8: Age of City
This is the ratio between the 1870 population (or nearest Census equivalent) and 1950 population. The source is *European Historical Statistics 1850–1970* (Mitchell 1975), where available, or failing that the *Encyclopaedia Britannica*: the figures from the first source are corrected for boundary changes wherever possible; those from the second of course are not. The hypothesis is that the 'older' the city, the lower the rate of subsequent growth; and that the 'older' the city, the greater the tendency to decentralisation. (American studies had suggested that both these associations were true.) This variable is not available for all 539 metropolitan areas.

Independent Variable 9: Distance from Capital
This is expressed in kilometres as the shortest road distance (including ferry routes where applicable) between metropolitan area cores and their respective national capitals. The hypothesis for growth is that the greater the distance from

the capital city, the lower the rate of growth (because of the disadvantages of a peripheral location in terms of poor access to markets and services, and low levels of information leading to lack of innovation and innovation diffusion). The hypothesis for shift is that the greater the distance from the capital, the lower the rate of decentralisation because of the lower rate of growth of the metropolitan system generally. As well as testing for distance to national capitals, this experiment tested for distance to 'regional capitals' (London, Copenhagen, Brussels, Rome, Frankfurt-am-Main) and for the 'European capital' of Brussels. The assumption here was that these higher-order centres may be becoming even more important than national capitals in their influence on growth, particularly through the location decisions of large corporations operating multinationally.

Each of the four dependent variables was tested against the relevant independent variables (six in the case of population growth and shift, seven in the case of employment growth and shift); scattergrams were plotted by the computer, and coefficients of determination (R^2 values) were produced together with tests of significance. The resulting correlation coefficients and R^2 values are summarised for each of the four dependent variables in Tables 5.1 to 5.8.

These tables also indicate the significance of the pairwise correlations, making use of the standard F test on the correlation coefficient. In most cases regression analysis is used to expand observed relationships from the sample population to the total population, and the F test indicates the levels of confidence which can be placed on the sample. In our study, however, this is not the case, as we are not dealing with samples, but with total populations. It could be argued, in fact, that 'significance' as such is a relatively meaningless concept for the way in which we have applied regression analysis. However, we have retained it for the presentation of the results, since it does take into account the number of cases involved. For, leaving aside questions of samples, our confidence in the validity of the relationships must increase in an absolute fashion with an increase in the number of metropolitan regions involved.

The Results Analysed: Population Change (Tables 5.1 and 5.2)
Straightaway, it can be said that the results fail to indicate very clear associations: the R^2 values are generally low, and they reveal no very consistent pattern. The hypotheses outlined earlier in the chapter would lead us to expect a negative correlation for each pairwise relationship (except for the dependent variable and latitude) and, as Table 5.1 shows, this is not always the case. In directional terms, city age and distance from capital give the best performance, although as Table 5.2 shows, rarely are these correlations significant. When they are significant, the R^2s are on the low side – Denmark providing the exception here. Population size gives hardly any values that would indicate clear association, and the conclusion must be that at this level of aggregation we cannot say that larger areas have grown more slowly than smaller ones. But this could be of importance, because it may indicate (as we already saw in Chapter 4) that in some countries a primate type of urban development is still in course of emergence,

Table 5.1   Correlation coefficients (R): population change 1950–60, 1960–70

	Population		Population density		Population concentration		Latitude		City age		Distance from capital	
	1950–60	1960–70	1950–60	1960–70	1950–60	1960–70	1950–60	1960–70	1950–60	1960–70	1950–60	1960–70
Europe	−0.03	−0.04	0.01	0.01	0.25[a]	0.24[a]	0.05	−0.01	−0.13[b]	−0.02	−0.08[c]	−0.14[a]
Atlantic Europe	−0.07	−0.19[c]	−0.07	—	0.29[a]	0.19[c]	−0.02	−0.28[a]	−0.36[a]	−0.19[c]	−0.08	−0.36[a]
Britain	−0.07	−0.19[c]	−0.08	—	0.29[a]	0.19[c]	−0.02	−0.29[a]	−0.34[a]	−0.17[c]	−0.07	−0.37[a]
Ireland	0.26	0.61	0.63	0.58	0.76	0.99[a]	0.91[a]	0.32	−0.93[c]	−0.64	−0.79	−0.41
Northern Europe	0.15	−0.16	0.27[c]	0.25[c]	0.56[a]	0.59[a]	−0.03	−0.14	0.19	0.03	0.12	−0.16
Sweden	0.39[c]	0.08	0.46[c]	0.25	0.58[b]	0.55[b]	−0.11	−0.03	−0.24	−0.47[c]	−0.48[c]	−0.36
Norway	−0.14	−0.06	0.06	−0.04	0.41	0.42	−0.61[c]	−0.65[c]	−0.13	−0.08	−0.27	−0.40
Denmark	0.02	−0.25	0.37	0.25	0.55[c]	0.71[c]	−0.27	−0.27	0.29	0.56	−0.66[c]	−0.81[a]
Western Europe	0.02	−0.01	0.11	−0.07	0.31[a]	0.37[a]	0.17[c]	−0.28[a]	−0.19[c]	−0.03	0.08	0.46[a]
Netherlands	−0.36	−0.58[b]	−0.10	−0.62[b]	−0.10	−0.44[c]	−0.75[c]	−0.18	−0.17	−0.01	−0.23	−0.25
Belgium	−0.13	−0.07	−0.09	—	−0.13	−0.07	0.34	0.45	−0.30	−0.07	0.23	−0.01
France	0.04	0.04	0.11	−0.02	0.35[a]	0.42[a]	0.13	−0.45[a]	−0.15	0.02	0.06	0.46[a]
Southern Europe	0.30[a]	0.25[b]	0.31[a]	0.18[c]	0.43	0.22[b]	—	0.07	−0.13	−0.20	0.03	−0.04
Spain	0.47[a]	0.38[b]	0.54[a]	0.48[a]	0.59[a]	0.41[b]	0.08	0.10	−0.08	−0.20	0.12	0.07
Portugal	0.33	−0.14	0.82[c]	0.23	−0.52	0.77	0.72	−0.24	0.48	−0.28	0.87	−0.36
Italy	0.26[b]	0.27[b]	0.37[a]	0.34[a]	0.41[a]	0.14	0.01	0.29[b]	−0.14	−0.08	0.18	−0.02
Central Europe	0.23[c]	0.01	0.37[a]	−0.24[b]	0.30[a]	−0.02	−0.22[c]	−0.41[a]	−0.13	0.18	−0.28[b]	−0.02
Germany	0.31[b]	0.13	0.39[a]	−0.26[c]	0.31[b]	−0.03	−0.22[c]	−0.38[a]	−0.18	0.27[c]	−0.58[a]	—
Switzerland	0.57[c]	−0.03	0.68[c]	−0.46	0.62[c]	0.06	0.49	−0.70[b]	−0.13	0.34	0.03	0.43
Austria	−0.29	−0.39	−0.29	−0.33	0.59[c]	0.28	−0.63[c]	−0.49[c]	−0.41	−0.45	0.55[c]	0.58[c]

Population change against independent variables

Notes: [a] Significant at 0.001   [b] Significant at 0.01   [c] Significant at 0.05

Table 5.2 Coefficients of determination (R^2): population change 1950–60, 1960–70

Population change against independent variables

	Population 1950–60	Population 1960–70	Population density 1950–60	Population density 1960–70	Population concentration 1950–60	Population concentration 1960–70	Latitude 1950–60	Latitude 1960–70	City age 1950–60	City age 1960–70	Distance from capital 1950–60	Distance from capital 1960–70
Europe	—	—	—	—	0.06	0.06	—	—	0.02	—	0.01	0.02
Atlantic Europe												
Britain	—	0.04	—	—	0.08	0.04	—	0.08	0.13	0.04	—	0.13
Ireland	—	0.04	—	—	0.08	0.98	—	0.08	0.12	0.03	—	0.14
Northern Europe												
Sweden	—	—	0.07	0.06	0.31	0.35	—	—	—	—	—	—
Norway	0.15	—	0.21	—	0.34	0.30	0.37	0.43	—	0.22	0.23	—
Denmark	—	—	—	—	0.30	0.50	0.83	—	0.86	—	0.44	0.46
Western Europe												
Netherlands	—	—	—	—	0.10	0.14	0.03	0.08	0.04	—	—	0.21
Belgium	—	0.34	—	0.38	—	0.19	0.56	—	—	—	—	—
France	—	—	—	—	0.12	0.18	—	0.20	—	—	—	0.21
Southern Europe												
Spain	0.09	0.06	0.10	0.03	0.18	0.05	—	—	—	—	—	—
Portugal	0.22	0.14	0.67	0.23	0.35	0.17	—	—	—	—	—	—
Italy	0.07	0.07	0.14	0.12	0.17	—	—	0.08	—	—	—	—
Central Europe												
Germany	0.05	—	0.14	0.06	0.09	—	0.05	0.17	—	—	0.08	—
Switzerland	0.10	—	0.15	0.07	0.10	—	0.05	0.49	—	0.08	0.34	—
Austria	0.32	—	0.46	—	0.38	—	0.40	0.24	—	—	0.30	0.34

Note: Only correlations significant at 0.05 have been included.

with the largest urban areas experiencing rapid growth. The results for the countries of Southern Europe would appear to support this, with correlations for population, population density and population concentration varying between 0.3 and 0.55. The decrease over time of many of these positive relationships would tend to support a theory of a reduction in the dominance of primacy in these countries. We can hypothesise that Southern Europe is at an earlier stage in the urban development sequence than Britain, the Netherlands and Belgium, for example, where negative correlations predominate. Population density gives slightly better results than population, especially for the Netherlands and Switzerland, although the instability over time of these particular relationships is disturbing. Population concentration gives largely positive results, with the best occurring in Northern and Southern Europe, while most of the correlations with latitude are negative. The exceptionally good results for Ireland are of course based on very few observations. City age is generally a poor predictor, the best correlations occurring in Atlantic Europe. Distance from capital gives some reasonable results, and again shows a similar spatial pattern to population with positive correlations in Southern Europe and negative correlations for the Netherlands, Belgium, Atlantic Europe and, additionally, northern Europe. Particularly disturbing, however, is the fact that there are instances in Table 5.1 where a significant value in one decade is not associated with a similar result for the same country in the other decade, indicating a distinct lack of stability in the associations.

Employment Change (Tables 5.3 and 5.4)
Again, the pairwise correlations for which data are available show very few associations of any strength. The most notable are for the Netherlands (employment concentration, latitude, city age and distance from capital) and for Switzerland (population, employment, employment concentration and city age). With the exception of the last correlation, these significant values are only present for 1950–60. As with population change, where a significant association appears for any country is one decade it is not repeated in the other. The conclusion, difficult to resist, is that employment change cannot readily be 'explained' by most of the factors posited in the tables.

Population Shift (Tables 5.5 and 5.6)
The relationships here are more striking. There are fairly strong associations between shift and population size for Sweden, Denmark and the Netherlands and in all these cases the relationship is negative as hypothesised: the bigger the metropolitan area, the greater the tendency to decentralisation. Even stronger correlations are observable for most countries with the density variable, and again they are always negative: the higher the density, the greater the tendency to outward shift. Similar, though fewer, relationships can be seen with population concentration, with the Netherlands again providing the strongest correlation. Latitude and city age have weak associations except for Ireland, where the small number of cases must be borne in mind, and Austria, where Vienna (a city

Table 5.3 Correlation coefficients (R): employment change 1950–60, 1960–70

Employment change against independent variables

	Population		Employment		Employment density		Employment concentration		Latitude		City age		Distance from capital	
	1950–60	1960–70	1950–60	1960–70	1950–60	1960–70	1950–60	1960–70	1950–60	1960–70	1950–60	1960–70	1950–60	1960–70
Europe	-0.05	-0.20[a]	-0.06	-0.05	-0.03	-0.10[c]	0.30[a]	-0.15[a]	0.15[b]	-0.11[c]	0.09	-0.07	-0.19[a]	0.01
Atlantic Europe														
Britain	-0.07	-0.15[c]	-0.06	-0.15[c]	-0.10	0.05	0.30[a]	0.28[a]	-0.01	-0.20[b]	-0.31[a]	-0.20[c]	-0.06	-0.26[a]
Ireland	-0.07	-0.15[c]	-0.06	-0.15[c]	-0.10	0.05	0.30[a]	0.28[a]	-0.01	-0.20[b]	-0.31[a]	-0.20[c]	-0.06	-0.26[a]
Northern Europe														
Sweden	na	0.12	na	0.11	na	0.28	na	0.51[b]	na	0.32	na	-0.40	na	-0.40[c]
Norway	na	0.12	na	0.11	na	0.28	na	0.51[b]	na	0.32	na	-0.40	na	-0.40[c]
Denmark	na	na	na	na	na	na	na	na	na	na	na	na	na	na
Western Europe														
Netherlands	-0.08	-0.11	-0.24	-0.10	-0.32[c]	-0.20	0.16	-0.15	-0.69[a]	0.07	0.43[c]	-0.05	-0.70[a]	-0.04
Belgium	0.19	-0.33	0.18	-0.33	0.38	-0.38	0.49[c]	-0.16	-0.66[a]	-0.24	-0.51[c]	-0.18	-0.55[b]	-0.40
France	na	-0.11	na	-0.09	na	-0.31	na	-0.16	na	0.55	na	0.05	na	-0.02
Southern Europe														
Spain	na	0.21[c]	na	0.25[c]	na	0.24[c]	na	0.28[b]	na	0.40[a]	na	-0.14	na	-0.38[a]
Portugal	na	na	na	na	na	na	ns	na	na	na	na	na	na	na
Italy	na	0.21[c]	na	0.25[c]	na	0.24[c]	na	0.28[b]	na	0.40[a]	na	-0.14	na	-0.11
Central Europe														
Germany	0.32[a]	-0.07	0.25[b]	-0.05	0.34[a]	-0.29[b]	0.45[a]	-0.05	-0.15	-0.59[a]	-0.10	0.31[b]	0.01	0.37[a]
Switzerland	0.40[a]	0.13	0.32[b]	0.17	0.41[a]	-0.27[b]	0.48[a]	0.01	0.08	-0.26[c]	-0.22	0.22	-0.43[a]	0.28[b]
Austria	0.58[c]	-0.13	0.58[c]	-0.12	0.49	-0.02	0.67[c]	0.28	0.10	-0.45	-0.07	0.61[c]	0.11	0.48
	na	-0.49[c]	na	-0.51[c]	na	-0.43	na	-0.07	na	-0.29	na	-0.13	na	0.17

Notes: na not available.

[a] Significant at 0.001.
[b] Significant at 0.01.
[c] Significant at 0.05.

Table 5.4 Coefficients of determination (R^2): employment change 1950-60, 1960-70

	Population		Employment		Employment density		Employment concentration		Latitude		City age		Distance from capital	
	1950-60	1960-70	1950-60	1960-70	1950-60	1960-70	1950-60	1960-70	1950-60	1960-70	1950-60	1960-70	1950-60	1960-70
Europe	—	0.04	—	—	—	0.01	0.09	0.02	0.02	0.01	—	—	0.04	—
Atlantic Europe														
Britain	—	0.02	—	0.02	—	—	0.09	0.08	—	0.04	0.01	0.04	—	0.07
Ireland	na	na	na	na	na	na	na	0.09	na	0.04	na	0.04	na	0.07
Northern Europe														
Sweden	na	na	na	—	na	—	na	0.26	na	—	na	—	na	0.16
Norway	na	na	na	na	na	na	na	0.26	na	na	na	na	na	0.16
Denmark	na	na	na	na	na	na	na	na	na	na	na	na	na	na
Western Europe														
Netherlands	—	—	—	—	0.10	—	0.24	—	0.48	—	0.18	—	0.49	—
Belgium	—	—	—	—	—	—	0.20	na	0.44	—	0.26	—	0.30	—
France	na	na	na	na	na	na	na	na	na	na	na	na	na	na
Southern Europe														
Spain	na	0.04	na	0.06	na	0.06	na	0.08	na	0.16	na	—	na	0.14
Portugal	na	na	na	na	na	na	na	na	na	na	na	na	na	na
Italy	na	0.04	na	0.06	na	0.06	na	0.08	na	0.16	na	—	na	0.01
Central Europe														
Germany	0.16	—	0.10	—	0.12	—	0.23	—	—	0.35	—	0.10	0.18	0.14
Switzerland	0.34	—	0.34	—	0.17	0.07	0.45	—	—	0.07	—	0.37	na	0.08
Austria	na	0.24	na	0.26	na	—	na	—	na	—	na	—	na	—

Notes: na not available.

Only correlations significant at 0.05 have been included.

C.6 xxxx Correlation coefficients (X) population shift 1950–60, 1960–70

Population shift against independent variables

	Population		Population density		Population concentration		Latitude		City age		Distance from capital	
	1950–60	1960–70	1950–60	1960–70	1950–60	1960–70	1950–60	1960–70	1950–60	1960–70	1950–60	1960–70
Europe	-0.12^b	-0.23^a	-0.28^a	-0.35^a	-0.24^a	-0.20^a	-0.19^a	-0.39^a	0.09^c	0.14^b	0.16^a	0.35^a
Atlantic Europe	-0.17^c	-0.25^b	-0.17^c	-0.13	-0.25^a	-0.14^a	-0.10	-0.05	0.16^c	0.10	-0.09	-0.17
Britain	-0.16^c	-0.24^b	-0.17^c	-0.13	-0.25^a	-0.13	-0.09	-0.02	0.13	0.04	-0.10	-0.01
Ireland	-0.59	-0.67	-0.82^c	-0.90^c	-0.44	-0.72	-0.83^c	-0.91^c	0.76	0.99^a	0.94^c	0.94^c
Northern Europe	-0.48^a	-0.68^a	-0.43^b	-0.67^a	-0.19	-0.50^a	0.12	0.24	-0.08	0.08	-0.32^c	-0.17
Sweden	-0.38^c	-0.82^a	-0.47^c	-0.81^a	-0.26	-0.55^a	0.30	0.19	0.25	0.34	0.04	-0.11
Norway	-0.25	-0.42	-0.52	-0.53	0.14	0.09	0.24	0.60^c	0.13	0.28	0.19	0.47
Denmark	-0.89^a	-0.85^a	-0.54^a	-0.96^a	0.09	-0.41	0.22	0.16	0.23	-0.27	-0.79^b	0.65^b
Western Europe	-0.18^c	-0.28^a	-0.46^a	-0.60^a	-0.16^c	-0.05	-0.42^a	-0.55^a	0.14	0.15	-0.07	-0.08
Netherlands	-0.73^a	-0.73^a	-0.74^a	-0.77^a	-0.70^a	0.72^a	0.25	0.16	0.44	0.58^c	0.55^b	0.61^b
Belgium	-0.19	-0.19	-0.15	-0.43	-0.19	-0.13	0.17	—	-0.15	-0.14	0.47	0.50^c
France	-0.12	-0.28^b	-0.31^b	-0.40^a	-0.27^b	-0.25^b	-0.10	-0.10	0.01	-0.18	-0.08	-0.06
Southern Europe	-0.20^c	-0.33^a	-0.36^a	-0.48^a	-0.11	-0.23^b	0.20^c	-0.19^c	0.09	—	-0.30^a	0.23^b
Spain	-0.17	-0.44^b	-0.43^b	-0.57^b	-0.09	-0.17	0.14	0.15	0.04	0.15	-0.27^b	-0.38^b
Portugal	-0.27	-0.27	0.52	-0.94^b	-0.33	0.37	0.47	-0.66	0.08	-0.29	0.17	-0.69
Italy	-0.15	-0.35^a	-0.59^a	-0.56^a	-0.20^c	-0.31^c	-0.01	-0.24^c	-0.01	-0.01	-0.23^c	-0.24^c
Central Europe	0.12	-0.38^a	-0.11	-0.18^c	-0.07	-0.17^c	0.29^b	-0.07	0.10	0.36^b	-0.05	0.02
Germany	0.12	-0.43^b	-0.17	-0.18^c	-0.07	-0.19	0.14	-0.19	0.21	0.43^b	0.24^c	0.10
Switzerland	-0.45	-0.68	-0.77^b	-0.21	-0.58	-0.60	-0.74	0.24	0.57	0.22	-0.18	-0.21
Austria	-0.23	-0.29	0.11	-0.24	-0.19	-0.07	0.11	0.08	0.72^b	0.36	-0.75^b	-0.36

Notes: ^a Significant at 0.001 ^b Significant at 0.01 ^c Significant at 0.05

— Correlation coefficient less than 0.01

Table 5.6 Coefficients of determination (R^2): population shift 1950–60, 1960–70

Population shift against independent variables

	Population		Population density		Population concentration		Latitude		City age		Distance from capital	
	1950–60	1960–70	1950–60	1960–70	1950–60	1960–70	1950–60	1960–70	1950–60	1960–70	1950–60	1960–70
Europe	0.01	0.05	0.08	0.12	0.06	0.04	0.04	0.15	0.01	0.02	0.03	0.12
Atlantic Europe												
Britain	0.03	0.06	0.03	—	0.06	0.02	—	—	0.03	—	—	—
Ireland	0.03	0.06	0.67	0.81	0.06	—	0.69	0.83	—	0.98	0.88	0.88
Northern Europe												
Sweden	0.23	0.46	—	0.45	—	0.25	—	—	—	—	0.10	—
Norway	0.14	0.67	0.22	0.66	—	0.42	—	0.36	—	—	—	—
Denmark	0.79	0.72	0.41	0.92	—	—	—	—	—	—	0.62	0.42
Western Europe												
Netherlands	0.03	0.08	0.21	0.36	0.49	0.52	0.18	0.30	—	0.34	0.30	0.37
Belgium	0.53	0.53	0.55	0.59	—	—	—	—	—	—	—	0.25
France	—	0.08	0.10	0.16	0.08	0.06	—	—	—	—	—	—
Southern Europe												
Spain	0.04	0.11	0.13	0.23	—	0.05	0.04	0.04	—	—	0.09	0.06
Portugal	—	0.20	0.19	0.32	—	—	—	—	—	—	0.07	0.14
Italy	—	0.12	0.35	0.88	0.04	0.10	—	0.06	—	—	0.06	0.06
Central Europe												
Germany	—	0.14	—	0.03	—	0.03	0.08	—	—	0.13	—	—
Switzerland	—	0.18	0.60	0.03	—	—	—	—	—	0.18	0.06	—
Austria	—	—	—	—	—	—	—	—	0.52	—	0.56	—

with an exceptionally high 1870–1950 ratio) was centralising in the 1950s. This relationship disappeared in the following decade. Distance from capital appears as a strong association in Denmark, the Netherlands and Austria where the relationship is negative – as it is in most of Southern and Central Europe; this indicates that the tendency to centralise increases with proximity to the capital. Conversely, most of Northern and Western Europe exhibits positive correlations, suggesting a growing tendency to decentralise in regions closer to the capital.

Employment Shift (Tables 5.7 and 5.8)
The observations here are fewer due to lack of employment data for several countries, particularly for the decade 1950–60. Nevertheless some reasonable relationships appear for population size, employment size and employment density (notably the Netherlands, Switzerland, Sweden and Austria, when available), and city age (Switzerland). The relationships are all negative, except for city age: thus, in these cases, employment decentralisation is associated with larger cities, denser cities and more concentrated cities in countries which exhibit a high degree of urbanisation. Here, then, our hypotheses are confirmed. For the variable city age, the significant results show centralisation to be positively associated with older-established cities.

The Impact of Government Policies
Finally, we wished to try to use regression analysis for a different purpose: to estimate, if possible, the impact of national governmental policies on urban change. As already noted in Chapter 4, all European governments have adopted policies that aim to try to divert growth from fast-growing prosperous regions to slower-growing less prosperous ones. Most of them have employed incentives to industrialists and other entrepreneurs to locate in the lagging areas, together with selective government investment in infrastructure. In addition, most governments have sought to channel financial aid from the centre to those local authorities deemed to be in need of separate support because of poor resources, or great needs, or a combination of the two. We wished to discover whether these transfers of resources had exerted any influence on patterns of urban and regional growth and change.

There was no need here to replicate the excellent studies, under way at the same time as our work, which describe in detail the patterns of regional aid in different European countries (for instance Allen *et al.* 1979; OECD 1979). They give a comprehensive factual review of the forms of aid, their limits in money terms, the conditions under which help is given, and the decision-making bodies responsible for them.

Because of this, the present project attempted something new: a *quantitative* assessment of the impact of central government expenditure on differential rates of growth in different urban areas. We determined to use the data base for population and employment growth as dependent variables in regression equations where the independent variable would be a measure of central government aid to particular areas. There were two obvious such kinds of aid in most Euro-

Table 5.7   Correlation coefficients (R): employment shift 1950–60, 1960–70

	Employment shift against independent variables												
	Population		Employment		Employment density		Employment concentration		Latitude		City age		Distance from capital	
	1950–60	1960–70	1950–60	1960–70	1950–60	1960–70	1950–60	1960–70	1950–60	1960–70	1950–60	1960–70	1950–60	1960–70
Europe	−0.09^c	na	−0.08	−0.04	−0.27^a	−0.19^a	−0.50^a	−0.34^a	−0.19^a	−0.13^b	−0.12^c	−0.03	0.15^b	0.20^a
Atlantic Europe														
Britain	−0.26^a	−0.13	−0.24^b	−0.12	−0.24^b	−0.19^c	−0.34^a	−0.34^a	0.04	0.04	0.19	0.19	−0.17^c	0.03
Ireland	−0.26^a	−0.13	−0.24^b	−0.12	−0.24^b	−0.19^c	−0.34^a	−0.31^a	0.04	0.04	0.19	0.19	−0.17^c	0.03
Northern Europe														
Sweden	na	−0.52^b	na	−0.52^b	na	0.58^b	na	−0.42^c	na	0.23	na	0.65^b	na	0.21
Norway	na	−0.52^b	na	−0.52^b	na	−0.58^b	na	−0.42^c	na	0.23	na	0.65^b	na	0.21
Denmark	na	na	na	na	na	na	na	na	na	na	na	na	na	na
Western Europe														
Netherlands	−0.31^c	−0.15	−0.16	−0.16	0.18	−0.07	−0.38^c	0.04	0.62^a	−0.10	−0.63^a	0.19	0.57^a	−0.01
Belgium	−0.72^a	−0.61^b	−0.71^a	−0.61^b	−0.69^a	−0.56^b	−0.41^c	−0.36	0.08	0.13	0.16	0.40	0.46^c	0.48
France	na	—	na	−0.01	na	0.33	na	0.22	na	−0.15	na	−0.02	na	−0.58
Southern Europe														
Spain	na	−0.12	na	−0.20^c	na	−0.54^a	na	−0.47^a	na	−0.42^a	na	−0.16	na	−0.41^a
Portugal	na	na	na	na	na	na	na	na	na	na	na	na	na	na
Italy	na	−0.12	na	−0.20^c	na	−0.54^a	na	−0.47^a	na	−0.42^a	na	−0.16	na	−0.18
Central Europe														
Germany	0.01	−0.33^a	0.01	−0.34^a	−0.23^c	−0.17^c	−0.22^c	−0.21^c	0.22^a	0.22^c	0.19	0.22^c	−0.11	−0.17^c
Switzerland	−0.05	−0.35^a	−0.05	−0.37^a	−0.30^b	−0.24^c	−0.22^c	−0.22^c	0.66^c	0.17	0.33^c	0.35^c	0.16	0.03
Austria	−0.50	−0.63^c	−0.50	−0.61^c	−0.68^c	−0.62^c	−0.55^c	−0.54^c	−0.52	−0.29	0.66^c	0.46	−0.29	−0.04

Notes: na not available.
^{a} Significant at 0.001.
^{b} Significant at 0.05.
— Correlation coefficient less than 0.01.

Employment shift against independent variables

	Population		Employment		Employment density		Employment concentration		Latitude		City age		Distance from capital	
	1950-60	1960-70	1950-60	1960-70	1950-60	1960-70	1950-60	1960-70	1950-60	1960-70	1950-60	1960-70	1950-60	1960-70
Europe	—	0.04	—	—	0.04	0.07	0.12	0.25	0.02	0.04	0.01	—	0.02	0.04
Atlantic Europe	—	0.07	—	0.06	0.04	0.06	0.12	0.10	0.02	0.02	0.04	—	0.03	—
Britain	—	0.07	—	0.06	0.04	0.06	0.12	0.10	0.02	0.02	0.04	—	0.03	—
Ireland	na	na	na	na	na	na	na	na	na	na	na	na	na	na
Northern Europe	na	0.27	na	0.27	na	0.34	na	0.18	na	—	na	0.42	na	na
Sweden	na	0.27	na	0.27	na	0.34	na	0.18	na	—	na	0.42	na	na
Norway	na	na	na	na	na	na	na	na	na	na	na	na	na	—
Denmark	na	na	na	na	na	na	na	na	na	na	na	na	na	na
Western Europe	0.10	—	na	—	—	—	0.14	—	0.38	—	0.40	—	0.32	—
Netherlands	0.52	0.37	0.50	0.37	0.48	0.31	0.17	—	—	—	—	—	0.21	0.23
Belgium	na	—	na	—	na	—	na	—	na	—	na	—	na	—
France	na	na	na	na	na	na	na	na	na	na	na	na	na	na
Southern Europe	na	—	na	0.24	na	0.29	na	0.22	na	0.18	na	—	na	0.17
Spain	na	na	na	na	na	na	na	na	na	na	na	na	na	na
Portugal	na	na	na	na	na	na	na	na	na	na	na	na	na	na
Italy	na	—	na	0.04	na	0.29	na	0.22	na	0.18	na	—	na	—
Central Europe	—	0.11	na	0.12	0.05	0.03	0.04	0.05	0.11	0.05	—	0.05	na	0.03
Germany	—	0.12	na	0.14	0.09	0.06	0.05	0.05	—	—	0.11	0.12	—	—
Switzerland	—	0.45	—	0.45	0.46	0.38	0.29	0.30	—	—	0.44	—	—	—
Austria	na	0.40	na	0.37	na	—	na	—	na	—	na	—	na	—

Notes: na   not available.

Only correlations significant at 0.05 have been included.

pean countries: first, *general central government aid* in the form of rate support grants and similar equalisation schemes, designed to boost the local tax income of poorer local authorities; and second, *specific schemes of aid to industry* either in capital or revenue support.

In the event, the data problems proved almost insuperable. We were left with a very limited number of potential statistical analyses:

- for *Great Britain*, of the impact of general government support (1960–70);
- for *Sweden*, of the impact of both general and specific industrial support (1963–70);
- for *West Germany*, of the impact of industrial support (for selected metropolitan areas only) (1970–73).

Thus, here was a further problem of the time periods to which these data related. Seldom did they correspond exactly to the time periods for which the dependent variables (population and employment) were available. In any event, some related to the post-1970 period for which employment data were not available. So, for the sake of standardisation, it was decided to use population change or shift as the sole dependent variable.

For each analysis, a standard procecure was used. Regression programmes were run using both linear and other functions, with some improvements in results in certain cases. Table 5.9 shows the results for each of the analyses.

Table 5.9 Government aid (1960–73†) and population growth (1970–5): regression results

	General aid versus population growth			Industrial aid versus population growth		
	Total Metro-politan area	*Core*	*Core/ ring differen-tial*	*Total metro-politan area*	*Core*	*Core/ ring differen-tial*
Great Britain	0.28	0.14	0.05	—	—	—
Sweden	0.02	0.03	0.03	—	—	—
	0.37*	0.07*	0.50*	—	—	—
Germany	—	—	—	0.04	0.02	0.08

* Results from fitting a polynomial in place of a straight-line function.
† Aid data dates vary from country to country.

Clearly, they are very poor. It is possible that with a better data base – and, above all, with a greater time-lag in the models – better results might have been forthcoming. This is however inherently doubtful. In many cases, aid is a response to perceived poor rates of growth, so that the relationship is both negative and is in causal terms the reverse of that postulated here. But in some of these cases aid does seem to be associated with high rates of growth in the time periods under study, while in others it does not. The fact is that the sources of regional growth and change appear too rich and too complex to be caught by the relatively crude statistical analysis that has been attempted here. So perhaps the chief lesson, and only value, of the exercise is to discourage other researchers from going much further down the same road – at least unless they can assemble a richer and more extensive data base than proved possible here. In the present state of European statistics on this subject area, that seems unlikely.

Some General Conclusions

In the original general design of the European Urban Systems study, the regression analyses occupied a central place. It was always hoped – and assumed – that they would show at least some strong and general relationships, confirming hypotheses that had been developed and tested elsewhere. True, in the overall design, some relationships were tested that were not so obvious and not so promising. But, for many of the tests, the results are surprising and disappointing. Few might have expected, for instance, that there would be such a weak relationship between rates of growth – whether for population or employment – and city size. It is surprising that there are so few associations between growth and latitude, or growth and distance from the capital city. The relationships for population or employment shifts are more numerous, but there are many cases almost invariably a majority – where strong associations are lacking. Thus it cannot be concluded from analysis at this level, for instance, that decentralisation of people or jobs is systematically associated with high densities or degree of central city concentration. And finally, the attempt to explain changes and shifts in terms of government aid proved almost wholly negative.

Leaving aside for one moment the general question of how to improve the analysis significantly, there are several points that arise from the results as presented above, all pointing to the complexity of European urban systems behaviour, and its ability to defy general rules. We take a number of examples, which can be followed in detail by close reference to the maps in Chapter 4.

1. It is generally not true that large size is associated with lower growth rates. In some of Europe, large metropolitan areas were growing rapidly in one or both decades. (This was particularly evident in southern Europe, and, to some extent, in western and central Europe.) Conversely, many smaller places were stagnating either because they were rural centres in declining peripheral regions, or older industrial cities.

2. It is not generally true that high growth tends to occur at the southern extemities. Countries where this might be expected (Sweden, Norway, France) in fact have complex patterns with more than one centre of high growth, generally far separated. Even where there is an association for a time, it seldom persists.

3. Similarly, the hypothesis regarding growth and distance from capital is not very effective. Though almost always the capital region shows high growth, this is not the case in Britain, Denmark and the Netherlands. And, in many cases, there are one or more regions peripheral to the capital which demonstrate very

high growth (Sweden, Denmark, the Netherlands, France, Spain, Italy, Germany, Austria, Britain).

4. Though, in some cases, decentralisation is associated with large size, high density and high degree of central core concentration, there are many exceptions. This is partly because the variable used for the analysis is the overall size or density of the metropolitan area. In retrospect it might have been better to use size or density of the core.

The general conclusion is that if the behaviour of Europe's urban systems is to be satisfactorily explained, the method will need to go to into greater depth. Attempts to increase the value and significance of the correlations already obtained were made by carrying out logarithmic transformations of both dependent and independent variables. These were largely successful but the operation did not appear to have much theoretical validity and did not greatly increase our understanding. Taking each pair of variables and cross-tabulating by frequency proved to be a useful exercise, however, and showed that the behaviour of our pairs of variables appeared to vary with position in the urban hierarchy. Thus, one of our future tasks must be to disaggregate by size-groups, perhaps using the rank-size plots referred to in the last chapter to indicate significant break points between size classes, and repeat the regression analysis at this finer level.

This type of analysis can only take us so far, however. In particular there needs to be a closer analysis of the employment (and income generating) base of each area. This was the approach used by Berry in his parallel analysis of the American urban system, and it was from the beginning an objective of the present study. In Chapter 6 we go on to describe how the analysis is undertaken.

Chapter 6
Towards Structural Explanations

The previous chapter demonstrated a negative conclusion: that in urban Europe, different rates of growth and change were not readily susceptible to statistical explanation in terms of conventional location variables. That suggests a need for a deeper approach. In the literature of regional analysis, a constant theme has been the likely significance of economic or industrial structure as an explanation of change. In the words of Frank Stilwell:

> Employment grows faster in some industries than in others. Given that the industrial composition of employment varies between regions, a causal relationship might reasonably be expected. It need not be suggested that any establishment in a given industry will grow at the same rate as the rest of that industry irrespective of the location of that establishment. (Stilwell 1969)

More precisely, regional analysts assume that the pattern of economic change in any region or area is a product of two sets of factors: one set operating more or less uniformly in all regions of the country concerned, another set operating specifically in that particular region. The first has commonly been called the *structural* or proportionality effect; it concerns the effect of changes in national economic structure, whereby some industries grow and others decline, the second is called the *differential* or local-factor effect (Perloff 1963; Stilwell 1969). Isolating the effect of these two sets of factors is the concern of *shift-share analysis*, on which a substantial literature now exists.

In essence the shift-share technique is easy to understand and to employ. The first step is to calculate the rate of economic growth (or decline) in a particular region or subset or set of regions, and also for the aggregate of the whole set (normally the national unit). This is usually done in terms of employment, for which data are commonly available, but output measures may be employed if data exist. The second step is to compare this regional rate with the national average rate of overall change, and to produce a regional difference which may be an excess (plus) or deficit (minus). Then this difference is split into the two components.

There are two ways of doing this. The simpler, known as *structural base standardisation*, takes the national aggregate figures of change for each sector of employment, and applies them to the regional total of employment in that sector at the start (or sometimes the mid-point) of the period. The resulting aggregate is said to be the *structural component*: the difference between this and the regional difference, earlier calculated, is the *differential component*. The more complex method, known as *national growth rate standardisation*, applies the same national growth rates to regional growth rates for each sector, to give a difference for each sector in each region; the aggregate of these differences becomes the structural element and the residue is again the differential component (Randall 1973). This clearly requires a larger data base, with figures of change for each sector in each region.

The problem, however, is that the results of the analysis prove to be highly sensitive to the way the data are used and in particular to their degree of disaggregation. Evidently, large regions will tend to be more heterogeneous than smaller ones; contrary tendencies will operate within the region, and will perhaps cancel each other out. Whatever the scale of region chosen, it is desirable that the regions should be as self-contained, in terms of economic organisation, as possible; regions into which large numbers of people travel to obtain services, for instance, can distort the analysis. (Functional urban regions, as used in the present study, provide the least unsatisfactory units from this viewpoint.) More seriously, a coarse breakdown of industrial sectors can tend to distort the analysis, because these again will tend towards heterogeneity. In general the coarser the sectors, the larger will be the size of the differential component; the structural element will tend to be lost, because of the effect of contradictory trends cancelling each other out. To take an obvious example: in many standard industrial classifications, the engineering industry is treated as an aggregate. If shift-share analysis is conducted on this basis, it will lose the fact that the composition of the industry will be different from one region to another; in one it may be dominated by growth elements (for instance, electronics), in another by declining elements (for instance, textile machinery). The differences, which should be reflected in the structural element, will in fact not appear there and will therefore show in the differential component. Other things being equal, it is always preferable to take the finest possible industrial classification. But this has to be balanced against data availability and cost of computation. And even a relatively fine breakdown will still contain heterogeneous headings. In any case, the finer the breakdown the greater the importance of the differential element; this is an inevitable feature of the nature of the technique.

There are other problems with the technique, and in particular with the implications that can be drawn from the analysis. By definition, it treats all sectors as equally important in every region, whereas, even at national level, but still more at regional level, the performance of one or two key sectors may be of paramount importance. More seriously, it fails to take account of the input–output relationships between the different industries, whereby expansion in one may really represent a derived demand from another. Again, because employment is usually the main measure (because of data availability) the technique may fail to distinguish the actual economic growth that is occurring in terms of output and productivity. And, by relating national and region changes to the same time scale, it may obscure time-lagged relationships (Randall 1973).

Use of Shift-share in This Study
These criticisms are by now well-known. Nevertheless the shift-share technique continues to be used because – particularly if its limitations are understood and accepted – it is at least a useful first stage of analysis of regional change, which has the overwhelming advantage that the necessary data are usually obtainable. This is why is has been used in the present study. We wished to use it to test two main questions: (i) to see whether different industrial structures were associated with differences in the overall rate of employment change as between one metropolitan area (treated as an aggregate) and another; and (ii) to see whether different industrial structures were associated with differences in the rate of internal employment shifts (centralisation or decentralisation) within metropolitan areas – concentrating here particularly on the rate of contraction of employment in the central core, that has been identified as a major policy problem in Great Britain.

The Choice of the Sample
While recognising the value of applying any further analysis to as much of the area, already reported in the previous chapters, as possible, several restrictive factors are immediately obvious. Given that shift-share technique relies on the availability of a disaggregated data base for at least two periods in time, many European countries are eliminated because of a deficiency in one or other or in both. Second, because our study has been primarily conducted according to groups of countries, we felt that any choice of countries for further research should preferably have regard to these groups. Third, the sheer size of the task involved – to process disaggregated employment data for each regional component – requires a matrix of gargantuan proportions: a situation which our resources could not handle. Fourth, the boundary change problem precludes the inclusion of regions where major modifications have occurred because of the invalid assumptions implied when employment sectors are proportionately allocated to regions in time point B according to their spatial distribution in time point A.

As a result, five countries were selected – one from each of the five major groups – although it is not suggested that any one of these is necessarily representative of any of the other countries in its group. In Atlantic Europe, Great Britain was the obvious choice because of its data availability, although Census data are only available for 1966 and 1971, hence restricting comparisons with the other four countries selected because of the five-year span rather than the ten years covered elsewhere. Additionally, the data are only available in 1966 by

SIC Orders and not by Minimum List Headings, thus requiring this to be the point of departure for the standardisation of the other industrial classifications.

In Northern Europe, only Sweden had any employment data for the two years desired, regardless of disaggregation. In Western Europe both Belgium and the Netherlands fulfilled the requirements of data availability, but Belgium was selected on two counts: first the small size of the building-blocks and the application of journey-to-work information to the original regionalisation means that the regions are more accurately defined in terms of the standard criteria; second fewer cores are overbounded, hence a finer core–hinterland differentiation results. All three countries of Central Europe have data for at least two dates, so the choice is wider. However, the Federal Republic of Germany was ultimately selected on the basis of its importance and interest to the researchers. We felt also that of the three, Germany provided the best core definitions because of the nature of the building-blocks involved; Austrian cores, for example, are far too overbounded for meaningful conclusions about intra-regional shifts to be made. Finally, only Italy in Southern Europe had any worthwhile disaggregated employment statistics and even these, as pointed out in an earlier chapter, must be approached cautiously. Nevertheless, the data are standard to two dates and thus permit the application of the technique, although we cannot pretend that international comparisons are necessarily more accurate than those presented in Chapter 4.

Within each country, further sampling was necessary: this time of the metropolitan regions themselves. Non-metropolitan regions were not considered purely because we had not distinguished a core in their definition, but there is no other reason why future research should not investigate their case. The metropolitan regions finally chosen from each country were mainly a function of practicality rather than the result of a rigorous sampling exercise. Thus, in Sweden and Germany regions were selected which had not been subject to dramatic boundary alterations between the two dates, although only modifications which affect the cores or region borders present problems. In these two countries *all* regions in this category were analysed. Great Britain was similarly treated, but boundary changes, 1966–71, were less significant. As the number of regions remaining, after those eliminated for changes, was too large for our modest resources, further selective procedures were introduced. Regions were classified according to various characteristics – size, rates of population and employment change 1950–70, types of population and employment shift 1950–70 and location according to Standard Region – and a sample selected with the widest ranges possible in each category.

Because of the smaller units comprising metropolitan regions in Belgium and Italy, that consequently require more prolonged data aggregations, fewer regions were sampled. In Belgium more consideration was given to relative locations in Flemish and French-speaking parts of the country while the choice of Italian areas logically required a selection from both the North and the Mezzogiorno. Moreover, only metropolitan regions from Lombardia, Campania and Calabria were analysed as it was originally thought (and subsequently found not to be the case) that small area data relating to government aid to industry might be available.

In summary, therefore, the analysis was conducted very much on countries and regions either where the required statistical base existed or where boundary changes were minimal. Moreover, our objective was to cover a diverse sample reflecting intra-national variations of socio-economic characteristics. Of course the ideal basis for shift-share analysis is universal coverage, but, as can be seen, in none of the countries under study is this feasible. Table 6.1 shows the extent of the sample and their regional characteristics in terms of 1950–70 population and employment changes and shifts.

Table 6.1   The sample for shift-share analysis

	Population Change 1950–60 (%)	Population Change 1960–70 (%)	Employment Change 1950–60 (%)	Employment Change 1960–70 (%)	Population Shift 1950–60 (type)	Population Shift 1960–70 (type)	Employment Shift 1950–60 (type)	Employment Shift 1960–70 (type)
A. *Great Britain*								
1. Reading	17.9	28.6	20.3	18.0	RD	RD	RD	RD
2. Slough	31.3	8.0	24.8	13.8	RD	RD	RC	RD
3. Swindon	18.6	14.4	17.9	13.6	RC	AD	RC	RD
4. Cambridge	21.8	29.2	22.2	28.2	RC	RD	AC	RD
5. Peterborough	9.4	11.8	8.1	8.0	RC	RC	RC	RC
6. Liverpool	4.2	−2.3	2.7	−4.0	RD	LD	AC	LD
7. Crewe	4.1	13.8	1.5	7.3	RD	AD	AC	AD
8. Carlisle	−0.5	−0.4	−4.7	2.8	LC	LC	LC	AC
9. Nottingham	7.7	7.7	7.6	0.1	RD	AD	RD	AD
10. Exeter	4.8	9.6	4.4	7.1	RC	RD	AC	RC
11. Yeovil	4.1	7.7	0.4	3.2	RC	RD	AC	AC
12. Darlington	−2.2	1.7	−6.3	3.7	LC	RD	LC	AD
13. Newcastle	2.6	−1.8	2.7	−2.6	AD	LD	AC	LD
14. Sunderland	3.7	0.6	0.2	−0.5	RC	AD	AC	LC
15. Southend	23.8	16.6	26.5	23.2	RD	AD	RD	RD
16. Cheltenham	13.7	11.5	23.1	13.4	RC	RD	RC	RC
17. Worcester	6.1	13.4	6.3	5.9	RC	RD	AC	RD
18. Stevenage	116.9	40.0	145.2	33.6	RC	RC	AC	AC
19. Watford	15.3	3.5	20.2	5.9	RD	RC	RD	RD
20. Bolton	−0.7	3.4	−0.6	−3.3	LD	AD	LD	LC
21. Wigan	−2.4	10.3	−1.3	4.6	LD	RD	LC	AC
22. Lincoln	4.2	7.8	2.6	5.8	RC	AD	AC	RD
23. Scunthorpe	8.6	8.5	11.6	4.0	RC	RD	AC	AC
24. Corby	18.9	16.0	19.3	7.8	AC	RC	RC	AC
25. Doncaster	9.5	5.5	7.3	−0.6	RD	AD	RC	LC
26. Mansfield	3.4	5.6	11.7	1.7	RC	RC	RC	AC
27. Stafford	12.0	21.1	13.4	9.0	AC	RD	AC	RD
28. Brighton	9.2	7.6	12.2	9.3	RD	AD	RD	RD
29. Hastings	3.5	10.0	0.2	11.5	RD	RD	AC	RC
30. Royal Leamington Spa	18.7	17.9	21.0	6.8	RD	RD	RD	RC
31. Kidderminster	9.3	19.3	7.2	16.2	RC	RD	AC	RC
32. Hull	3.6	2.0	6.6	0.7	RD	AD	RD	AD
33. Leeds	1.7	4.0	1.4	−3.7	RD	AD	RD	AD
34. Newport	5.4	5.0	2.5	5.5	RD	RD	AC	AD
35. Merthyr Tydfil	−3.0	−4.7	15.5	−9.2	LD	LD	RC	LC
36. Swansea	0.1	1.0	−1.8	0.6	AC	AC	LC	AC
37. Port Talbot	5.3	3.7	5.1	0.9	RC	AD	AC	AC
38. Aberdeen	−2.5	−0.6	−1.6	2.6	LC	LD	LC	RC
39. Edinburgh	2.4	4.6	3.1	3.1	RD	AD	AC	AD

Table 6.1 – *continued*

	Population Change 1950–60 (%)	Population Change 1960–70 (%)	Employment Change 1950–60 (%)	Employment Change 1960–70 (%)	Population Shift 1950–60 (type)	Population Shift 1960–70 (type)	Employment Shift 1950–60 (type)	Employment Shift 1960–70 (type)
40. Glasgow	0.9	−3.1	−1.1	−8.9	AD	LD	LD	LD
41. Motherwell	2.4	3.2	4.6	4.2	RC	RD	AC	RD
B. Sweden								
1. Malmö/Lund	6.8	13.0	5.9	8.2	AC	RC	AC	AC
2. Västerås	16.8	14.8	13.0	10.0	RC	RC	RC	AC
3. Norrköping	1.1	6.0	−4.2	1.3	AC	RC	LC	AC
4. Örebro	1.4	7.3	0.5	2.1	AC	RC	AC	AC
5. Helsingborg	4.4	9.9	3.7	6.1	RC	RD	RC	RC
6. Eskilstuna	5.1	10.4	4.3	4.8	RC	RC	AC	AC
7. Gävle	7.5	6.0	5.6	−0.2	RC	RC	RC	LC
8. Karlstad	4.4	−2.1	−0.4	−8.2	RC	LC	LC	LC
9. Södertälje	17.6	50.0	15.4	26.3	RC	RC	AC	AC
10. Trollhättan	6.1	7.2	4.1	2.2	AC	AC	AC	AC
C. Belgium								
1. Antwerpen	12.7	6.3	na	6.7	RD	AD	na	RD
2. Gand	13.5	2.8	na	−0.1	RC	AD	na	LC
3. Charleroi	5.6	−0.2	na	−10.3	RD	LD	na	LC
4. Leuven	9.8	8.1	na	10.1	AD	AD	na	AC
5. Oostende	13.4	5.8	na	3.6	RC	RC	na	RC
6. Verviers	−0.0	3.0	na	−6.6	LD	AD	na	LD
D. Italy								
1. Milano	28.9	23.4	na	15.3	RC	RD	na	RD
2. Napoli	15.2	11.4	na	−1.1	RC	RD	na	LC
3. Brescia	2.8	10.0	na	9.5	AC	RC	na	RC
4. Bergamo	9.2	15.3	na	11.3	RC	RD	na	AD
5. Salerno	10.8	6.5	na	−8.0	RC	RC	na	LC
6. Como	11.1	16.3	na	5.4	RC	RC	na	AD
7. Pavia	1.6	2.9	na	−6.5	AC	AC	na	LC
8. Varese	23.8	24.3	na	12.8	RC	RD	na	RD
9. Reggio Calabria	3.2	2.1	na	−12.5	AC	AC	na	LC
10. Busto Arsizio	22.8	16.7	na	2.7	RD	RC	na	AD
11. Cremona	−10.8	−6.7	na	−10.1	LC	LC	na	LC
12. Vigevano	10.0	2.9	na	−13.3	AC	AC	na	LD
13. Cosenza	−1.6	−1.7	na	−18.3	LC	LC	na	LC
14. Lecco	10.1	12.8	na	2.3	RC	RD	na	AD
15. Legnano	18.1	18.2	na	−1.1	RD	RD	na	LD
16. Catanzaro	0.7	−4.2	na	−32.3	AC	LC	na	LD
17. Caserta	10.8	2.3	na	−14.9	AC	AC	na	LC
E. Germany								
1. Freiburg i.B.	18.8	15.6	−5.8	6.0	RC	RD	LC	RC
2. Heidenheim	7.8	10.2	−4.0	2.1	RC	RC	LC	RD
3. Karlsruhe	15.8	14.0	−2.0	8.4	RC	RD	LC	RC
4. Pforzheim	20.9	19.0	7.5	0.1	RC	RD	AC	AD
5. Ravensburg	13.8	17.0	−5.3	6.0	RD	RC	LC	RC
6. Stuttgart	27.0	18.9	16.8	8.9	RD	RD	RC	RD
7. Ulm	10.2	13.6	−5.5	6.1	RC	RD	LC	RC
8. Aschaffenburg	9.3	15.1	−2.0	0.6	RC	RD	LC	AD
9. Augsburg	7.2	10.8	−3.9	6.4	RC	RD	LC	RD
10. Bamberg	−0.4	4.9	−15.4	−1.8	LD	AD	LC	LC
11. Bayreuth	−4.4	2.7	−17.7	−2.0	LC	RC	RC	LC
12. Coburg	−1.7	2.5	−11.5	−4.6	LC	AD	LC	LC
13. Hof	−5.0	−1.8	−16.8	−8.0	LD	LD	LD	LC
14. Kempten	−0.8	9.5	−6.6	6.7	LC	RD	LC	RC
15. Landshut	−9.1	7.1	−23.4	3.4	LC	RD	LC	AD
16. München	14.2	21.1	6.2	12.4	RC	RC	AC	RD

Table 6.1 – *continued*

	Population Change 1950–60 (%)	Population Change 1960–70 (%)	Employment Change 1950–60 (%)	Employment Change 1960–70 (%)	Population Shift 1950–60 (type)	Population Shift 1960–70 (type)	Employment Shift 1950–60 (type)	Employment Shift 1960–70 (type)
17. Nürnberg	5.1	9.1	−8.8	3.3	AC	RD	LC	RC
18. Schweinfurt	−0.7	7.3	−16.3	−1.5	LC	RD	LC	LC
19. Straubing	−10.3	5.9	−22.6	−0.6	LC	RD	LC	LC
20. Weiden i.d.O.	1.0	5.0	−7.7	−5.3	AC	RD	LC	LC
21. Würzburg	4.3	6.9	−12.6	−3.4	AC	RD	LC	LC
22. Bremen	3.9	5.2	3.9	0.1	AC	RD	AC	RD
23. Bremerhaven	−0.3	2.4	−9.1	−2.3	LC	AD	LC	LC
24. Hamburg	6.4	5.2	14.3	−0.2	AC	AD	AC	LD
25. Darmstadt	16.3	18.6	11.8	4.8	RC	RD	AC	AD
26. Frankfurt a.M.	20.6	17.3	18.5	10.5	RC	AD	RC	RC
27. Fulda	−3.6	5.7	−17.5	−4.9	LC	RD	LC	LC
28. Giessen	2.9	9.9	−10.4	0.0	RC	RC	LC	LC
29. Kassel	−1.6	6.9	−13.6	−5.0	LC	RD	LC	LC
30. Marburg a.d.L.	0.9	11.5	−14.1	1.2	AC	RD	LC	AC
31. Braunschweig	9.8	1.1	6.2	−5.8	AC	AD	AC	LC
32. Celle	−5.8	6.5	−12.9	6.0	LC	AD	LC	AD
33. Emden	−0.8	10.8	2.2	−0.4	LC	RD	AC	LC
34. Hameln	−11.3	0.2	−8.2	−4.0	LC	AD	LC	LC
35. Hannover	5.9	7.9	9.2	4.6	AC	AD	AC	RD
36. Hildesheim	−3.1	2.4	−3.8	−3.2	LC	AD	LC	LC
37. Oldenburg	−2.3	12.2	−8.4	5.9	LC	RD	LC	RC
38. Wilhelmshaven	−7.3	7.1	−1.5	−0.6	LC	RD	LC	LC
39. Wolfsburg	10.3	14.5	6.1	14.4	AC	RC	AC	AC
40. Saarbrücken	11.7	5.2	0.9	−3.7	RC	AD	RC	LD

Key: LC Centralisation during loss.
AC Absolute centralisation.
RC Relative centralisation.
RD Relative decentralisation.
AD Absolute decentralisation.
LD Decentralisation during loss.
na not available.

Industrial Classifications and the Standardisation of Data

As outlined earlier, the shift-share technique is inherently sensitive to the level of disaggregation of the sectoral data with various observers advocating disaggregation as far down as individual industries or even individual firms. However, the flexibility of the method is such that the degree of disaggregation must reflect the purpose for which the analysis is intended, despite the acknowledgement that no one level can overcome the problems of industrial misallocation. Accordingly, we aimed at a broader approach than is usual: rather than concentrating on manufacturing industry, which, after all, can never present a mutually exclusive regional synthesis, we decided to analyse across the board at a macro-sectoral level. The achievement of this end, however, requires the standardisation of data according to one industrial classification if any semblance of international comparability is to result.

As we have seen throughout this book, there is very little compatibility among countries in data sources. The same is true of disaggregated employment statistics. Even though the United Nations recommendations on statistical practices

(United Nations 1958, 1969) are often followed, they are very open to individual interpretations – hence the necessity for careful standardisation. Our point of departure, as stated above, was the 1966 sample Census of Great Britain as the level of disaggregation is only by SIC orders of industry. All other countries in the sample have the required three or even four-digit industrial classifications to enable standardisation to the British basis, although even between two dates within one country can different classifications be officially used. For example, the Belgian statistics required a two-stage process: first a standardisation between 1961 and 1970 data (ISIC and NACE – the latter is the 'Nomenclature des Activités de la Communauté Européenne') and second a standardisation to the 1958 Standard Industrial Classification of Great Britain upon which the 1966 British data are based (Great Britain: Central Statistical Office 1958)

Lesser difficulties are posed by the classifications of Italy, Sweden and the Federal Republic of Germany. All are based on the ISIC, and although minor inconsistencies exist among dates or among countries the data from these three nations are more easily adjustable to the Project's norm. All data are taken from the respective national Censuses of the five countries in the sample, although the British data are unpublished. Rather than bore the reader with further technicalities, reference should be made to the fuller commentary contained in another report (Hall and Hay 1979) where complete details of the standardisation and data sources are described.

Thus, the analysis was conducted upon the ten standard sectors of employment by place of work and, although we fully recognise the concealed variations within each sector, our emphasis, as in the preceding chapters, must be upon international comparability rather than upon detailed intra-regional or national analysis of individual industries. The results of the next section are presented on this basis and thus should be viewed in context.

The Analysis

The results of the analysis for each region are set out in Table 6.2. Essentially it consists of three parts. The first deals with the regional aggregate, and attempts to answer a question: how far does industrial structure explain the overall regional performance? The second deals only with the core of each region, and attempts to answer the question: how far does the industrial structure of the core explain the performance of that core? The third analysis is slightly more complex, because it seeks to examine the differential performance between the core and ring for each region or, in other words, the difference between core rates of growth and ring rates of growth. It seeks therefore to answer the question: how far does different industrial structure in the core from that of the ring explain the differential performance of the core as against the ring? The analysis logically gives the answer in terms of three elements:

1. A figure for the overall percentage difference in growth (or decline) of total employment in the region in relation to the national average change (R/ND). This is then broken down into elements, which in turn sum up to it;

2. A structural component (SC) representing the effect of industrial (strictly, employment) structure at the start of the period; and
3. A differential component (DC) representing the residual, that is the effect of different rates of growth in any industry in that region compared to the national total.

Table 6.2 presents this threefold analysis for each sample region and additionally gives a mean figure and the deviation around the mean for the total of sample regions in each country.

Table 6.2 Shift-share analysis: employment change

	Entire region			Core only			Core/ring differential		
	R/ND	SC	DC	R/ND	SC	DC	R/ND	SC	DC
A. *Great Britain* (1965–70)									
1. Reading	6.3	1.4	5.0	6.8	1.7	5.1	0.9	0.6	0.3
2. Slough	0.2	1.1	−1.0	3.5	0.9	2.6	8.7	−0.6	9.3
3. Swindon	4.9	1.1	3.9	4.6	1.1	3.5	−0.6	0.1	−0.7
4. Cambridge	4.4	0.4	4.0	10.0	2.1	8.0	9.1	2.7	6.4
5. Peterborough	3.8	−0.8	4.6	6.0	0.6	5.5	3.4	2.1	1.3
6. Liverpool	−4.8	1.1	−5.9	−9.3	1.3	−10.7	−18.5	1.0	−19.5
7. Crewe	6.4	−0.1	6.5	5.6	0.5	5.1	−1.2	0.9	−2.1
8. Carlisle	0.1	−0.2	0.3	6.9	1.8	5.1	12.4	3.6	8.8
9. Nottingham	−0.3	−2.3	2.0	−1.6	0.4	−2.1	−3.7	5.4	−8.1
10. Exeter	3.9	−0.2	4.1	8.6	2.0	6.6	7.7	3.6	4.1
11. Yeovil	1.5	0.7	0.8	10.3	0.9	9.4	−0.7	0.6	−1.3
12. Darlington	4.1	−0.4	4.4	−1.1	0.1	−1.2	−7.9	0.7	−8.7
13. Newcastle	−2.0	−1.6	−0.5	−6.7	0.7	−7.4	−11.0	5.2	−16.2
14. Sunderland	−3.5	−5.4	2.0	−4.4	−1.0	−3.4	−2.2	11.0	−13.2
15. Southend	6.5	1.3	5.3	−1.0	1.9	−2.9	−23.9	2.1	−25.9
16. Cheltenham	6.8	1.6	5.3	4.7	3.1	1.6	−4.9	3.6	−8.5
17. Worcester	1.6	0.7	0.9	0.5	1.4	−0.9	−2.1	1.3	−3.4
18. Stevenage	12.8	0.8	12.0	12.9	0.0	12.9	0.3	−1.6	1.9
19. Watford	−4.3	0.4	−4.8	−11.3	0.3	−11.7	−40.1	−0.6	−39.5
20. Bolton	0.2	−0.4	0.6	−0.8	−0.1	−0.8	−5.7	−1.6	−7.3
21. Wigan	−1.8	−0.3	−1.5	1.6	0.1	1.5	9.5	1.2	8.4
22. Lincoln	1.9	0.3	1.7	−3.1	1.5	−4.6	−7.4	1.8	−9.2
23. Scunthorpe	7.3	−0.8	8.1	12.4	0.1	12.2	9.9	1.3	8.0
24. Corby	2.6	−1.2	3.8	6.7	−0.4	7.1	12.4	2.4	10.0
25. Doncaster	−2.3	−5.8	3.5	7.5	−0.1	7.6	14.7	8.5	6.2
26. Mansfield	−3.1	−7.2	4.1	−3.5	−0.6	−2.9	−0.6	10.8	−11.4
27. Stafford	0.5	1.0	−0.6	−4.5	1.3	−5.8	−22.4	1.4	−23.8
28. Brighton	1.5	1.1	0.4	−1.3	1.9	−3.2	−7.7	2.1	−9.8
29. Hastings	3.1	0.5	2.6	4.6	1.7	2.9	1.2	−0.9	2.2
30. Royal Leamington Spa	4.9	0.9	4.0	7.0	1.4	5.6	3.8	0.8	3.0
31. Kidderminster	6.7	−1.8	8.5	11.9	−1.5	13.4	14.1	0.7	13.4
32. Hull	−1.2	.6	−1.8	−5.4	1.1	−6.5	−15.1	1.7	−16.8
33. Leeds	−3.1	−0.9	−2.2	−4.4	0.1	−4.5	−4.0	2.7	−6.7
34. Newport	−4.7	−1.8	−2.8	−13.4	0.9	−14.3	−13.4	4.2	−17.5
35. Merthyr Tydfil	1.0	−2.0	3.0	9.0	−1.8	10.8	19.9	0.4	19.5
36. Swansea	2.3	−1.7	4.0	2.8	0.8	2.1	1.0	4.5	−3.5
37. Port Talbot	4.1	−3.1	7.2	19.8	−0.5	20.4	21.8	3.5	18.3
38. Aberdeen	0.9	−0.8	1.7	1.5	1.3	0.2	1.5	4.8	−3.4
39. Edinburgh	−3.0	−0.3	−2.7	−4.0	0.0	−4.0	−2.8	0.9	−3.8
40. Glasgow	−1.0	−0.1	−0.9	−2.3	1.5	−3.8	−4.8	5.9	−10.7
41. Motherwell	1.1	−1.2	2.3	1.1	0.4	0.8	0.1	2.9	−2.8
Mean	1.6	−0.6	2.2	2.2	0.7	1.5	−1.1	2.6	−3.7
Standard deviation	3.855	1.922	3.641	6.992	0.822	7.203	11.922	2.751	11.94

Table 6.2 – *continued*

	Entire region			Core only			Core/ring differential		
	R/ND	SC	DC	R/ND	SC	DC	R/ND	SC	DC
B. *Sweden* (1960–70)									
1. Malmö-Lund	3.6	1.6	2.0	12.5	8.3	4.3	21.4	16.0	5.5
2. Västerås	7.1	0.7	6.3	18.8	6.2	12.6	19.6	9.2	10.5
3. Norrköping	–2.7	1.4	–4.1	4.2	5.5	–1.3	–3.2	–4.2	1.0
4. Örebro	–9.6	–0.5	–9.1	11.9	7.7	4.2	30.5	11.7	18.8
5. Helsingborg	4.5	1.2	3.3	5.2	7.5	–2.3	1.2	10.2	–9.0
6. Eskilstuna	.1.2	1.0	0.2	13.0	6.0	7.0	19.3	8.2	11.1
7. Gävle	–5.5	1.2	–6.7	6.6	7.3	–0.8	19.7	10.0	9.6
8. Karlstad	–12.7	–2.9	–9.7	33.9	9.4	24.5	55.3	14.6	40.7
9. Södertälje	31.8	2.9	28.9	39.5	6.7	32.7	22.0	10.9	11.0
10. Trollhättan	0.7	5.0	–4.3	40.0	4.4	35.6	55.3	–0.9	56.2
Mean	1.8	1.2	0.7	18.6	6.9	11.7	24.1	8.6	15.5
Standard deviation	11.636	1.936	10.688	13.316	1.375	13.532	18.253	6.040	17.858
C. *Belgium* (1960–70)									
1. Antwerpen	4.6	2.6	2.0	–0.9	4.4	–5.3	–11.4	3.7	–15.2
2. Gent	–2.6	–0.9	–1.6	1.7	4.0	–2.3	7.3	8.5	–1.2
3. Charleroi	–7.9	–4.3	–3.6	–4.1	2.4	–6.5	5.6	10.0	–4.3
4. Leuven	7.8	2.7	5.1	18.7	6.9	11.8	21.3	8.2	13.2
5. Oostende	2.2	1.9	0.3	2.2	5.0	–2.7	0.1	5.7	–5.5
6. Verviers	–28.1	–1.4	–26.6	–16.3	3.6	–20.0	14.8	6.4	8.4
Mean	–4.0	0.1	–4.1	0.2	4.4	–4.2	6.3	7.1	–0.8
Standard deviation	11.900	2.545	10.427	16.259	1.379	10.366	10.412	2.065	9.332
D. *Italy* (1960–70)									
1. Milano	21.8	22.0	–0.2	20.9	23.4	–2.4	–2.4	3.7	–6.1
2. Napoli	0.1	1.9	–1.8	–0.6	16.7	–17.4	–1.3	25.9	–27.3
3. Brescia	8.9	8.6	0.3	14.6	23.8	–9.2	7.6	20.3	–12.6
4. Bergamo	7.1	14.2	–7.0	–10.6	20.5	–31.1	–24.2	8.6	–32.9
5. Salerno	–8.2	–12.8	4.6	18.9	10.9	8.0	33.7	29.5	4.2
6. Como	4.5	11.6	–7.1	–3.5	19.4	–23.0	–11.8	11.5	–23.5
7. Pavia	–5.8	5.8	–11.6	–5.2	23.1	–28.3	0.9	28.1	–27.1
8. Varese	–12.5	20.3	–32.8	6.3	21.2	–14.9	24.7	1.1	23.6
9. Reggio Calabria	–16.2	–4.5	–11.7	–10.7	4.8	15.5	14.5	24.5	–10.0
10. Busto Arsizio	6.3	21.7	–15.4	–2.4	22.9	–25.3	–18.2	2.6	–20.8
11. Cremona	–7.5	–2.0	–5.5	–0.8	14.8	–15.6	9.5	23.8	–14.3
12. Vigvano	–10.2	8.9	–19.1	–11.5	19.4	–30.9	–2.9	23.0	–25.8
13. Cosenza	–14.7	–17.7	3.0	–3.5	8.1	–11.6	12.6	29.1	–16.5
14. Lecco	–3.5	22.4	–25.9	–3.4	29.5	–32.9	0.2	11.5	–11.3
15. Legnano	0.7	24.1	–23.4	–9.4	27.4	–36.7	–18.4	6.0	–24.3
16. Catanzaro	–18.8	–11.3	–7.5	–0.9	8.5	–9.4	25.3	27.9	–2.6
17. Caserta	–13.2	–19.3	6.1	22.2	3.8	18.4	39.3	25.7	13.7
Mean	3.6	5.5	–9.1	1.2	17.5	16.3	5.2	17.8	–12.6
Standard deviation	10.518	14.274	10.800	10.937	7.580	14.361	17.809	10.079	14.929
E. *Germany* (1960–70)									
1. Freiburg im Breisgau	10.0	–0.1	10.1	13.0	4.5	8.6	3.9	5.9	–1.9
2. Heidenheim	3.7	0.8	2.9	–1.2	1.2	–2.4	–8.0	0.6	–8.6
3. Karlsruhe	10.9	2.0	8.9	–3.7	4.1	–7.8	–24.5	3.6	–28.1
4. Pforzheim	2.3	0.7	1.6	–6.7	0.3	–6.9	–15.9	–0.7	–15.1
5. Ravensburg	11.2	0.5	10.7	10.9	0.9	9.9	–0.3	0.6	–1.0
6. Stuttgart	5.7	1.3	4.4	–6.1	2.9	–9.0	–20.4	2.7	–23.0
7. Ulm/Neu Ulm	8.6	0.4	8.3	7.3	2.0	5.3	–2.3	2.8	–5.0
8. Aschaffenburg	5.7	–3.2	9.0	–8.0	–1.7	–6.3	–22.5	2.5	–25.1
9. Augsburg	22.4	–0.1	22.5	–3.8	0.8	–4.6	–71.0	2.2	–73.2
10. Bamberg	–0.4	0.5	–0.9	–4.4	1.7	–6.1	–13.2	4.0	–17.2
11. Bayreuth	0.1	–1.4	1.5	–3.2	3.3	–6.5	–5.9	8.3	–14.2
12. Coburg	–6.4	–3.1	–3.3	–5.2	2.5	–7.6	1.6	7.3	–5.6
13. Hof	–11.2	–5.5	–5.6	–7.3	–2.7	–4.6	4.8	3.5	1.3

Table 6.2 – *continued*

	Entire region			Core only			Core/ring differential		
	R/ND	SC	DC	R/ND	SC	DC	R/ND	SC	DC
14. Kempten	1.2	−1.0	2.2	14.4	0.0	14.3	15.5	1.2	14.2
15. Landshut	−17.1	1.0	−18.0	−7.3	5.4	−12.7	11.8	5.4	6.4
16. München	14.6	2.3	12.3	4.5	3.2	1.3	−36.7	3.5	−40.0
17. Nürnberg	2.0	1.5	0.5	−1.9	3.0	−4.9	7.3	−0.6	7.8
18. Schweinfurt	5.3	3.2	2.1	5.1	5.7	−0.6	5.5	1.6	3.9
19. Straubing	10.3	−1.3	11.6	1.5	1.2	0.3	−11.8	3.4	−15.1
20. Weiden i.d.O.	−5.7	−3.6	−2.1	−6.1	−0.8	−5.3	−0.8	5.2	−6.0
21. Würzburg	2.1	1.1	1.0	0.5	4.3	−3.8	−2.8	5.5	−8.3
22. Bremen	−0.5	1.7	−2.2	−6.8	2.0	−8.8	−19.1	0.8	−19.9
23. Bremerhaven	−1.1	3.5	−4.6	−6.6	4.6	−11.2	−12.9	2.5	−15.4
24. Hamburg	−5.5	2.3	−7.8	−10.2	2.5	−12.7	−25.1	1.2	−26.3
25. Darmstadt	13.6	0.8	12.8	2.3	2.3	0.0	−25.7	3.4	−29.2
26. Frankfurt a.M.	7.1	1.7	5.4	4.0	2.7	1.4	−6.2	1.9	−8.1
27. Fulda	0.5	−3.8	4.4	−2.8	−1.7	−1.2	−4.7	3.0	−7.7
28. Giessen	9.6	1.3	8.3	14.6	3.9	10.7	6.9	3.6	3.3
29. Kassel	2.2	0.9	1.3	−9.6	3.5	−13.1	−20.2	4.4	−24.7
30. Marburg a.d.L.	10.8	1.7	9.2	5.9	8.4	−2.5	6.1	8.4	−14.5
31. Braunschweig	−7.4	1.3	−8.7	−10.2	2.5	−12.7	−6.3	2.5	−8.9
32. Celle	0.1	−3.6	3.7	−6.0	3.4	−9.4	−13.1	14.8	−27.9
33. Emden	10.6	2.9	7.7	16.4	3.6	12.8	7.6	0.9	6.7
34. Hameln	−2.0	−0.5	−1.5	−1.9	2.0	−3.9	0.2	4.1	−3.9
35. Hannover	3.0	0.7	2.3	−3.6	2.5	−6.1	−16.7	4.5	−21.2
36. Hildesheim	−1.2	1.4	−2.6	2.0	4.9	−2.9	6.3	6.9	−0.6
37. Oldenburg	15.6	1.7	13.9	4.9	3.4	1.5	−22.5	3.5	−26.0
38. Wilhelmshaven	1.7	3.1	−1.4	0.5	3.6	−3.1	−2.2	0.9	−3.1
39. Wolfsburg	19.0	1.7	17.3	38.1	5.9	32.2	36.6	8.0	28.6
40. Saarbrücken	−5.3	−3.1	−2.1	−10.8	4.3	−15.1	−7.4	9.9	−17.3
Mean	3.7	0.3	3.4	0.3	2.7	−2.3	−7.9	3.8	−11.7
Standard deviation	7.924	2.158	7.603	9.407	2.182	9.002	16.927	6.519	16.736

Looking first at the *whole region* analysis, it is immediately clear that the differential component appears generally stronger than the structural one. In Britain the structural component is mildly negative, but a stronger differential element gives a positive anomaly overall. In Sweden alone of the five countries the structural element appears stronger than the differential. In both Belgium and Germany the structural element has virtually a nil effect on average, and the anomaly (negative for Belgium, positive for Germany) is explained almost wholly in terms of the differential component.

By looking at the simple standard deviation around the mean of the sample, some index of the relative performances of each factor is given, remembering though that it is a sample and that the figures for Great Britain are quinquennial rather than the decennial rates used elsewhere. This said, high internal variability is evident everywhere in the differential component, but is smaller for the structural component. The exception is Italy, with a large standard deviation around the structural component mean; sample regions in the North generally are strongly positive in this regard as opposed to the reverse in the Mezzogiorno – as would be expected.

Turning to the *core* performance, the results are more complex. In Britain the mean anomaly is relatively small and positive; the differential element provides a larger part of the explanation. The same is true for the much larger positive anomaly in Sweden. In Belgium, however, a very small anomaly is produced by a positive structure component and a negative differential component of about the same amount. The same is true of Italy and Germany save that in Italy both the structural and differential components are very large.

Again, the mean figures disguise internal variability and again the structural component in Italy provides the most noticeable contrast to the other countries in this respect with the Mezzogiorno scoring weakly. Overall, the variability in the core differential component is higher still, perhaps suggesting that, at this level of disaggregation, the employment mix of cores is only significant in southern Italy. Here, it should be recalled, agrarian urban settlements were still prevalent as late as the 1960s, but were responding rapidly to government-induced diversification by the end of the decade.

In many ways the most interesting analysis is the third one, which explores the core–ring difference in performance. For Britain it shows a negative figure overall (indicating that the core performance is poorer than that of the rings, as might be expected from the analysis earlier in this book). However the surprising point is that the structure element is positive: the weak core performance is due to the poorer growth of individual industries there as compared with the ring. For Sweden, Belgium and Italy, in contrast, the core performance was positive, indicating a better overall growth record than the rings. Structure provided the bulk of the explanation in Belgium and in Italy, but not in Sweden. Lastly, in Germany the cores again show a negative difference; and again, as in Britain, the structure component is strongly negative.

We are forced to conclude from this analysis that overall in the 1960s the weaker performance of the cores in Britain and Germany – as compared with the rings – was not due to an unfavourable economic structure. Structure did, however, help to explain the stronger performance in Belgium and Italy, though not in Sweden.

To select a few individual cases for further analysis is of course arbitrary. But some are of particular interest. Within Britain, for instance, Liverpool had an outstanding negative core–ring difference, but the main explanation was the differential performance of individual industries. The same goes for the less spectacular negative differences exhibited by other large cities such as Newcastle, Leeds, Glasgow and Hull. In Sweden the strength of the structure element is seen in a few fast-growing central cores, such as Malmö–Lund but there too, overall the differential component emerges as much the stronger in the majority of cases. In Belgium, Antwerp is similar to some large British cities: its negative difference in relation to the ring is explained chiefly in terms of the differential. In Italy the relative strength of the structure component emerges chiefly in the small- and middle-sized centres, where it may represent mainly the decline of agriculture in the hinterlands. The very large negative anomalies for many German cores, including some large cities (Munich, Hamburg) are almost everywhere a result of the differential component, as are some of the bigger positive anomalies occurring in smaller core cities. This may partly result from the coarse nature of the employment classification, however. It is surprising for instance to find the strong positive anomaly in the core city of Wolfsburg (home of Volkswagen) explained mainly by the differential component.

Thus the figures can be related to the earlier analyses of Chapter 4, with the results largely predictable. In Italy, where the urban development sequence (particularly in the Mezzogiorno) was at an earlier stage of evolution than elsewhere, structure even at a coarse ten sector level was found to be more significant than in the rest of the sample. Next, Sweden which it will be remembered had the most rapidly changing urban systems revealed a strong core influence overall, with high core–ring differences evident in both components. Here, decentralisation of employment was virtually nil by 1970. Belgium showed less dramatic differences between expected and observed employment changes, but notable are the performances of the two predominantly French areas sampled, reflecting not only the decline of the economic base, but also perhaps the effects of less intervention than would be evident in other countries. In West Germany, the average figures are low, but the standard deviations from these averages show surprising inequalities between regions. Most significant are the strongly negative results for regions close to the DDR – indeed many regions which feature in the Federal aid programmes of recent years. The British figures, however, are less variable than those of the four countries, perhaps in part reflecting the difference in time-spans analysed. But, again many areas which had negative overall population and employment changes and shifts also display a negative differential as between core and ring – though this seems to be explained much more by the differential rather than the structural component.

Yet many anomalies to the above generalisations lead us to conclude that much more analysis is needed – either by further disaggregation or by modifications to the technique. However, two points can be made: first, as various commentators have prescribed, shift-share analysis can be useful as a first examination of regional employment data, perhaps leading to the identification of areas or sectors of employment for further analysis. Second, it appears to provide a useful basis for comparative research; although we agree that regional policy measures should not be based solely on the evidence of such a controversial statistical test, it is interesting that some of our results correspond to those which we intuitively expected. Indeed, many areas receiving government assistance in these five countries gave results which differed from those non-aided areas.

What perhaps emerges from this exceedingly complex piece of statistical manipulation, therefore, is the importance of the fineness of the classification in any share-shift analysis. Had we been able to use a finer classification, then – as explained at the start of this chapter – we might have been able to ascribe a bigger importance to economic structure. But that would have taken resources far in excess of those available for this study.

Chapter 7
Overview

In this final chapter, we try to bring together the main conclusions of the study. We go back to the original hypotheses posed in Chapter 2, and try in particular to answer the question: how far do European urban trends follow the model established in North America? We try to suggest some explanations for the observed trends, and in particular for some of the more important divergences between European and American patterns. Lastly, we ask what directions research in this general area might now fruitfully follow.

The 'American Hypotheses'
Abundant recent American research, outlined in Chapter 1 of this book (Berry 1973; Berry in Berry 1976; Berry and Dahmann 1977; Beale 1977; Alonso 1978; McCarthy and Morrison 1977, 1979; Sternlieb and Hughes 1975, 1977) leads to the conclusion – summarised at the start of Chapter 2 – that there, urban growth is passing:

1. *Downwards* through the urban hierarchy from larger to smaller urban systems;
2. *Outwards* within metropolitan areas from cores to rings;
3. *Outwards* from metropolitan to non-metropolitan areas – that is, from urban to rural areas;
4. *Across* from older industrialised and urbanised regions dominated by manufacturing (the Northeast, the Midwest) to newly industrialising and urbanising regions, dominated by service industry (the South, the West).

Together, these trends have led some American observers to postulate that in the early 1970s urbanisation in America has passed through a 'clean break' (Vining and Strauss 1977; Vining and Kontuly 1978; Vining in Kawashima 1980): the traditional pattern of rural-to-urban migration – dominant since the Industrial Revolution – is being reversed, as Americans move in increasing numbers from the metropolitan areas to quite remote, sparsely populated rural areas. Others have doubted the evidence, stressing that the main migration streams were still into those non-metropolitan areas close to the metropolitan boundaries – representing a continuation of the long-evident wave motion, that earlier took millions from central cities to suburban rings within the metropolitan areas themselves. This theory of the 'clean break' became a central research question of the European Urban Systems study.

Having stated the questions, we can now straightaway answer them: at least down to 1970, Europe did not demonstrate any general tendency to deconcentration on the American model. Rather, it presents a varied, even confused picture in which different parts of the continent were behaving in very different ways. And, as far as any generalisations are possible, they seem to be almost the reverse of North American ones.

Thus not only did the great majority of Europeans live in metropolitan areas as we have defined them: that proportion actually increased, from 86 per cent in 1950 to over 88 per cent in 1970. The non-metropolitan areas were almost static in population, and actually had slightly fewer people in 1970 than in 1950. The only parallel with American experience is that there was some decentralisation within metropolitan areas: the metropolitan rings had a decreasing share of the total population in the 1950s but an increasing share in the 1960s, when their aggregate population growth (15.4 million) was actually greater than that of the cores. Thus it can be said that while in the 1950s population in Europe was concentrating into metropolitan cores, by the 1960s it was deconcentrating into metropolitan rings.

However, the early 1970s saw quite new tendencies, and it was in this period, it must be remembered, that the Americans identified their 'clean break'. Somewhat unsatisfactory evidence – that excludes five of the fourteen countries in the study, for lack of data – suggests that after 1970 the process of decentralisation accelerated. The urban cores, which had had as much as two-thirds of the population growth in the 1950s, had less than one-half in the 1960s and a negligible share in the 1970s. The rings took only one-third of total net growth in the 1950s, more than one-half in the 1960s – and the whole of the net growth in the 1970–75 period. However, there is a most important caveat: on balance, population was still leaving non-metropolitan areas for metropolitan areas, which were steadily increasing their share of total population in the nine countries.

Our areas, it must be stressed, were more widely bounded than the Standard Metropolitan Statistical Areas used in the American analyses. But this means merely that they include what the American workers call contiguous non-metropolitan areas. They do, of course, exclude the non-contiguous areas, which have been taking a large share of American growth in the 1970s. In other words, the results strongly support the hypothesis that there has been a continuation of the outward wave movement, already evident in many parts of Europe in the 1960s. They do not support the notion of the 'clean break' as writers such as Vining and Kontuly have defined it: the drift to the remoter rural areas is not yet evident in Europe.

The evidence for employment trends is more limited than that for population. For the 1950s a majority of European countries failed to return data for employment at place of work, and for the 1970s figures are virtually non-existent until publication of the 1980–81 round of Censuses. The available evidence for the 1950–70 period suggests that a very high proportion of total employment, between 98 and 99 per cent, has been concentrated in the metropolitan areas. For the same group of countries, the proportion of employment in the metropolitan cores increased in the 1950s but decreased marginally by the 1960s, indicating that the movement off the land and into the cities was progressively replaced by a process of local outward decentralisation. But it must be stressed that this group of countries included the more heavily urbanised ones, where in general decentralisation processes set in earlier than elsewhere.

It is also clear, however, that these overall trends concealed important differences between one part of Europe and another. In Atlantic Europe (Great Britain plus Ireland) there was a strong tendency towards decentralisation of population on the American model, and by the 1960s populations in some urban cores, especially the biggest, were falling. Notable too in these biggest metropolitan areas was the fact that – again on the American model – the loss transferred itself from the core to the whole area, so that London, Manchester and Liverpool were actually recording declines overall. During the early 1970s this trend accelerated, with massive losses from the cores and gains in the rings; non-metropolitan areas continued to decline, so that even here there was a lack of support for the 'clean break' hypothesis. Employment – where data are available only for Britain – was centralising into the cores in the 1950s but was decentralising in the 1960s, admittedly with a large minority of exceptions in both cases.

However, on the European mainland the experience has been rather different. Northern Europe (Sweden, Norway and Denmark) showed a much weaker degree of metropolitan development than did Atlantic Europe, with less than 80 per cent living in metropolitan areas in 1970 (against 94 per cent in atlantic Europe); within metropolitan areas there was some decentralisation of population in the 1960s, with the rings claiming some 64 per cent of total growth. Employment, available only for Sweden, continued to be concentrated almost exclusively in the metropolitan cores. In the 1970s the suburban trend strengthened as core populations actually fell overall. It appears then that Scandinavia may be following the British trends with a time-lag of about ten years.

Of all our five regional divisions, that we call Western Europe (Belgium, the Netherlands, Luxembourg, France) is the least homogeneous and the most difficult to describe in short compass. Overall, metropolitan areas grew at the expense of non-metropolitan ones, and within them the majority of the growth (nearly 64 per cent in the 1950s, nearly 54 per cent in the 1960s) was in the cores. But while in both decades the Netherlands and Belgium were decentralising population from cores to rings, in France the tendency was strongly towards centralisation. Then however came a 'clean break': excluding Luxembourg, the overall core share of growth fell dramatically from 53 per cent in the 1960s to 20 per cent in the early 1970s, while the ring share rose from 40 to 69 per cent and the non-metropolitan share rose from 6 to over 11 per cent. But while this trend was very marked in the Benelux countries, in France between 1970 and

1975 the growth of the cores still outstripped that of the rings. Significant however for France was the sharp acceleration of growth in non-metropolitan areas, which were taking 15 per cent of the total growth by the early 1970s.

Southern Europe (Spain, Portugal and Italy) presents a simpler case – and in many ways an interesting one – because it so completely contradicts the American experience. Here, was an even stronger tendency than in France to centralisation: the proportion of total population living in metropolitan areas rose rapidly – though even by 1970 it was still less than 80 per cent – and the cores took over 80 per cent of total growth in both the 1950s and 1960s. In fact, non-metropolitan areas lost people heavily, and this trend actually intensified during the 1960s. Here as elsewhere, however, the 1970s witnessed a break – though of a rather different character than elsewhere. The figures for Spain and Italy show that indeed the cores continued to grow and to increase their total share of population. But the rate of core growth dramatically slowed, and the rings by this time were growing twice as fast; they accounted for virtually all the net growth, the more modest core gains being offset by continued non-metropolitan losses. If there were a break here, it was certainly not transferring people back into remoter rural areas. Employment data in this region are available only for Italy in the 1960s: they show sharp losses in non-metropolitan areas and in metropolitan rings, with modest gains in the cores.

Lastly, in Central Europe (the Federal Republic of Germany, Switzerland, Austria) there was an exceptionally high concentration of people in metropolitan areas: the cores took nearly two-thirds of total growth in the 1950s but less than one-third in the 1960s. (In this region, unfortunately, virtually no comparable data exist for the post-1970 period.) Employment, in contrast, centralised throughout: in the 1950s the rings showed heavy losses, while by the 1960s the cores were still accounting for more than half the total growth. But this overall picture – just as in the case of adjacent western Europe – conceals important differences between one country and another: by the 1960s Switzerland and Austria were decentralising both people and jobs – a pattern comparable to that of Britain – while in Germany people were decentralising but their jobs were still centralising. In this respect, Germany seems to have been typical of a whole group of countries elsewhere in Europe – Sweden, the Netherlands and Belgium, for instance.

Closer analysis shows that the pattern of growth was highly concentrated geographically. Western, Southern and Central Europe were growing faster than Atlantic or Northern Europe, but this in turn reflects the fact that seventeen relatively small zones, accounting for a mere 8.5 per cent of the area of the fourteen countries, accounted for no less than 54 per cent of total growth between 1950 and 1970. Fourteen of them were located within an extended 'Golden Triangle', the corners of which were North Holland, Madrid and Rome. Outside this triangle, the only areas of above-average growth were the Stockholm area, the Valencia area and the area north and west of London – and the last two of these were only just beyond the boundaries of the Golden Triangle. There were two particular kinds of concentration. First, axial areas of growth along the Rhine valley, the Rhône–Saône valleys and the Côte d'Azur: most of this was in medium-sized cities outside the older industrial areas, though these areas were not yet exhibiting absolute decline. Second, southern Europe: here the growth was concentrated in the biggest cities such as Madrid, Barcelona, Bilbao, Valencia, Milan, Turin and Rome. Here there is superficial evidence for a 'drift to the sunbelt', but the causal mechanism is very different from that observed in the United States; it is a process of primary migration from the land and into the cities, drawn by better job prospects and higher real wage levels.

In all this, there is no firm evidence of a real decline in Europe's industrial heartland. Though some areas – northern England and central Scotland, the southern Belgian–northern French coalfield, the Ruhr region – have shown structural weaknesses in the 1960s, there have been counteracting patterns of industrial growth in the English Midlands, the eastern Randstad, the Cologne–Bonn area and the upper Rhine region. Here, growth has been based on a firm foundation of expanding industries such as electrical and chemical industries, and some higher-order service industries such as banking, insurance and finance.

While these growth areas are geographically central, the areas of lower growth or decline tend to have been nationally peripheral: they include much of Scotland, Wales and northern England; most of rural Ireland; the London area; the northern Jutland area of Denmark; northern Norway and Sweden; southern and eastern Belgium; western and central France; central and north-western Spain; much of Portugal; parts of central and northern Italy; the Mezzogiorno (down to 1970); the upland periphery of Germany, especially the areas adjacent to the DDR and Czechoslovakia, and eastern Austria. Though a few of these are large urban regions, most are based on quite small towns (50 000–100 000) in remoter rural areas. It appears that only in Britain – and to a limited degree in the Franco–German coalfield and the Ruhrgebiet – is there serious evidence of the decline of older industrial–urban regions.

Thus in the period from 1950 to 1975 the European urban system was failing to operate like the American. The tendency was still for population to move from rural to urban areas, not the reverse. The industrial heartland was still strong, and the remoter rural areas were still losing. There was a drift to the sunbelt, but for reasons quite different from those obtaining in the United States. Even the movement from central urban core to suburban ring was more tardy than in North America, with Atlantic Europe in the van and southern Europe in the rear of the process.

There is however another important respect in which the European trends are different. One of the American trends was downwards through the urban hierarchy: larger urban systems tended to stagnate or decline, while smaller ones grew. This conforms to the well-known geographical rule, whereby – as industrialisation and urbanisation proceeds – the system of cities moves progressively form a primate distribution to a rank-size one. We have seen that in a few parts of Europe – most notably Great Britain – there was already a close approximation to a rank-size distribution by 1950, and that this maintained stability during the following quarter-century. But other countries had a pattern that was strongly primate or semi-primate (that is, with two or three dominant urban systems); and in a number of cases, this pattern actually reinforced itself over the quarter-century as the largest urban systems showed strong growth. This pattern was most marked where urban growth was most rapid: in western Europe it led to increases in metropolitan areas in the size range above 325 000, while in southern and central Europe it led to big gains in the areas with 500 000 and more. Spain, Italy and Germany in particular showed very vigorous growth at the very top of the urban hierarchy.

So in general, the hypotheses derived from American experience do not perform well in Europe. In particular, the hypothesis of the 'clean break' receives little support. Independent work by Peter Gordon, using the Reading–IIASA data set, confirms this (Gordon in Kawashima 1980). He uses the same technique as was employed by Vining and Strauss (1977) as evidence for the 'clean break': the so-called Hoover index, which measures the sum of differences between the proportion of a country's total population living in any given sub-area, and the proportion of the country's total area that is taken up by that sub-area. For a number of European countries and for Japan Gordon calculates the Hoover index for 1950–60 and for 1960–70 using a number of different units: whole metropolitan areas, cores, hinterlands and non-metropolitan areas. He then studies the changes between the first decade and the second. The evidence strongly supports the notion of a wave motion, not a clean break. A large group of European countries show increasing concentration except in the cores, where there is clear evidence for spillover of growth into the rings in the larger urban areas. A limited group – Britain, the Netherlands, Switzerland, Belgium, Austria and Poland – display deconcentration at all scales. An even more limited group – Spain, Italy, Finland and Japan – display continuing concentration at all scales. This evidence, using an entirely different technique from ours, provides interesting confirmation of our findings. It is also in accord with the notion of stages of concentration and deconcentration, which we develop below.

The evidence, then, does not support the American hypotheses. When we sought deeper causal explanations of the differences, however, we experienced disappointment. Systematic statistical analysis of the patterns – both of comparative growth and comparative internal shift – reveals that no one factor has very good explanatory power. Rates of growth are not systematically related to geographical position – whether this is measured by latitude (the sunbelt hypothesis) or distance from national or regional capital. Nor are they related very systematically to size or density – though the latter is particularly difficult to measure because of possible overbounding of some of the areas. Nor are rates of internal shift, of concentration or deconcentration, related systematically to variations in core density or age of the central city. However the statistical manipulations were varied to try to identify better relationships the results still proved bafflingly poor.

There was only one kind of analysis that proved fruitful in analysing the patterns of internal shift. It does not aim to provide explanatory power, but rather to establish a systematic ordering of the pattern of change. It hypothesises that as the process of industrialisation–urbanisation proceeds, urban areas in particular countries move fairly regularly from one stage to another on a concentration–deconcentration spectrum: first, centralisation during loss (as people leave rural rings at a rate faster than central cities can absorb them in that local region); then absolute centralisation; then relative centralisation; then, as the critical pivotal point is passed, relative decentralisation; then, as cores begin to lose people, absolute decentralisation; lastly, in older or larger urban regions, decentralisation during loss. Our detailed analysis at the end of Chapter 4 shows that indeed such a sequence appears to occur in the great majority of cases, but that some parts of Europe – Atlantic, Northern and Central Europe – are more advanced in their passage through it than are parts of Western Europe or most of Southern Europe.

We can now summarise the entire evidence in this way. In most of the ways that the process could be measured, Europe down to 1975 was not de-urbanising. An already urban continent was undergoing further urbanisation. This process was especially marked in Western, Southern and Central Europe. People were moving off the land and into the urban areas. Indeed, in many countries there was actually a movement up the urban hierarchy, with growth of medium-sized cities in Western Europe and of bigger cities in Southern and Central Europe. In the more rural areas, the cities could not absorb the outflow from the land, which passed on into the larger urban areas. The fast-growing areas were quite highly concentrated in the industrial 'Golden Triangle' or on the Mediterranean shores. There was little evidence then of the decline of the industrial heartland of Europe. Though there was an apparent drift to the sunbelt, as the Mediterranean cities grew, the main cause was quite different in kind from the equivalent American phenomenon: it was the primary migration of people off the land into their first industrial jobs. Lastly, though Atlantic Europe was exhibiting decentralisation of people and jobs in the 1960s, and some nations in mainland Europe were beginning to decentralise their residential populations from cores to rings, generally jobs were still centralising while in France and southern Europe population was still flooding into central cores too. Even in the early 1970s, though generally population was leaving the core cities, in France and in southern Europe this transition point had not been passed.

The evident reason for these very different trends is that – at least down to 1970, and even down to 1975 – most of Europe was at an earlier stage of industrial and urban evolution than either the United States or Great Britain, the European country that most closely conformed to the American model. People were still flooding off the land and into the cities. Within the extended European Economic Community, 17.0 million persons (17.1 per cent of the workforce) were still in primary industries (agriculture, forestry, fishing) in 1950; by 1972 the figure was down to 9.7 million (9.4 per cent) (Salt and Clout 1976, pp. 34–5). Naturally, these new arrivals concentrated first in the central core cities where housing and jobs were available. The suburbanisation process set in later, perhaps due to lower per capita incomes compared with North America, and perhaps even due to different social preferences for central city as against suburban life-styles.

The most likely hypothesis is that the main differences are related to stage of industrial–urban evolution; and that as this proceeds, Europe will more and more follow the American–British path. But the patterns may not be exactly parallel, for at least two main reasons. First, cultural styles are different: France and the Mediterranean countries have a quite different preference for higher-density, inner city apartment-house living compared with the Anglo–American suburban tradition. Second, and even more important, much of Europe's urban population is still only one or two generations removed from the land, in a way that is simply not true for either Great Britain or the United States. Many urban families have ancestral farmhouses in the countryside to which they can return – whether for summer, for weekends, or for retirement, or for an escape from urban pressures to a simpler life-style. The return migration to Italy's Mezzogiorno, which is such a striking new feature of the 1970–75 analysis, offers a foretaste of what could happen if a prolonged recession were to limit job opportunities in the larger industrial cities of Europe.

Some Open Questions

The results summarised above represent the conclusion of stage one of our study. In a second stage, we went on to try to deepen the analysis, in two ways. First, we took a sample of metropolitan areas in five countries (Britain, Sweden, Belgium, Italy, Germany) and made a more intensive analysis of their employment structure in terms of major industrial sectors. By applying the familiar techniques of shift-share analysis, we sought to establish whether different rates of growth – and of internal shift, from core to ring or vice-versa – could be 'explained' by industrial structure. For each area, using a standardised industrial classification, we made a threefold analysis: first, to see whether differences in overall rates of growth could be thus explained; second, to see whether rates of change in the core areas could be explained; and third, to see whether differences in core versus ring performance could be interpreted in terms of structure. The results, reported in Chapter 6, do not suggest that structure is a very important explanation. In all three analyses, far more important overall was the so-called differential component – the residual that is left after the structural influence is accounted for. There are exceptions to this – for instance Italy, where the influence of structure appears more important. Almost certainly, this represents the very heavy weight of declining employment in primary industry, especially agriculture, in many Italian metropolitan areas as late as the 1960s. But elsewhere, this influence was not so strong.

Secondly, we hoped to measure the effect of national planning and other public policies. Since the 1950s almost all European countries have exercised at least nominal control over the pattern of urban growth: in some (Great Britain, Sweden, the Netherlands, Germany) this control has been fairly effective. Great Britain comprehensively since 1945, France and the Netherlands more partially since the 1950s, have sought to steer employment out of their congested national capital regions by a combination of direct movement of government jobs and restrictions on private employers, plus incentives to private industry to move either short distances to local growth centres, or longer distances to lagging regions. Almost every country has sought to promote growth in peripheral regions, usually through some combination of governmental infrastructure investments and incentives to private industrialists. By the mid-1970s, as already recorded at the end of Chapter 4, national–regional policies of various kinds covered no less than three-fifths of the area and more than two-fifths of the population of the enlarged European Economic Community; and these national efforts have been supplemented since 1975 by the European Regional Fund (Romus in Vaizey 1975, pp. 125–31; Clout 1976, pp. 54–5; Allen 1979, *passim*). And nearly all countries have sought to allocate central or regional funds among local authorities, to reflect differences in needs or resources or both.

However, looked at more closely these policies have some evident limitations as effective instruments. The most important is that the regional policies, in particular, tend to be spatially very coarse: they do not distinguish very clearly between one part of a region and another. Most of them are concerned to shift growth from one major region of the country to another – generally from large metropolitan areas that are regarded as overgrown and congested (London, Paris, the Dutch Randstad) to lagging areas: either to rural regions, or to older industrial regions. Only on a very limited scale, in certain countries, have there been policies to secure local out-migration from larger urban areas – or from their congested inner cores – to local growth centres in the form of planned new towns or urban satellites. Another is that – especially at this more local scale – it is not easy to measure the strength of the policy instruments, because they may consist of a mixture of regulation and financial incentives. Both these incentives, and the more general schemes for central-to-local government subsidy, are in practice highly technical in character and difficult to interpret.

Despite these obvious limitations, we originally wanted to try to discover whether these policies had exerted any effect on the pattern of geographical change or on the rate of internal shift between central cores and suburban rings. In this, we were largely frustrated by lack of comparative data for small areas within our sample countries. The very limited statistical analysis we were able to perform gave no basis for a belief that regional policies or patterns of transfer of fiscal resources between local authorities had influenced patterns of change. But it is far from conclusive; and it may be that further work in this area would be justified.

There are other fields of work, identified at the start of the European urban systems study as appropriate for a second state study, where no work at all has yet been started: the study of quality of life indices in various urban areas and within these same urban areas; the study of energy flows and balances within urban areas of different size and character, which has now become an area of the greatest practical importance to policy-makers; and the development of general models of development of the national and international urban system. In this last area, IIASA have determined that they will begin a study – based probably on four sample countries, two from western Europe and two from eastern Europe – in the summer of 1979. This will represent the logical continuation of stage one of the study, as originally planned as long ago as 1975.

Meanwhile, the study reported here has thrown up a number of additional areas that would certainly be worthy of further analysis. The eastern European results, recently reported to IIASA (Kawashima 1980), should be standardised and incorporated into the analysis. Population change could profitably be dis-aggregated into its natural increase and net migration components, and gross migration flows could even be identified. The IIASA models, which will incorporate a demographic component, will certainly do this for the four sample countries. The non-metropolitan areas, considered as simple aggregates for the purposes of the present study, could profitably be studied in more detail in order to provide a parallel to the many studies of non-metropolitan growth completed or under way in the United States. The consequences of urban growth for the provision of infrastructure and services, both in the urban areas themselves and in the depopulating countryside, would certainly merit closer study. As planned from the start, much of this work could and should be done in a variety of loosely cooperating research centres, which would deepen the Reading–IIASA data base in a variety of ways. And lastly, the data base itself should certainly be updated at the 1980–81 round of Censuses, perhaps through the agency of the Statistical Office of the European Communities which has commissioned a study by the present authors on problems of comparable definition of urban agglomerations (Hall, Hay and Sammons 1979).

The real test of the European Urban Systems study, then, will be whether fellow researchers are encouraged to join in a continuing programme of work, thus developing a tradition of urban research within a common data framework as has long been standard in the United States. That in turn would permit international co-operation between scholars in different continents to compare urban trends world-wide within a rigorous definitional framework. Thus the present book represents not the end of a study, but merely the end of the beginning.

Appendices

Table A.1   Great Britain: population 1950–75

Population data for 1950, 1960, 1970 and 1975

Areal unit	1950 Total	1950 % of total	1960 Total	1960 % of total	1970 Total	1970 % of total	1975 Total	1975 % of total
Core	26 155 464	53.39	26 665 070	51.87	25 991 849	47.99	25 363 655	46.58
Ring	21 077 570	43.03	23 011 691	44.77	26 354 112	48.65	27 305 133	50.15
Non-metropolitan	1 755 616	3.58	1 727 969	3.36	1 822 003	3.36	1 781 208	3.27
Total	48 988 650	100.00	51 404 730	100.00	54 167 964	100.00	54 449 996	100.00

Population change 1950–60, 1960–70 and 1970–75

Areal unit	1950–60 Absolute change	1950–60 % change	1950–60 % of total	1960–70 Absolute change	1960–70 % change	1960–70 % of total	1970–75 Absolute change	1970–75 % change	1970–75 % of total
Core	509 606	1.95	21.10	−673 221	−2.52	−24.36	−628 194	−2.42	−222.74
Ring	1 934 121	9.18	80.04	3 342 421	14.52	120.96	951 021	3.61	337.20
Non-metropolitan	−27 647	−1.57	−1.14	94 034	5.44	3.40	−40 795	2.24	−14.46
Total	2 416 080	4.93	100.00	2 763 234	5.37	100.00	282 032	0.52	100.00

Table A.2   Great Britain: employment 1950–70

Employment data for 1950, 1960 and 1970

Areal unit	1950 Total	1950 % of total	1960 Total	1960 % of total	1970 Total	1970 % of total
Core	13 510 731	60.95	14 383 617	61.86	13 980 800	58.93
Ring	8 011 344	36.14	8 241 697	35.45	9 097 538	38.35
Non-metropolitan	645 301	2.91	626 123	2.69	646 213	2.72
Total	22 167 376	100.00	23 251 437	100.00	23 724 551	100.00

Employment change 1950–60 and 1960–70

	1950–60			1960–70		
Areal unit	Absolute change	% change	% of total	Absolute change	% change	% of total
Core	872 886	6.46	80.52	− 402 817	− 2.80	− 85.14
Ring	230 353	2.88	21.25	855 841	10.38	180.90
Non-metropolitan	− 19 178	− 2.97	− 1.77	20 090	3.21	4.25
Total	1 084 061	4.89	100.00	473 114	2.03	100.00

Table A.3 Ireland: population 1950–70

Population data for 1950, 1960 and 1970

	1950		1960		1970	
Areal unit	Total	% of total	Total	% of total	Total	% of total
Core	1 166 332	26.95	1 168 073	27.51	1 167 959	25.89
Ring	1 497 278	34.60	1 538 758	36.24	1 824 358	40.45
Non-metropolitan	1 663 719	38.45	1 538 679	36.24	1 518 096	33.66
Total	4 327 329	100.00	4 245 510	100.00	4 510 413	100.00

Population change 1950–60 and 1960–70

	1950–60			1960–70		
Areal unit	Absolute change	% change	% of total	Absolute change	% change	% of total
Core	1741	0.15	− 2.13	− 114	− 0.01	− 0.04
Ring	41 480	2.77	− 50.70	285 600	18.56	107.81
Non-metropolitan	− 125 040	− 7.52	152.83	− 20 583	− 1.34	− 7.77
Total	− 81 819	− 1.89	100.00	264 903	6.24	100.00

Table A.4 Ireland: employment 1950–70

	1950		1960		1970	
Areal unit	Total	% of total	Total	% of total	Total	% of total
Core	na	na	na	na	202 826	36.85
Ring	na	na	na	na	255 142	46.36
Non-metropolitan	na	na	na	na	92 431	16.79
Total	na	na	na	na	550 399	100.00

na – not available.

Table A.5   Sweden: population 1950–75

	Population data for 1950, 1960, 1970 and 1975							
	1950		*1960*		*1970*		*1975*	
Areal unit	*Total*	*% of total*	*Total*	*% of total*	*Total*	*% of total*	*Total*	*% of total*
Core	2 310 730	32.78	2 707 232	36.32	3 007 183	37.23	2 781 272	33.89
Ring	3 026 994	42.94	3 011 320	40.39	3 329 347	41.22	3 668 112	44.69
Non-metropolitan	1 711 593	24.28	1 736 256	23.29	1 740 375	21.55	1 758 082	21.42
Total	7 049 317	100.00	7 454 808	100.00	8 076 905	100.00	8 207 466	100.00

	Population change 1950–60, 1960–70 and 1970–75								
	1950–60			*1960–70*			*1970–75*		
Areal unit	*Absolute change*	*% change*	*% of total*	*Absolute change*	*% change*	*% of total*	*Absolute change*	*% change*	*% of total*
Core	396 502	17.16	97.78	299 951	11.08	48.22	− 225 911	− 7.51	− 173.03
Ring	− 15 674	− 0.52	− 3.87	318 027	10.56	51.12	338 765	10.18	259.47
Non-metropolitan	24 663	1.44	6.08	4 119	0.24	0.66	17 707	1.02	13.56
Total	405 491	5.75	100.00	622 097	8.34	100.00	130 561	1.62	100.00

Table A.6   Sweden: employment 1950–70

	Employment data for 1950, 1960 and 1970					
	1950		*1960*		*1970*	
Areal unit	*Total*	*% of total*	*Total*	*% of total*	*Total*	*% of total*
Core	na	na	1 358 855	41.01	1 519 883	45.41
Ring	na	na	1 244 966	37.57	1 147 609	34.28
Non-metropolitan	na	na	709 995	21.42	679 843	20.31
Total	na	na	3 313 816	100.00	3 347 335	100.00

	Employment change 1950–60 and 1960–70					
	1950–60			*1960–70*		
Areal unit	*Absolute change*	*% change*	*% of total*	*Absolute change*	*% change*	*% of total*
Core	na	na	na	161 028	11.85	480.40
Ring	na	na	na	− 97 357	− 7.82	− 290.45
Non-metropolitan	na	na	na	− 30 152	− 4.25	− 89.95
Total	na	na	na	33 519	1.01	100.00

na – not available.

Table A.7   Norway: population 1950–75

Population data for 1950, 1960, 1970 and 1975

	1950		1960		1970		1975	
Areal unit	Total	% of total	Total	% of total	Total	% of total	Total	% of total
Core	927 503	28.29	1 028 306	28.63	1 091 055	28.16	1 102 090	27.47
Ring	1 385 301	42.25	1 527 341	42.53	1 710 986	44.17	1 816 177	45.27
Non-metropolitan	965 635	29.45	1 035 578	28.84	1 071 990	27.67	1 093 818	27.26
Total	3 278 439	100.00	3 591 225	100.00	3 874 031	100.00	4 012 085	100.00

Population change 1950–60, 1960–70 and 1970–75

	1950–60			1960–70			1970–75		
Areal unit	Absolute change	% change	% of total	Absolute change	% change	% of total	Absolute change	% change	% of total
Core	100 803	10.87	32.23	62 749	6.10	22.19	11 035	1.01	7.99
Ring	142 040	10.25	45.41	183 645	12.02	64.94	105 191	6.15	76.20
Non-metropolitan	69 943	7.24	22.36	36 412	3.52	12.88	21 828	2.04	15.81
Total	312 786	9.54	100.00	282 806	7.87	100.00	138 054	3.56	100.00

Table A.8   Norway: employment 1950–70

	1950		1960		1970	
Areal unit	Total	% of total	Total	% of total	Total	% of total
Core	na	na	na	na	569 191	38.06
Ring	na	na	na	na	552 813	36.97
Non-metropolitan	na	na	na	na	373 441	24.97
Total	na	na	na	na	1 495 445	100.00

na – not available.

Table A.9   Denmark: population 1950–75

| | *Population data for 1950, 1960, 1970 and 1975* | | | | | | | |
| | *1950* | | *1960* | | *1970* | | *1975* | |
Areal unit	*Total*	*% of total*	*Total*	*% of total*	*Total*	*% of total*	*Total*	*% of total*
Core	1 721 021	40.17	1 818 104	39.68	1 851 861	37.51	1 799 158	35.60
Ring	1 862 039	43.47	2 050 526	44.75	2 362 532	47.85	2 522 391	49.90
Non-metropolitan	700 743	16.36	713 102	15.57	723 185	14.64	732 868	14.50
Total	4 283 803	100.00	4 581 732	100.00	4 937 578	100.00	5 054 417	100.00

| | *Population change 1950–60, 1960–70 and 1970–75* | | | | | | | |
| | *1950–60* | | | *1960–70* | | | *1970–75* | | |
Areal unit	*Absolute change*	*% change*	*% of total*	*Absolute change*	*% change*	*% of total*	*Absolute change*	*% change*	*% of total*
Core	97 083	5.64	32.59	33 757	1.86	9.49	− 52 703	−2.85	−45.11
Ring	188 487	10.12	63.27	312 006	15.22	87.68	159 859	6.77	136.82
Non-metropolitan	12 359	1.76	4.14	10 083	1.41	2.83	9 683	1.34	8.29
Total	297 929	6.95	100.00	355 846	7.77	100.00	116 839	2.37	100.00

Table A.10   Denmark: employment 1950–70

| | *1950* | | *1960* | | *1970* | |
Areal unit	*Total*	*% of total*	*Total*	*% of total*	*Total*	*% of total*
Core	na	na	na	na	907 078	43.40
Ring	na	na	na	na	882 055	42.20
Non-metropolitan	na	na	na	na	301 047	14.40
Total	na	na	na	na	2 090 180	100.00

na – not available.

Table A.11   Netherlands: population 1950–75

Population data for 1950, 1960, 1970 and 1975

	1950		1960		1970		1975	
Areal unit	Total	% of total	Total	% of total	Total	% of total	Total	% of total
Core	4 286 489	42.94	4 711 437	41.25	4 764 420	36.54	4 560 837	33.34
Ring	5 046 566	50.56	5 991 890	52.47	7 468 379	57.28	8 261 262	60.38
Non-metropolitan	649 263	6.50	717 030	6.28	806 635	6.19	859 093	6.28
Total	9 982 318	100.00	11 420 357	100.00	13 039 434	100.00	13 681 192	100.00

Population change 1950–60, 1960–70 and 1970–75

	1950–60			1960–70			1970–5		
Areal unit	Absolute change	% change	% of total	Absolute change	% change	% of total	Absolute change	% change	% of total
Core	424 948	9.91	29.55	52 983	1.12	3.27	−203 583	−4.27	−31.72
Ring	945 324	18.73	65.74	1 476 489	24.64	91.19	792 883	10.62	123.55
Non-metropolitan	67 767	10.44	4.71	89 605	12.50	5.53	52 458	6.50	8.17
Total	1 438 039	14.41	100.00	1 619 077	14.18	100.00	641 758	4.92	100.00

Table A.12   Netherlands: employment 1950–70

Employment data for 1950, 1960 and 1970

	1950		1960		1970	
Areal unit	Total	% of total	Total	% of total	Total	% of total
Core	1 647 240	44.89	1 893 281	46.74	1 893 794	45.90
Ring	1 778 871	48.48	1 912 585	47.22	1 994 034	48.33
Non-metropolitan	243 371	6.63	244 448	6.04	238 290	5.78
Total	3 669 482	100.00	4 050 314	100.00	4 126 118	100.00

Employment change 1950–60 and 1960–70

	1950–60			1960–70		
Areal unit	Absolute change	% change	% of total	Absolute change	% change	% of total
Core	246 041	14.94	64.61	513	0.03	0.68
Ring	133 714	7.52	35.11	81 449	4.26	107.45
Non-metropolitan	1077	0.44	0.28	−6158	−2.52	−8.12
Total	380 832	10.38	100.00	75 804	1.87	100.00

Table A.13   Belgium and Luxembourg: population 1950–70

Population data for 1950, 1960, 1970 and 1975

Areal unit	1950a Total	% of total	1960a Total	% of total	1970a Total	% of total	1950b Total	% of total	1960b Total	% of total	1970b Total	% of total	1975b Total	% of total
Core	2 127 787	24.34	2 215 435	23.31	2 202 869	22.06	2 065 791	24.45	2 143 782	23.33	2 126 710	22.04	2 066 279	21.06
Ring	6 456 089	73.86	7 126 016	74.97	7 620 624	76.30	6 227 093	73.69	6 882 780	74.90	7 356 937	76.25	7 605 191	77.50
Non-metropolitan	157 339	1.80	163 332	1.72	164 469	1.65	157 339	1.86	163 332	1.77	164 469	1.70	141 682	1.44
Total	8 741 215	100.00	9 504 783	100.00	9 987 962	100.00	8 450 223	100.00	9 189 894	100.00	9 648 116	100.00	9 813 152	100.00

Population change 1950–60, 1960–70 and 1970–75

Areal unit	1950–60a Absolute change	% change	1960–70a Absolute change	% change	% of total	1950–60b Absolute change	% change	% of total	1960–70b Absolute change	% change	% of total	1970–75b Absolute change	% change	% of total
Core	87 648	4.12	−12 566	−0.57	−2.60	77 991	3.77	10.54	−17 072	−2.84	−36.62	−60 431	−2.84	−36.62
Ring	669 927	10.38	494 608	6.94	102.37	655 687	10.53	88.65	474 157	6.89	103.48	248 254	3.37	150.42
Non-metropolitan	5993	3.81	1137	0.70	0.24	5993	3.81	0.81	1137	0.70	0.25	−22 787	−13.85	−13.81
Total	763 568	8.74	483 179	5.08	100.00	739 671	8.75	100.00	458 222	4.99	100.00	165 036	1.71	100.00

Notes: a Belgium and Luxembourg.
b Belgium only.

Table A.14   Belgium and Luxembourg: employment 1950–70

Employment data for 1950, 1960 and 1970

Areal unit	1950 Total	% of total	1960 Total	% of total	1970 Total	% of total
Core	na	na	1 357 849	39.95	1 401 254	37.63
Ring	na	na	1 995 583	58.71	2 278 875	61.20
Non-metropolitan	na	na	45 524	1.34	43 559	1.17
Total	na	na	3 398 956	100.00	3 723 688	100.00

Employment change 1950–60 and 1960–70

Areal unit	1950–60 Absolute change	% change	% of total	1960–70 Absolute change	% change	% of total
Core	na	na	na	43 405	3.20	13.37
Ring	na	na	na	283 292	14.20	87.24
Non-metropolitan	na	na	na	− 1965	−4.32	−0.61
Total	na	na	na	324 732	9.55	100.00

na   not available

Table A.15   France: population 1950–75

Population data for 1950, 1960, 1970 and 1975

Areal unit	1950 Total	% of total	1960 Total	% of total	1970 Total	% of total	1975 Total	% of total
Core	16 329 328	39.46	19 798 036	43.60	23 749 339	46.73	24 541 823	46.61
Ring	16 171 592	39.08	16 593 106	36.54	17 671 241	34.78	18 441 566	35.02
Non-metropolitan	8 876 194	21.45	9 019 855	19.86	9 396 570	18.49	9 672 413	18.37
Total	41 377 144	100.00	45 410 997	100.00	50 817 150	100.00	52 655 802	100.00

Population change 1950–60, 1960–70 and 1970–75

Areal unit	1950–60 Absolute change	% change	% of total	1960–70 Absolute change	% change	% of total	1970–75 Absolute change	% change	% of total
Core	3 468 708	21.24	85.99	3 951 303	19.96	73.09	792 484	3.34	43.10
Ring	421 514	2.61	10.45	1 078 135	6.50	19.94	770 325	4.36	41.90
Non-metropolitan	143 661	1.62	3.56	376 715	4.18	6.97	275 843	2.94	15.00
Total	4 033 883	9.75	100.00	5 406 153	11.90	100.00	1 838 652	3.62	100.00

Table A.16   France: employment 1950–70

Areal unit	1950 Total	1950 % of total	1960 Total	1960 % of total	1970 Total	1970 % of total
Core	na	na	8 430 597	44.82	na	na
Ring	na	na	7 013 841	37.29	na	na
Non-metropolitan	na	na	3 366 678	17.90	na	na
Total	na	na	18 811 116	100.00	na	na

na – not available.

Table A.17   Spain: population 1950–75

Population data for 1950, 1960, 1970 and 1975

Areal unit	1950 Total	1950 % of total	1960 Total	1960 % of total	1970 Total	1970 % of total	1975 Total	1975 % of total
Core	7 783 025	29.22	9 539 464	32.53	12 514 117	38.32	13 525 261	40.28
Ring	12 094 292	45.41	12 673 096	43.22	14 025 687	42.95	15 148 250	45.10
Non-metropolitan	6 758 730	25.37	7 112 104	24.25	6 113 890	18.73	4 908 023	14.62
Total	26 636 047	100.00	29 324 664	100.00	32 656 694	100.00	33 581 534	100.00

Population change 1950–60, 1960–70 and 1970–5

Areal unit	1950–60 Absolute change	1950–60 % change	1950–60 % of total	1960–70 Absolute change	1960–70 % change	1960–70 % of total	1970–5 Absolute change	1970–5 % change	1970–5 % of total
Core	1 756 439	22.57	65.33	2 974 653	31.18	89.35	1 011 144	8.08	108.98
Ring	578 804	4.79	21.53	1 352 591	10.67	40.63	1 122 563	8.00	120.98
Non-metropolitan	353 374	5.23	13.14	– 998 214	– 12.94	– 29.98	– 1 205 867	– 19.72	– 129.96
Total	2 688 617	10.09	100.00	3 329 030	11.35	100.00	927 840	2.84	100.00

Table A.18   Spain: employment 1950–70*

Areal unit	1950 Total	1950 % of total	1960 Total	1960 % of total	1970 Total	1970 % of total
Core	na	na	na	na	3 163 970	50.43
Ring	na	na	na	na	2 434 145	38.80
Non-metropolitan	na	na	na	na	675 359	10.76
Total	na	na	na	na	6 273 474	100.00

Notes: * Excludes agricultural employment.
         na – not available.

Table A.19   Portugal: population 1950–70

| | *Population data for 1950, 1960 and 1970* | | | | | |
| | 1950 | | 1960 | | 1970 | |
Areal unit	*Total*	*% of total*	*Total*	*% of total*	*Total*	*% of total*
Core	1 283 363	16.41	1 431 563	17.35	1 449 846	18.29
Ring	4 102 599	52.45	4 414 286	53.50	4 468 774	56.39
Non-metropolitan	2 436 030	31.14	2 405 923	29.16	2 006 475	25.32
Total	7 821 992	100.00	8 251 772	100.00	7 925 095	100.00

| | *Population change 1950–60 and 1960–70* | | | | | |
| | 1950–60 | | | 1960–70 | | |
Areal unit	*Absolute change*	*% change*	*% of total*	*Absolute change*	*% change*	*% of total*
Core	148 200	11.55	34.48	18 283	1.28	− 5.60
Ring	311 687	7.60	72.52	54 488	1.23	− 16.68
Non-metropolitan	− 30 107	− 1.24	− 7.01	− 399 448	− 16.60	122.28
Total	429 780	5.49	100.00	− 326 677	− 3.96	100.00

Table A.20   Portugal: employment 1950–70

| | 1950 | | 1960 | | 1970 | |
Areal unit	*Total*	*% of total*	*Total*	*% of total*	*Total*	*% of total*
Core	na	na	na	na	743 498	24.88
Ring	na	na	na	na	1 534 672	51.36
Non-metropolitan	na	na	na	na	709 885	23.76
Total	na	na	na	na	2 988 055	100.00

na – not available.

Table A.21   Italy: population 1950–75

Population data for 1950, 1960, 1970 and 1975

	1950		1960		1970		1975	
Areal unit	*Total*	*% of total*	*Total*	*% of total*	*Total*	*% of total*	*Total*	*% of total*
Core	13 735 066	29.14	16 850 223	33.79	19 382 129	36.09	19 448 662	35.10
Ring	21 549 823	45.72	21 608 185	43.33	22 930 929	42.70	24 325 008	43.90
Non-metropolitan	11 851 007	25.14	11 409 355	22.88	11 395 218	21.22	11 634 652	21.00
Total	47 135 896	100.00	49 867 763	100.00	53 708 276	100.00	55 408 322	100.00

Population change 1950–60, 1960–70 and 1970–5

	1950–60			1960–70			1970–5		
Areal unit	*Absolute change*	*% change*	*% of total*	*Absolute change*	*% change*	*% of total*	*Absolute change*	*% change*	*% of total*
Core	3 115 157	22.68	114.03	2 531 906	15.03	65.93	66 533	0.34	3.91
Ring	58 362	0.27	2.14	1 322 744	6.12	34.44	1 394 079	6.08	82.00
Non-metropolitan	−441 652	−3.73	−16.17	−14 137	−0.12	−0.37	239 434	2.10	14.09
Total	2 731 867	5.80	100.00	3 840 513	7.70	100.00	1 700 046	3.17	100.00

Table A.22   Italy: employment 1950–70

Employment data for 1950, 1960 and 1970

	1950		1960		1970	
Areal unit	*Total*	*% of total*	*Total*	*% of total*	*Total*	*% of total*
Core	na	na	6 451 998	36.06	6 980 738	39.36
Ring	na	na	7 380 833	41.25	7 146 152	40.29
Non-metropolitan	na	na	4 061 287	22.70	3 610 455	20.36
Total	na	na	17 894 118	100.00	17 737 345	100.00

Employment change 1950–60 and 1960–70

	1950–60			1960–70		
Areal unit	*Absolute change*	*% change*	*% of total*	*Absolute change*	*% change*	*% of total*
Core	na	na	na	528 740	8.19	−337.26
Ring	na	na	na	−234 681	−3.18	149.69
Non-metropolitan	na	na	na	−450 832	−11.10	287.57
Total	na	na	na	−156 773	−0.88	100.00

na – not available.

Table A.23   Federal Republic of Germany: population 1950–75

Population data for 1950, 1960, 1970 and 1975

	1950		1960		1970		1975	
Areal unit	Total	% of total	Total	% of total	Total	% of total	Total	% of total
Core	15 221 130	31.12	18 403 603	34.51	19 185 584	32.86	na	na
Ring	33 683 105	68.88	34 918 511	65.49	39 194 469	67.14	na	na
Non-metropolitan	0	0.00	0	0.00	0	0.00	0	0.00
Total	48 904 235	100.00	53 322 114	100.00	58 380 053	100.00	59 801 942	100.00

Population change 1950–60, 1960–70 and 1970–5

	1950–60			1960–70			1970–5		
Areal unit	Absolute change	% change	% of total	Absolute change	% change	% of total	Absolute change	% change	% of total
Core	3 182 473	20.91	72.04	781 981	4.25	15.46	na	na	na
Ring	1 235 406	3.67	27.96	4 275 958	12.25	84.54	na	na	na
Non-metropolitan	0	0.00	0.00	0	0.00	0.00	0	0.00	0.00
Total	4 417 879	9.03	100.00	5 057 939	9.49	100.00	1 421 889	2.44	100.00

na – Separate core and Ring figures not available.

Table A.24   Federal Republic of Germany: employment 1950–70

Employment data for 1950, 1960 and 1970

	1950		1960		1970	
Areal unit	Total	% of total	Total	% of total	Total	% of total
Core	8 344 118	34.19	10 505 845	42.08	10 873 669	42.97
Ring	16 061 508	65.81	14 458 914	57.92	14 431 015	57.03
Non-metropolitan	0	0.00	0	0.00	0	0.00
Total	24 405 626	100.00	24 964 759	100.00	25 304 684	100.00

Employment change 1950–60 and 1960–70

	1950–60			1960–70		
Areal unit	Absolute change	% change	% of total	Absolute change	% change	% of total
Core	2 161 727	25.91	386.62	367 824	3.50	108.21
Ring	– 1 602 594	–9.98	–286.62	– 27 899	–0.19	–8.21
Non-metropolitan	0	0.00	0.00	0	0.00	0.00
Total	559 133	2.29	100.00	339 925	1.36	100.00

Table A.25   Switzerland: population 1950–70

	1950		*1960*		*1970*	
		Population data for 1950, 1960 and 1970				
Areal unit	*Total*	*% of total*	*Total*	*% of total*	*Total*	*% of total*
Core	1 267 801	25.21	1 451 822	25.26	1 479 795	22.23
Ring	3 432 230	68.24	3 936 555	68.48	4 768 958	71.64
Non-metropolitan	329 404	6.55	359 986	6.26	408 135	6.13
Total	5 029 435	100.00	5 748 363	100.00	6 656 888	100.00

	1950–60			*1960–70*		
		Population change 1950–60 and 1960–70				
Areal unit	*Absolute change*	*% change*	*% of total*	*Absolute change*	*% change*	*% of total*
Core	184 021	14.51	25.60	27 973	1.93	3.08
Ring	504 325	14.69	70.15	832 403	21.15	91.62
Non-metropolitan	30 582	9.28	4.25	48 149	13.38	5.30
Total	718 928	14.29	100.00	908 525	15.80	100.00

Table A.26   Switzerland: employment 1950–70

	1950		*1960*		*1970*	
		Employment data for 1950, 1960 and 1970				
Areal unit	*Total*	*% of total*	*Total*	*% of total*	*Total*	*% of total*
Core	722 075	31.90	877 218	33.14	1 015 175	32.36
Ring	1 412 369	62.39	1 616 766	61.09	1 938 056	61.79
Non-metropolitan	129 169	5.71	152 643	5.77	183 489	5.85
Total	2 263 613	100.00	2 646 627	100.00	3 136 720	100.00

	1950–60			*1960–70*		
		Employment change 1950–60 and 1960–70				
Areal unit	*Absolute change*	*% change*	*% of total*	*Absolute change*	*% change*	*% of total*
Core	155 143	21.49	40.51	137 957	15.73	28.15
Ring	204 397	14.47	53.37	321 290	19.87	65.56
Non-metropolitan	23 474	18.17	6.13	30 846	20.21	6.29
Total	383 014	16.92	100.00	490 093	18.52	100.00

Table A.27   Austria: population 1950–70

	1950		1960		1970	
		Population data for *1950, 1960 and 1970*				
Areal unit	*Total*	*% of total*	*Total*	*% of total*	*Total*	*% of total*
Core	2 766 972	40.15	2 863 304	40.48	2 967 089	39.79
Ring	4 124 852	59.85	4 210 503	59.52	4 489 314	60.21
Non-metropolitan	0	0.00	0	0.00	0	0.00
Total	6 891 824	100.00	7 073 807	100.00	7 456 403	100.00

	Population change 1950–60 and 1960–70					
	1950–60			1960–70		
Areal unit	*Absolute change*	*% change*	*% of total*	*Absolute change*	*% change*	*% of total*
Core	96 332	3.48	52.93	103 785	3.62	27.13
Ring	85 651	2.08	47.07	278 711	6.62	72.87
Non-metropolitan	0	0.00	0.00	0	0.00	0.00
Total	181 983	2.64	100.00	382 596	5.41	100.00

Table A.28   Austria: employment 1950–70

	1950		1960		1970	
		Employment data for 1950, 1960 and 1970				
Areal unit	*Total*	*% of total*	*Total*	*% of total*	*Total*	*% of total*
Core	na	na	1 533 336	52.84	1 520 029	50.01
Ring	na	na	1 368 282	47.16	1 519 671	49.99
Non-metropolitan	na	na	0	0.00	0	0.00
Total	na	na	2 901 618	100.00	3 039 700	100.00

	Employment change 1950–60 and 1960–70					
	1950–60			1960–70		
Areal unit	*Absolute change*	*% change*	*% of total*	*Absolute change*	*% change*	*% of total*
Core	na	na	na	− 13 307	− 0.87	− 9.64
Ring	na	na	na	151 389	11.06	109.64
Non-metropolitan	na	na	na	0	0.00	0.00
Total	na	na	na	138 082	4.76	100.00

na – not available.

Table A.29   Italy: population sequential shifts 1950–60–70

		LC	AC	RC	RD	AD	LD
	LC	10	8	5	0	0	0
Type	AC	4	11	9	1	0	0
of	RC	1	2	18	9	0	0
shift 1950–60	RD	0	0	2	4	0	0
	AD	0	0	0	0	0	0
	LD	0	0	0	0	0	0

Type of shift 1960–70

LC–LC	Messina, Ferrara, Piacenza, Arezzo, Cremona, Mantova, Siena, Cosenza, Faenza, Rovigo.
LC–AC	Parma, Perugia, Foggia, La Spezia, Pescara, Pesaro, Asti, Cuneo.
LC–RC	Padova, Reggio nell'Emilia, Udine, Lucca, Cesena.
AC–AC	Modena, Forlì, Pavia, Alessandria, Reggio di Calabria, Terni, Sassari, Vigevano, Carpi, Imola, Caserta.
AC–RC	Bologna, Verona, Brescia, Vicenza, Pisa, Rimini, Trento, Treviso, Pordenone.
AC–RD	Firenze.
RC–RC	Roma, Bari, Taranto, Cagliari, Prato, Ravenna, Livorno, Salerno, Bolzano, Novara, Como, Ancona, Brindisi, Lecce/Surbo, Latina, Biella, Ivrea, San Remo.
RC–RD	Milano, Torino, Napoli, Genova, Venezia, Bergamo, Varese, Pistoia, Lecco.
RD–RD	Trieste, Legnano, Gallarate, Carrara.

Table A.30   Italy: population sequential shifts 1960–70–75

	LC	AC	RC	RD	AD	LD
LC	0	1	2	7	2	3
AC	1	2	6	5	3	4
RC	0	1	4	14	14	1
RD	0	0	0	6	6	2
AD	0	0	0	0	0	0
LD	0	0	0	0	0	0

Type of shift 1960–70 (row labels)

Type of shift 1970–75

LC–AC	Rovigo.
LC–RC	Arezzo, Grosseto.
AC–AC	Terni, Asti.
AC–RC	Forlì, Foggia, Reggio di Calabria, Carpi, Siracusa, Imola.
AC–RD	Modena, Perugia, Pescara, Pesaro, Sassari.
RC–RC	Prato, Latina, Biella, Pordenone.
RC–RD	Roma, Bari, Brescia, Taranto, Cagliari, Ravenna, Salerno, Rimini, Trento, Busto Arsizio, Cesena, Brindisi, Lecce/Surbo, Ivrea.
RC–AD	Bologna, Verona, Padova, Livorno, Reggio nell'Emilia, Vicenza, Bolzano, Novara, Udine, Como, Ancona, Treviso, Lucca, Savona.
RD–RD	Milano, Varese, Pistoia, Lecco, Gallarate, Carrara.
RD–AD	Torino, Napoli, Firenze, Venezia, Bergamo, Legnano.
RD–LD	Genova, Trieste.

Table A.31 Spain: population sequential shifts 1950–60–70

		LC	AC	RC	RD	AD	LD
	LC	4	2	1	0	0	0
	AC	2	4	4	0	0	0
Type of shift 1950–60	RC	1	4	9	5	1	0
	RD	0	1	3	0	0	0
	AD	0	0	0	0	0	0
	LD	0	0	0	0	0	0

Type of shift 1960–70

LC–LC Lugo, Jaén, Orense, Albacete.
LC–AC Burgos, Santiago de Compostela.
LC–RC Alicante.
AC–AC Zargoza, Logroño, Salamanca, Almería.
AC–RC Vigo, La Coruña, Pamplona, Palma de Mallorca.
RC–RC Sevilla, Málaga, Vitoria, Santander, Huelva, Castellón, Tarragona, Gerona, Lérida.
RC–RD Madrid, Barcelona, Bilbao, San Sebastián, Alcoy.
RC–AD Murcia.

Table A.32   Spain: population sequential shifts 1960–70–75

		LC	AC	RC	RD	AD	LD
	LC	6	0	0	1	0	0
	AC	5	3	2	1	0	0
Type of shift 1960–70	RC	2	1	12	2	0	0
	RD	0	0	0	4	1	0
	AD	0	1	0	0	0	0
	LD	0	0	0	0	0	0

Type of shift 1970–75

LC–LC   León, Lugo, Badajoz, Orense, Palencia, Albacete.
AC–AC   Zaragoza, Valladolid, Salamanca.
AC–RC   Cartagena, Santiago de Compostela.
AC–RD   Almería.
RC–RC   Valencia, Vigo, Avilés–Gijón, Pamplona, Alicante, Vitoria, Santander, Huelva, Castellón, Tarragona, Gerona, Palma de Mallorca.
RC–RD   Málaga, Cádiz.
RD–RD   Madrid, Barcelona, Bilbao, San Sebastián.
RD–AD   Alcoy.

Table A.33   France: population sequential shifts 1950–60–70

		LC	AC	RC	RD	AD	LD
	LC	1	3	1	0	0	0
	AC	2	15	29	1	0	0
Type of shift 1950–60	RC	0	1	24	3	0	0
	RD	0	2	1	1	1	0
	AD	0	0	0	0	0	1
	LD	0	0	0	0	0	0

Type of shift 1960–70

LC–LC   Périgueux.

LC–AC   Saint Brieuc, Laval, Vichy.

LC–RC   Cherbourg.

AC–AC   Brest, Lorient, Douai, Cambrai, St. Quentin, Nevers, Bourges, Le Mans, Niort, Poitiers, Limoges, Roanne, Albi, Béziers, Montluçon.

AC–RC   Rennes, Caen, Le Havre, Rouen, Amiens, Chartres, Calais, Reims, Châlons-sur-Marne, Troyes, Epinal, Colmar, Besançon, Dijon, Chalon-sur-Saône, Tours, Blois, Orléans, Angers, Bordeaux, Clermont-Ferrand, St. Etienne, Grenoble, Chambéry, Annecy, Tarbes, Toulouse, Montpellier, Nîmes.

AC–RD   Cannes.

RC–RC   Arras, Evreux, Beauvais, Dunkerque, Maubeuge, Charleville–Mézières, Nancy, Mulhouse, Belfort, Montbéliard, St. Nazaire, Nantes, La Rochelle, Lyon, Valence, Bayonne–Biarritz, Pau, Perpignan, Avignon, Aix-en-Provence, Toulon, Lille, Thionville–Longwy, Strasbourg.

RC–RD   Paris, Boulogne-sur-Mer, Nice.

RD–RD   Marseille.

RD–AD   Forbach.

AD–LD   Bruay-en-Artois.

Table A.34 France: population sequential shifts 1960–70–75

		LC	AC	RC	RD	AD	LD
	LC	0	1	1	1	0	0
	AC	7	2	9	1	0	2
Type of shift 1960–70	RC	4	5	28	13	4	1
	RD	0	1	2	1	1	0
	AD	0	0	0	0	1	0
	LD	0	0	0	0	1	0

Type of shift 1970–75

LC–AC Châteauroux.
LC–RC Périgueux.
AC–AC Limoges, Roanne.
AC–RC Lorient, Saint Brieuc, St. Quentin, Bourges, Le Mans, Niort, Poitiers, Angoulême, Laval.
AC–RD Brest.
RC–RC Le Havre, Amiens, Chartres, Dunkerque, Châlons-sur-Marne, Troyes, Nancy, Metz, Epinal, Colmar, Mulhouse, Chalon-sur-Saône, Tours, Blois, Orléans, Angers, Nantes, Lyon, Valence, Grenoble, Chambéry, Annecy, Bayonne–Biarritz, Pau, Montpellier, Avignon, Aix-en-Provence, Toulon.
RC–RD Arras, Rennes, Rouen, Evreux, Beauvais, Belfort, Besançon, Dijon, St. Nazaire, La Rochelle, Bordeaux, Toulouse, Strasbourg.
RC–AD St. Etienne, Perpignan, Nîmes, Lille.
RD–RD Paris.
RD–AD Marseille.
AD–AD Forbach.

Table A.35   Belgium and Luxembourg: population sequential shifts 1950–60–70

		LC	AC	RC	RD	AD	LD
	LC	o	o	o	o	o	o
	AC	o	o	o	o	o	o
Type	RC	o	o	2	2	1	o
of shift	RD	o	o	o	2	2	1
1950–60	AD	o	o	o	1	2	o
	LD	o	o	o	o	1	o

Type of shift 1960–70

RC–RC   Brugge, Oostende.
RC–RD   Kortrijk, Sint Niklaas.
RC–AD   Gand.
RD–RD   Mechelen, Hasselt.
RD–AD   Antwerpen, Namur.
RD–LD   Charleroi.
AD–AD   Liège, Leuven.

Table A.36   Belgium: population sequential shifts 1960–70–75

		LC	AC	RC	RD	AD	LD
	LC	o	o	o	o	o	o
	AC	o	o	o	o	o	o
Type	RC	o	o	o	2	o	o
of shift	RD	o	o	o	1	4	o
1960–70	AD	o	o	o	o	6	o
	LD	o	o	o	o	1	o

Type of shift 1970–75

RC–RD   Brugge, Oostende.
RD–RD   Hasselt.
RD–AD   Bruxelles, Mechelen, Kortrijk, Sint Niklaas.
AD–AD   Antwerpen, Liège, Gand, Leuven, Namur, Verviers.

Table A.37   The Netherlands: population sequential shifts 1950–60–70

		LC	AC	RC	RD	AD	LD
	LC	o	o	o	o	o	o
	AC	o	o	o	o	o	o
Type of shift 1950–60	RC	o	o	2	5	o	o
	RD	o	o	o	9	3	o
	AD	o	o	o	o	o	o
	LD	o	o	o	o	o	o

Type of shift 1960–70

RC–RC   Deventer–Apeldoorn, Emmen.
RC–RD   Groningen, Breda, s'Hertogenbosch, Leeuwarden, Venlo.
RD–RD   Utrecht, Eindhoven, Arnhem, Nijmegen, Tilburg, Enschede, Maastricht, Zwolle, Amersfoort.
RD–AD   Amsterdam, Rotterdam, Den Haag.

Table A.38   The Netherlands: population sequential shifts 1960–70–75

		LC	AC	RC	RD	AD	LD
	LC	o	o	o	o	o	o
	AC	o	o	o	o	o	o
Type of shift 1960–70	RC	o	o	o	2	o	o
	RD	o	o	o	5	9	o
	AD	o	o	o	o	3	o
	LD	o	o	o	o	o	o

Type of shift 1970–75

RC–RD   Deventer–Apeldoorn, Emmen.
RD–RD   Nijmegen, Enschede, s'Hertogenbosch, Zwolle, Amersfoort.
RD–AD   Utrecht, Eindhoven, Groningen, Arnhem, Tilburg, Breda, Maastricht, Leeuwarden, Venlo.
AD–AD   Amsterdam, Rotterdam, Den Haag.

Table A.39   Sweden: population sequential shifts 1950–60–70

		LC	AC	RC	RD	AD	LD
	LC	1	1	1	0	0	0
Type	AC	1	2	7	1	0	0
of	RC	1	0	4	1	0	0
shift 1950–60	RD	0	0	0	1	0	0
	AD	0	0	0	0	0	0
	LD	0	0	0	0	0	0

Type of shift 1960–70

LC–LC   Karlskrona.
LC–AC   Växjö.
LC–RC   Umeå.
AC–AC   Trollhättan, Luleå.
AC–RC   Malmö, Norrköping, Örebro, Uppsala, Linköping, Borås, Halmstad.
AC–RD   Helsingborg.
RC–RC   Västerås, Jönköping, Eskilstuna, Södertälje.
RC–RD   Göteborg.
RD–RD   Stockholm.

Table A.40   Sweden: population sequential shifts 1960–70–75

		LC	AC	RC	RD	AD	LD
	LC	0	0	0	0	2	1
Type	AC	0	0	0	0	3	0
of	RC	2	0	0	2	6	3
shift 1960–70	RD	0	0	0	0	3	0
	AD	0	0	0	0	0	0
	LD	0	0	0	0	0	0

Type of shift 1970–75

RC–RD   Uppsala, Umeå.
RC–AD   Malmö, Linköping, Jönköping, Eskilstuna, Halmstad, Södertälje.
RD–AD   Stockholm, Göteborg, Helsingborg.

Table A.41   Denmark: population sequential shifts 1950–60–70

		LC	AC	RC	RD	AD	LD
	LC	0	0	0	0	0	0
	AC	0	0	3	1	0	0
Type	RC	0	0	7	0	0	0
of shift	RD	0	0	0	0	0	0
1950–60	AD	0	0	0	0	1	0
	LD	0	0	0	0	0	0

Type of shift 1960–70

AC–RC   Randers, Vejle, Horsens.
AC–RD   Helsingør.
RC–RC   Århus, Odense, Ålborg, Esbjerg, Herning, Kolding, Roskilde.
AD–AD   København.

Table A.42   Denmark: population sequential shifts 1960–70–75

		LC	AC	RC	RD	AD	LD
	LC	0	0	0	0	0	0
	AC	0	0	0	0	0	0
Type	RC	0	0	1	7	2	0
of shift	RD	0	0	0	1	0	0
1960–70	AD	0	0	0	0	1	0
	LD	0	0	0	0	0	0

Type of shift 1970–75

RC–RC   Kolding.
RC–RD   Århus, Odense, Ålborg, Esbjerg, Randers, Herning, Horsens.
RC–AD   Vejle, Roskilde.
RD–RD   Helsingør.
AD–AD   København.

Table A.43   Norway: population sequential shifts 1950–60–70

		LC	AC	RC	RD	AD	LD
	LC	o	o	o	o	o	o
	AC	o	o	o	o	o	o
Type	RC	o	1	4	o	o	o
of shift							
1950–60	RD	o	o	1	2	2	o
	AD	o	o	o	o	o	o
	LD	o	o	o	o	o	o

Type of shift 1960–70

RC–RC   Trondheim, Porsgrunn-Skien, Kristiansand, Ålesund.
RD–RD   Oslo, Stavanger.
RD–AD   Bergen, Frederikstad.

Table A.44   Norway: population sequential shifts 1960–70–75

		LC	AC	RC	RD	AD	LD
	LC	o	o	o	o	o	o
	AC	o	o	1	o	o	o
Type	RC	o	o	1	4	o	o
of shift							
1960–70	RD	o	o	o	1	1	o
	AD	o	o	o	1	1	o
	LD	o	o	o	o	o	o

Type of shift 1970–75

AC–RC   Tromsø.
RC–RC   Porsgrunn–Skien.
RC–RD   Trondheim, Drammen, Kristiansand, Ålesund.
RD–RD   Stavanger.
RD–AD   Oslo.
AD–AD   Frederikstad.

Table A.45 Germany: population sequential shifts 1950–60–70

		LC	AC	RC	RD	AD	LD
	LC	0	0	4	12	8	0
	AC	0	0	2	6	3	0
Type of shift 1950–60	RC	0	0	9	16	6	0
	RD	1	1	3	3	1	0
	AD	0	1	0	0	0	0
	LD	0	0	0	0	1	1

Type of shift 1960–70

LC–RC   Tübingen–Reutlingen, Bayreuth, Rosenheim, Koblenz.
AC–RC   Ingolstadt, Wolfsburg.
AC–RD   Nürnberg–Fürth–Erlangen, Weiden, Würzburg, Bremen, Marburg, Osnabrück.
RC–RC   Heidenheim, Heilbronn, Villingen–Konstanz, München, Giessen, Düren, Lüdenscheid, Paderborn, Mainz–Wiesbaden.
RC–RD   Freiburg, Karlsruhe, Pforzheim, Ulm–Neu Ulm, Aschaffenburg, Augsburg, Darmstadt, Aachen, Bocholt, Dortmund, Köln, Krefeld, Mönchengladbach, Münster, Siegen, Ludwigshafen–Heidelberg–Mannheim.
RC–AD   Amberg, Frankfurt, Bielefeld, Bochum, Düsseldorf, Saarbrücken.
RD–RD   Stuttgart, Wuppertal, Pirmasens.
RD–AD   Duisburg.

Table A.46   Germany: population sequential shifts 1960–70–75*

		LC	AC	RC	RD	AD	LD
	LC	0	0	0	0	0	1
	AC	0	0	1	0	0	1
Type	RC	0	0	2	2	2	0
of shift 1960–70	RD	0	1	2	2	7	2
	AD	0	0	1	0	2	0
	LD	0	0	0	0	0	0

Type of shift 1970–75

AC–RC   Kaiserslautern.
RC–RC   Paderborn, Mainz–Wiesbaden.
RC–RD   Rosenheim, Bonn.
RC–AD   Heidenheim, Koblenz.
RD–RD   Aschaffenburg, Regensburg.
RD–AD   Stuttgart, Schweinfurt, Bremen, Darmstadt, Kassel, Ludwigshafen–Heidelberg–Mannheim, Lübeck.
RD–LD   Dortmund, Wuppertal.
AD–AD   Hamburg, Kiel.
Note: * Partial analysis only.

Table A.47 Austria: population sequential shifts 1950–60–70

	LC	AC	RC	RD	AD	LD
LC	0	0	2	0	0	0
AC	0	0	0	0	1	0
RC	0	0	4	4	0	0
RD	0	0	0	2	0	0
AD	0	0	0	0	0	0
LD	0	0	0	0	0	0

Type of shift 1950–60 *(row label)*

Type of shift 1960–70

LC–RC   Steyr, Wiener Neustadt.
RC–RC   Graz, Leoben, Linz, Villach.
RC–RD   Klagenfurt, Salzburg, St. Polten, Wels.
RD–RD   Bregenz, Innsbruck.

Table A.48 Switzerland: population sequential shifts 1950–60–70

	LC	AC	RC	RD	AD	LD
LC	0	0	0	0	0	0
AC	0	0	1	0	0	0
RC	0	0	0	4	1	0
RD	0	0	0	3	2	0
AD	0	0	0	0	0	0
LD	0	0	0	0	0	0

Type of shift 1950–60 *(row label)*

Type of shift 1960–70

AC–RC   Fribourg.
RC–RD   Aarau–Olten, St. Gallen, Neuchâtel–Biel, Lausanne.
RC–AD   Genève.
RD–RD   Basle, Luzern, Lugano–Bellinzona.
RD–AD   Zürich, Bern.

Table A.49   Great Britain: population sequential shifts 1950–60–70

		LC	AC	RC	RD	AD	LD
	LC	2	0	2	2	0	2
	AC	1	1	2	3	1	0
Type of shift 1950–60	RC	1	0	22	26	5	1
	RD	0	0	2	18	18	1
	AD	0	0	1	5	4	4
	LD	0	0	1	3	6	4

Type of shift 1960–70

LC–LC   Carlisle, Perth
LC–RC   Rochdale, Shrewsbury.
AC–AC   Swansea.
AC–RC   Corby, Hereford.
AC–RD   Bury, Huddersfield, Stafford.
RC–RC   Ashford, Aylesbury, Basildon, Basingstoke, Crawley, East Kilbride, Ellesmere Port, Falkirk, Gloucester, Harlow, Harrogate, Hemel Hempstead, King's Lynn, Maidenhead, Mansfield, Milton Keynes, Peterborough, Stevenage, Telford, Thurrock, Torbay.
RC–RD   Bedford, Cambridge, Canterbury, Chatham, Chelmsford, Cheltenham, Chester, Colchester, Coventry, Derby, Exeter, Great Yarmouth, Ipswich, Kidderminster, Kilmarnock, Letchworth, Loughborough, Maidstone, Motherwell, Redditch, Rugby, Scunthorpe, Teesside, Woking, Worcester, Yeovil.
RC–AD   Cardiff, Lincoln, Port Talbot, Sunderland, Swindon.
RD–RD   Bath, Eastbourne, Guildford, Hastings, High Wycombe, Luton, Newport, Northampton, Nuneaton, Oxford, Reading, Royal Leamington Spa, St. Albans, Slough, Southampton, Taunton, Widnes, Worthing.
RD–AD   Birmingham, Blackpool, Bournemouth, Brighton, Bristol, Burton-on-Trent, Crewe, Doncaster, Edinburgh, Grimsby, Hull, Kirkcaldy, Leeds, Leicester, Nottingham, Sheffield, Southend, Wakefield.
RD–LD   Liverpool.
AD–AD   Portsmouth, Preston, Stoke, York.
AD–LD   Glasgow, London, Manchester, Newcastle.
LD–LD   Burnley, Greenock, Merthyr Tydfil, Rhondda.

Table A.50 Great Britain: population sequential shifts 1960–70–75

		LC	AC	RC	RD	AD	LD
	LC	1	0	1	1	0	1
	AC	0	0	0	1	0	0
Type of shift 1960–70	RC	1	1	14	11	1	2
	RD	0	0	14	29	10	4
	AD	1	0	3	12	13	5
	LD	0	0	0	0	1	11

Type of shift 1970–75

LC–LC Ayr.

LC–RC Dunfermline.

AC–RD Swansea.

RC–RC Basildon, Basingstoke, Crawley, East Kilbride, Ellesmere Port, Harlow, Harrogate, Mansfield, Milton Keynes, Peterborough, Rochdale, Southport, Telford, Thurrock.

RC–RD Ashford, Aylesbury, Corby, Falkirk, Gloucester, Hemel Hempstead, Hereford, King's Lynn, Maidenhead, Shrewsbury, Torbay.

RC–AD Chesterfield.

RD–RD Bedford, Cambridge, Chatham, Chelmsford, Cheltenham, Chester, Eastbourne, Great Yarmouth, Guildford, Hastings, Kilmarnock, Lancaster, Leigh, Letchworth, Loughborough, Luton, Motherwell, Northampton, Royal Leamington Spa, Rugby, Scarborough, Stafford, Taunton, Teesside, Widnes, Woking, Worcester, Worthing, Yeovil.

RD–AD Bath, Coventry, Darlington, Exeter, Ipswich, Norwich, Reading, Scunthorpe, Slough, Southampton.

RD–LD Barnsley, Derby, Dewsbury, Newport.

AD–AD Blackpool, Bournemouth, Bristol, Cardiff, Edinburgh, Grimsby, Hull, Lincoln, Port Talbot, Preston, Southend, Stoke, York.

AD–LD Barrow, Birmingham, Brighton, Nottingham, Sheffield.

LD–LD Burnley, Glasgow, Greenock, Halifax, Liverpool, London, Manchester, Merthyr Tydfil, Newcastle, Rhondda, Whitehaven.

Bibliography

Allen, K. *et al.* (1979), *Regional Incentives in the European Community: A Comparative Study*. Brussels: Commission of the European Communities.

Alonso, W. (1978), The Current Halt in the Metropolitan Phenomenon. In Leven (ed.), (1978), *The Mature Metropolis*.

Batty, M. (1976), *Urban Modelling: Algorithms, Calibrations, Predictions*. Cambridge: Cambridge University Press.

Beale, C. (1977), The recent Shift of U.S. Population to Non-Metropolitan Areas. *International Regional Science Review*, *2*, pp. 113–22.

Belgium: INS (Institut National de Statistique) (1975), *Données Par Secteurs Statistiques des Communes*. Recensement de la Population 1970, Vol. 13. Brussels: INS.

Benjamin, B. (1976), Europe's Population. *New Society*. *37*, pp. 502–3.

Berry, B. J. L. (1970), The Geography of the United States in the Year 2000. *Transactions of the Institute of British Geographers*. *51*, pp. 21–53.

Berry, B. J. L. (1973), *Growth Centers in the American Urban System*, 2 vols. Cambridge, Mass: Ballinger.

Berry, B. J. L. (ed.), (1976), *Urbanization and Counter-Urbanization*. Urban Affairs Annual Reviews, *11*, Beverly Hills and London: Sage.

Berry, B. J. L. (1976), The Counterurbanization Process: Urban America since 1970. In Berry (ed.), (1976), *Urbanization and Counter-Urbanization*.

Berry, B. J. L. and Dahmann, D. C. (1977), Population Redistribution in the United States in the 1970s. *Population and Development Review*. *3*, pp. 443–71.

Berry, B. J. L. and Gillard, Q. (1977), *The Changing Shape of Metropolitan America: Commuting Patterns, Urban Fields and Decentralization Processes 1960–1970*. Cambridge, Mass: Ballinger.

Biraben, J. N. and Duhourcau, F. (1973), La Redistribution Géographique de la Population de l'Europe Occidentale de 1961 à 1971. *Population*. *6*, pp. 1158–69.

Bobek, H. (1966), Aspekte der Zentralörtlichen Gliederung Österreichs. *Berichte zur Raumforschung und Raumplanung*. *10*, pp. 114–29.

Bobek, H. (1975), Zentrale Orte und ihre Bereiche – Neuerhebung 1973. *Österreich-Atlas*, 6. Lieferung. Vienna: Österreichische Akademie der Wissenschaften, Kommission für Raumforschung.

Böhning, W. R. (1974), Migration of Workers as an Element of Employment Policy. *New Community*. *3*, pp. 6–25.

Bourne, L. S. (1975), *Urban Systems: Strategies for Regulation.* Oxford: Clarendon Press.

Bourne, L. S. (1978), *Emergent Realities of Urbanization in Canada: Some Parameters and Implications of Declining Growth.* Centre for Urban and Community Studies, Research Paper No. 96. University of Toronto.

Bourne, L. S. and Logan, M. I. (1976), Changing Urbanization Processes at the Margin: The Examples of Australia and Canada. In Berry (ed.), (1976), *Urbanization and Counter-Urbanization.*

Boustedt, O. (1960), *Stadtregionen in der Bundesrepublik Deutschland.* Forschungs- und Sitzungsberichte der Akademie für Raumforschung und Landesplanung, Band 14, Bremen-Horn: Die Akademie.

Boustedt, O. (1968), *Stadtregionen in der Bundesrepublik Deutschland 1961.* Forschungs- und Sitzungsberichte der Akademie für Raumforschung und Landesplanung, Band 32, Hanover: Die Akademie.

Boyden, S. V. (1979), *The Ecology of a City and its People: The Case of Hong Kong.* Reading: W. H. Freeman.

Buchanan, C. and Partners (1968), *Regional Development in Ireland*: Technical Volume 1. Dublin: Regional Studies in Ireland.

Buursink, J. (1971), *Centraliteit en Hierarchie: De Theorie der Centrale Plaatsen en Enkele Nederlandse Industriegebieden.* Assen: Van Gorcum.

Buursink, J. and Keuning, H. J. (1972), Stedelijke Verzorgingsgebieden 1969. In *Atlas van Nederland* (1972). The Hague: Staatsdrukkerij.

Cafiero, S. and Busca, A. (1970), *Lo Sviluppo Metropolitano in Italia.* SVIMEZ. Rome: Giuffré.

Cameron, G. and Wingo, L. (eds.), (1973), *Cities, Regions and Public Policy.* Baltimore: Johns Hopkins.

Charré, J. G. and Coyaud, L. M. (1969–73), *Les Villes Françaises,* 4 vols. Paris: Centre de Recherche d'Urbanisme.

Chisholm, M. and Manners, G. (eds.), (1971), *Spatial Policy Problems of the British Economy.* Cambridge: Cambridge University Press.

Clout, H. (1976), *The Regional Problem in Western Europe.* Cambridge: Cambridge University Press.

Coombs, S. *et al.* (1978), *The Standard Metropolitan Labour Area Concept Revisited.* Discussion Paper No. 17, CURDS, University of Newcastle-upon-Tyne.

Coombs, S. *et al.* (1979), *Defining Functional Urban Areas for Use in the 1981 Census.* Paper presented at Institute of British Geographers Conference, 1979, CURDS, University of Newcastle-upon-Tyne.

Davis, K. (1969), *World Urbanization 1950–1970.* Vol. 1. *Basic Data for Cities, Countries and Regions.* Berkeley: International Population and Urban Research.

Denmark: Landsplanudvalgets Sekretariat (1974), Pendling og Arbejdskraftoplande 1970. *Landsplan Information,* January, No. 2.

Department of the Environment (1976), *British Cities: Urban Population and Employment Trends 1951–71.* DOE Research Report 10. London: Department of the Environment.

Drewett, R. Goddard, J. and Spence, N. (1976), Urban Britain: Beyond Containment. In Berry (ed.), (1976), *Urbanization and Counter-Urbanization.*

Enache, M. and Holtier, S. (1980), Functional Urban Regions in Romania. In Kawashima (ed.), (1980), *Urbanization Processes: Experiences of Western and Eastern Countries.*

Forbes, J. (1970), Towns and Planning in Ireland. In Stephens and Glasscock (eds.), (1970), *Irish Geographical Studies in Honour of E. Estyn Evans.*

France: Bottin (1976), *Départements.* Paris: Bottin Directories.

France: INSEE (Institut National de Statistique et des Etudes Economiques) (1970). *Les Zones de Peuplement Industriel ou Urbain.* Paris: INSEE.

France: La Documentation Française (1973), La Carte Scolaire. *Notes et Etudes Documentaires, 3958.*

Germany: BROB (Bundesminister für Raumordnung, Bauwesen und Städtebau) (1975), *Raumordnungsberichte 1974.* Schriftenreihe Raumordnung, 06.004.

Glickman, N. J. (1978), *The Growth and Management of the Japanese Urban System.* New York: Academic Press.

Gordon, P. (1980), Deconcentration without a 'Clean Break'. In Kawashima (ed.), (1980), *Urbanization Processes: Experiences of Western and Eastern Countries.*

Great Britain: Central Statistical Office (1958) *Standard Industrial Classification.* London: HMSO.

Grigorov, N. (1980), Human Settlement Systems: Analysis and Tendencies of Development. In Kawashima (ed.), (1980), *Urbanization Processes: Experiences of Western and Eastern Countries.*

Hall, P. (1971), Spatial Structure of Metropolitan England and Wales. In Chisholm and Manners (eds.), (1971), *Spatial Policy Problems of the British Economy.*

Hall, P. *et al.* (1973), *The Containment of Urban England.* London: George Allen and Unwin.

Hall, P. (1974), *Urban and Regional Planning.* Harmondsworth: Penguin.

Hall, P. (1977), *The World Cities,* Second Edition. London: Weidenfeld and Nicolson.

Hall, P. and Hall, M. (1977), *Urban Regionalisation of France 1968.* Working Paper 10. Reading: University, Geography Department.

Hall, P., Hansen, N. and Swain, H. (1975a), *Urban Systems: A Comparative Analysis of Structure, Change and Public Policy.* Research Memorandum RM–75–35. Laxenburg: International Institute for Applied Systems Analysis.

Hall, P., Hansen, N. and Swain, H. (1975b), *Status and Future Directions of the Comparative Urban Region Study: A Summary of Workshop Conclusions.* Research Memorandum RM–75–59. Laxenburg: International Institute for Applied Systems Analysis.

Hall, P. and Hay, D. (1977), *Urban Regionalisation of Ireland 1971.* Working Paper 11. Reading: University, Geography Department.

Hall, P. and Hay, D. (1979), *Employment Change and Government Policy: Some Implications for European Cities.* Final Report to the SSRC. Reading: University Geography Department.

Hall, P., Hay, D. and Sammons, R. (1979), *Compilation of Statistics of Large Towns for Community Countries: Interim Report.* Reading: University, Geography Department.

Hall, P. and Metcalfe, D. (1978), The Declining Metropolis: Patterns, Problems, and Policies in Britain and Mainland Europe. In Leven (ed.), (1978), *The Mature Metropolis.*

Hampl, M., Jezek, J. and Kuehnl, K. (1980), *Socio-Geographic Regionalization of the Czech Socialist Republic.* (1980), *Urbanization Processes: Experiences of Western and Eastern Countries.*

Hay, D. and Hall, P. (1976a), *Urban Regionalisation of Great Britain 1971.* Working Paper 1. Reading: University, Geography Department.

Hay, D. and Hall, P. (1976b), *Urban Regionalisation of Sweden 1970.* Working Paper 2. Reading: University, Geography Department.

Hay, D. and Hall, P. (1976c), *Urban Regionalisation of Denmark 1970.* Working Paper 3. Reading: University, Geography Department.

Hay, D. and Hall, P. (1977a), *Urban Regionalisation of Belgium 1970.* Working Paper 4. Reading: University, Geography Department.

Hay, D. and Hall, P. (1977b), *Urban Regionalisation of Norway 1970.* Working Paper 5. Reading: University, Geography Department.

Hay, D. and Hall, P. (1977c), *Urban Regionalisation of Portugal 1970*. Working Paper 6. Reading: University, Geography Department.

Hay, D. and Hall, P. (1977d), *Urban Regionalisation of the Netherlands 1970*. Working Paper 7. Reading: University, Geography Department.

Hay, D. and Hall, P. (1977e), *Urban Regionalisation of Italy 1971*. Working Paper 8. Reading: University, Geography Department.

Hay, D. and Hall, P. (1977f), *Urban Regionalization of Spain 1970*. Working Paper 9. Reading: University, Geography Department.

Heinzmann, J. (1980), The Structure and Dynamics of the Settlement Systems in the German Democratic Republic. In Kawashima (ed.), (1980), *Urbanization Processes: Experiences of Western and Eastern Countries*.

Hirvonen, M. (1980), On the Urban Change in Finland. In Kawashima (ed.), (1980), *Urbanization Processes: Experiences of Western and Eastern Countries*.

Hoch, I. (1973), Income and City Size. In Cameron and Wingo (eds.), (1973), *Cities, Regions and Public Policy*.

Italy: SOMEA (1973), *Atlante Economico-Commerciale delle Regione d'Italia*. Rome: Istituto dell'Enciclopedia Italiana.

Italy: TECNECO (1973), *Prima Relazione sulla Situazione Ambientale del Paese*. Firenze: TECNECO.

Italy: UICCIAA (1968), *La Carta Commerciale d'Italia*. 2nd edn. Milan: Guiffré.

Italy: UICCIAA (1975), *Le Aree Socio-Economiche in Italia*. Milan: Franco Angeli.

Japan Center for Area Development Research (1974), *Seminar on the International Comparative Study of Megalopolis*, 1973. Tokyo: The Center.

Kawashima, T. (1977), *Changes in the Spatial Population Structure of Japan*. Research Memorandum RM–77–25. Laxenburg: International Institute for Applied Systems Analysis.

Kawashima, T. (ed.), (1980), *Urbanization Processes: Experiences of Western and Eastern Countries*, 2 vols. Oxford: IIASA–Pergamon.

Kennett, S. (1978), *Exploding the Myth of Rapidly Expanding Urban Systems in Britain: Implications for the Adoption of Functional Areas in the 1981 Census*. Graduate School of Geography Discussion Paper No. 70. London School of Economics.

Kirwan, R. (1979), *The Inner City in the United States*. (Inner City Working Papers.) London: Social Science Research Council.

Klemmer, P. *et al.* (1975), *Regionale Arbeitsmärkte: Ein Abgrenzungsvorschlag für die Bundesrepublik Deutschland*. Bochum: Studienverlag Brockmeyer.

Korcelli, P. (1977), *An Approach to the Analysis of Functional Urban Regions: A Case Study of Poland*. Research Memorandum RM–77–52. Laxenburg: International Institute for Applied Systems Analysis.

Kroner, G. (1970), Die Bestimmung zentraler Orte durch die Bundesländer. *Information*. *20, No. 4*, pp. 97–109.

Lacko, L. *et al.* (1980), Functional Urban Regions in Hungary. In Kawashima (ed.), (1980), *Urbanization Processes: Experiences of Western and Eastern Countries*.

Leven, C. (ed.), (1978), *The Mature Metropolis*. Lexington, Mass: Lexington Books.

Lichtenberger, E. (1976), The Changing Nature of European Urbanization. In Berry (ed.), (1976), *Urbanization and Counter-Urbanization*.

McCarthy, K. F. and Morrison, P. A. (1977), The Changing Demographic and Economic Structure of Non-Metropolitan Areas in the United States. *International Regional Science Review 2*, pp. 123–42.

McCarthy, K. F. and Morrison, P. A. (1979), *The Changing Demographic and Economic Structure of Non-Metropolitan Areas in the United States*. R–2399–EDA. Santa Monica: Rand Corporation.

Merlin, P. (1971), L'Exode Rural. *Cahiers de l'Institut National d'Etudes Demographiques*, 59.

Mitchell, B. R. (1975), *European Historical Statistics, 1850–1970*. London: Macmillan.

Morrison, P. A. (1978), *Overview of Demographic Trends affecting the Nation's Future*. Testimony before the Joint Economic Committee, U.S. Congress, 31 May 1978. P.6128. Santa Monica: Rand Corporation.

Netherlands: CBS (Centraal Bureau Voor de Statistiek) (1977), *Uitkomsten voor Nodaal Gebied*. 14e. Algemene Volkstelling 1971. The Hague: Staatsdrukkerij.

Neundörfer, L. (1964), *Atlas of Social and Economic Regions of Europe*. Baden–Baden: August Lutzeyer.

OECD (1979), *Report on the Role of Industrial Incentives in Regional Development*. Paris: OECD (mimeo).

O'Farrell, P. N. (1970), A Multivariate Model of the Spacing of Urban Centres in the Irish Republic. In Stephens and Glasscock (eds.), (1970), *Irish Geographical Studies in Honour of E. Estyn Evans*.

Perloff, H. S. (1963), *How a Region Grows*. Supplementary Paper No. 17, New York: Committee for Economic Development.

Portugal: Secreteriado Téchnico (1969), *A Rede Urbana do Continente: Hierarquia e Funcionamento*. Lisboa: Secreteriado Technico, Presidência do Conselho.

Portugal: CEP (Centro de Estudos de Planeamento) (1977), *Estudo para a Delimitacão de Regios-Plano*. Lisboa: CEP.

Pred, A. R. (1977), *City Systems in Advanced Economies: Past Growth, Present Processes and Future Development Options*. London: Hutchinson.

Pred, A. R. and Törnqvist, G. (1973), *Systems of Cities and Information Flows*. Lund Series in Geography, Series B, 38. Lund: Lunds Universitet.

Randall, J. N. (1973), Shift-Share as a Guide to the Employment Performance of West Central Scotland. *Scottish Journal of Political Economy. 20*, pp. 1–26.

Rodwin, L. (1970), *Nations and Cities*. Boston: Houghton Mifflin.

Romus, P. (1975), Regional Policy in the European Economic Community. In Vaizey (ed.), (1975), *Economic Sovereignty and Regional Policy*.

Salt, J. and Clout, H. (eds.), (1976), *Migration in Post-War Europe: Geographical Essays*. Oxford: Oxford University Press.

Sant, M. (ed.), (1974), *Regional Policy and Planning for Europe*. Farnborough, Hants: Saxon House, D. C. Heath.

Schmitz, J. (1966), *Stedelijke Agglomeraties met 100,000 en meer Inwoners*. Nederlands Centraal Bureau voor de Statistiek, Maandschrift, October, pp. 1042–8.

Schuurmans, F. S. (1974), *Gebiedsindeling van Nederland ten Behoeve van het Onderzoek naar Regionale Arbeitsmarkten*. Interimrapporten Censusmonografien. Amsterdam: SISWO.

Sherrill, K. (1976), *Functional Urban Regions in Austria*. Research Memorandum RM–76–71. Laxenburg: International Institute for Applied Systems Analysis.

Sherrill, K. (1977), *Functional Urban Regions and Central Place Regions in the Federal Republic of Germany and Switzerland*. Research Memorandum RM–77–17. Laxenburg: International Institute for Applied Systems Analysis.

Shyrock, H. (1957), The Natural History of Standard Metropolitan Areas. *American Journal of Sociology. 63*, pp. 163–70.

Simmons, J. W. (1974, *The Growth of the Canadian Urban System*. University of Toronto, Centre for Urban and Community Studies, Research Paper 69. Toronto: The Centre.

Smart, M. W. (1974), *Labour Market Areas: Uses and Definition*. Progress in Planning, 2, Part 4. Oxford: Pergamon.

Smith, D. (1973), *The Geography of Social Well-Being in the United States.* New York: McGraw Hill.

Smith, D. (1977), *Human Geography: A Welfare Approach.* London: Edward Arnold.

Spain: Cámaras de Comercio, Industria y Navegación (1963), *Atlas Comercial de España.* Madrid: Camaras de Comercio.

Spain: Ministerio de la Vivienda (1974), *Metra Seis Delimitación de Areas Metropolitanas de Madrid.* Madrid: Ministerio de la Vivienda.

Spain: Ministerio de Obras Publicas (1970), *Mapa de Tráfico 1970.* Madrid: Dirección General de Carreteras y Caminos Vecinales.

Spain: SIE (Sociedad de Investigación Económica) (1976), *Esquema Nacional de Ordenación del Territorio.* Madrid: SIE.

Sternlieb, G. and Hughes, J. (1975), *Post-Industrial America: Metropolitan Decline and Inter-Regional Job Shifts.* New Brunswick, New Jersey: Rutgers University.

Sternlieb, G. and Hughes, J. (1977), New Regional and Metropolitan Realities of America. *Journal of the American Institute of Planners. 43,* pp. 227–41.

Stephens, N. and Glasscock, R. E. (eds.), (1970), *Irish Geographical Studies in Honour of E. Estyn Evans.* Belfast: Queen's University.

Stilwell, F. J. B. (1969), Regional Growth and Structural Adaption. *Urban Studies. 6,* pp. 162–78.

Sweden: Kungl Arbetsmarknadstyrelsen (1958), *Befolkning och Näringsliv.* Stockholm: SOU.

Sweden: Kungl Arbetsmarknadstyrelsen (1960), *Samhällsservice och Localiseringsverksamhet.* Stockholm: SOU.

Sweden: Kungl Arbetsmarknadstyrelsen (1961), *Arbetsmarknadstyrelsens Regionindelning 1961: A- och B-Regioner.* Stockholm: SOU.

Sweden: SCB (Statistika Centralbyrån) (1966), Regionala Indelningar i Statistikredovisningen. *Meddelanden i Samordningsfrågor, 2.*

Sweden: SCB (1968), Regionala Indelningar i Statistikredovisningen. *Meddelanden i Samordningsfrågor. 4.*

Sweden: SCB (1972), *Folk-och Bostadräkningen 1970.* Vol. 2, Stockholm: SOU.

Tagliacarne, G. (1973), *Atlante delle Aree Commerciale d'Italia.* Milan: Mondadori Espansione.

Törnqvist, G. (1980), Contact Potentials in the European Urban System. In Kawashima (ed.), (1980), *Urbanization Processes: Experiences of Western and Eastern Countries.*

United Nations (1976), *Demographic Yearbook 1975.* New York: United Nations.

United Nations (Statistical Office) (1958). *Principles and Recommendations for National Population Censuses,* Series M, No. 27. New York: United Nations.

United Nations (Statistical Office) (1969), *Principles and Recommendations for the 1970 Population Censuses.* Series M, No. 44, Second Printing. New York: United Nations.

United States, Bureau of the Budget (1964), *Standard Metropolitan Statistical Areas.* Washington DC: Government Printing Office.

Vaizey, J. E. (ed.), (1975), *Economic Sovereignty and Regional Policy.* Dublin: Gill and Macmillan.

Van der Haegen, H. and Pattyn, M. (1979), Les Régions Urbaines Belges. *Bulletin de Statistique, 3,* pp. 235–49.

Van der Haegen, H. and Van Waelvelde, W. (1974), Bilans de Main-d'Oeuvre et Mouvement des Migrants Alternantes. *Bulletin de Statistique. 6, No. 3.*

Vining, D. R. Jr. (1980), Recent Dispersal from the Industrial World's Core Regions. In Kawashima (ed.), (1980), *Urbanization Processes: Experiences of Western and Eastern Countries.*

Vining, D. R. Jr. and Kontuly, T. (1977), Increasing Returns to City Size in the Face of an Impending Decline in the Sizes of Large Cities: Which is the Bogus Fact? *Environment and Planning. A, 9*, pp. 59–62.

Vining, D. R. Jr. and Kontuly, T. (1978), Population Dispersal from major Metropolitan Regions: An international Comparison. *International Regional Science Review. 3*, pp. 49–73.

Vining, D. R. Jr. and Strauss, A. (1977), A Demonstration that the Current Deconcentration of Population in the United States is a Clean Break with the Past. *Environment and Planning. A, 9*, pp. 751–8.

Wickham, S. (1969), *L'Espace Industriel Européen*. Paris: Calmann-Lévy.

Wilson, A. G. (1972), *Papers in Urban and Regional Analysis*. London: Pion.

Index

Page references in italics, e.g. *50*, refer to maps. A number of minor references on most of the
intervening pages is shown thus: 20–30 *passim*